THE
COSMIC GURU

RANDOLPH C. PHELPS

Artwork by Kaleigh Phelps kyleighphelps@gmail.com

Printed in the United States of America

First Printing, 2017
ISBN-10: 0-9977440-2-2
ISBN-13: 978-0-9977440-2-6
Cristo Morpho

Luella Dunn — Family photo courtesy of Carl Williams.

"Scream for Help" — Self-portrait by Randolph C. Phelps.

The Guru — This is an artist's rendition of Swami Sri Yukteswar. Copyright 2006. Permission granted by www.astrogems.com.

About the Author — Photo taken by Don R. Whipple, Whipple Photography, Newport, VT.

*I dedicate this book to
all of my spiritual teachers.*

This book contains material with sexual content
in the form of pornography and casual relationships.
It reveals the underlying issues, causes, and treatments
of sexual addiction. I make every effort to present
it in a clean and approachable fashion.

Author's Preface

My story is the truth as I see it, carefully written with an awareness of sensitive topics while holding myself to be honest, in a context of believing "the truth will set you free."

I invite readers to set an intention as they read The Cosmic Guru. I offer my story in large part with the hope that it might guide you on an inner journey of your own. Toward the end of these chapters, a guided meditation will offer a space in which readers will receive either a word of wisdom, a vision, or the healing they considered while reading my story. The meditation will allow the words to fully absorb into the heart. It was originally designed to activate for readers who have read Swan Song and The Cosmic Guru or Ten Minutes, Ten Days, Ten Years.

Swan Song is crucial part of my memoirs because it allows the reader to submerge in the true meaning of love. In essence, it is a continuation of my story after The Cosmic Guru. If you enjoy reading The Cosmic Guru, then I recommend you read Swan Song. It is about a conscious relationship, complete with all the complexities and challenges.

Contents

Prologue

Two police cruisers slip silently down the middle of the long dirt driveway toward my family's three-story brick home. Pine trees, 100 feet tall, are staggered along either side of the driveway as if javelins were thrown down from heaven, just missing these intruders. I peer out to see them through a small side window beside our white front door.

I run upstairs, out of breath, and enter my sister's bedroom. Vinyl wallpaper covered with foot-long red roses surrounds me on all sides, but this situation does not smell sweet. Panicked, I open the second story window that faces the river.

In the distance, under a cluster of pine trees, is a granite platform covered with pine needles. A prior owner in the late 1800s built it as his throne. I imagine him sitting like a dignified statue gazing down upon the waterfall while he contemplated life's intricate ways.

If I could jump out far enough, I could grab a branch of the giant pine tree near the house. I squat like a bird on the window ledge, pausing to ask myself, *"Is this the right moment to allow The Guru to have full control of my body?"* It seems like a reasonable solution and an easy way to escape this predicament, but deep down my soul suspects that to surrender itself to another spirit is breaking some sacred spiritual ethic. But then again, why not?

Ten minutes earlier, I was sitting in the lotus position on top of a four-foot-long, gold-framed antique mirror that I had taken down from the bathroom wall and positioned on the edges of the tub. It felt as though The Guru sharing my body for the past ten days was ready to blast out of my third eye. I had positioned the Waterpik shower-massager to direct a strong half-inch beam of water toward my third eye, which I was intently focusing upon. I became distracted by anticipating a jolt as The Guru departed, and I was suddenly overcome by fear. I envisioned a sudden blow of pain that might throw me into the shower wall with tremendous force. I found myself beginning to scream as long and loudly as is humanly possible in one breath. Although this eased my fears of imminent bodily harm, it didn't occur to me that my screaming would raise the concern of my mother, who immediately called the police.

Perching on the windowsill with my heart beating rapidly, I make my plea. "Guru, take over complete control and get me out of this situation!"

What happens next is hard to explain. It's as though I am looking through a periscope. I can't see anything to the left or right unless I turn and face that direction. Jumping to the tree branch seems more challenging now, but begins to look more realistic when it comes into focus through my tunnel vision. I leap from the window ledge and catch hold of the branch.

Life is looking better, I fantasize about taking a nice easy float down to the soft, pine needle-bedding ... but before this happens, I hear a *crack!* and a *snap!* My descent suddenly turns into a crash landing. My ankles feel slightly sprained, but they still function. Deciding to run, I discover it's not that easy with tunnel vision. I see a foot here, a branch there ... *look out for that tree!* I make a quick left turn. There's a steep, fifty-foot descent to the river. I find myself airborne, somewhere near the granite platform, floating or flying, a big rock heading my way. I feel the impact, hard against my skull. Blood trickles down my cheek. I feel numb, sick, and woozy.

Time passes: ten minutes ... ten days ... or ten years? As if in a dream, I stand up and wade through the waist-high ferns. I feel like a cornered warrior, forced to retaliate.

I come back to something resembling reality when a tranquilizer is injected into my hip. This wakes me up from one dream and puts me into another. I first notice the smell of hot vinyl seats. Then I realize that I am locked in the back of a police car and have pepper spray in my eyes and a black mesh sack over my head. I feel blood on my face and hands, and my ribs feel cracked or broken. It's painful to breathe. My right shoulder has a bloody scrape where I was dragged on the ground. I feel chains on my lap that lead to a set of handcuffs around my wrists and a pair of ankle cuffs below. I have been captured like a prisoner.

But this is *not* fiction. These events are real. What happened during those ten minutes after I crashed into the rock until I was brought back to reality in the police car? I reveal the unusual events during the ten days preceding this scene, and the amazing spiritual journey that unfolded during the ten years thereafter.

I have given pseudonyms to the key characters. This allows some discretion, and the fun names reveal a bit about each person's distinguishing trait.

My Dad . . . . *The Lion*

My Mom . . . . *The Lamb*

My Brother . . . . *Gadget*

My Sister . . . . *Priceless*

Grandmother (maternal) . . . . *Lily*

Grandmother (paternal) . . . . *Hosanna*

Grandfather (paternal) . . . . *Buck*

Favorite Barefoot Aunt . . . . *Fuzzy Bear*

Adopted Aunt . . . . *Gigi*

My Ex-wife . . . . *Forevermore*

First Girlfriend . . . . *Sarah Lee*

Rental Tenant . . . . *Lizzy*

Acupuncturist . . . . *Frenzy*

Psychiatrist . . . . *Debbie Goldfinger*

New York Travel Companion . . . . *Cleopatra*

Teacher of Native American Traditions . . *My Native Brother*

Martial Arts Instructor . . . . *Mr. R.I.P.* (a.k.a. *Pastor R.I.P.*)

Liberty University Housemate . . . . *Cowboy*

Female Spiritual Friend . . . . *Helen Keller*

Magog Sailing Partner . . . . *Veronica Vogue*

College Girlfriends . . . . *Nani & Glitter*

Hometown Teenage Friends . . . . *Judas Priest & Cheap Trick*

Part 1: The Cosmic Guru

"Author W.Y. Evans-Wentz described his impression of Sri Yukteswar in the preface to Yogananda's Autobiography of a Yogi: Sri Yukteswar was of gentle mien and voice, of pleasing presence, and worthy of the veneration, which his followers spontaneously accorded to him. Every person who knew him, whether of his own community or not, held him in the highest esteem. I vividly recall his tall, straight, ascetic figure, garbed in the saffron-colored garb of one who has renounced worldly quests, as he stood at the entrance of the hermitage to give me welcome. His hair was long and somewhat curly, and his face bearded. His body was muscularly firm, but slender and well-formed, and his step energetic." (8)

"Sri Yukteswar's face can be seen on the cover of The Beatles' album Sgt. Pepper's Lonely Hearts Club Band (1967). It appears on the upper left of the crowd behind The Beatles." (Wikipedia)

FINDING THE STONE

THE WORMY APPLE GANG

As a 10 year old, life is a dream. I am a boy. I spend part of the summer at my grandparents' dairy farm in Kirby, Vermont. My siblings, cousins, and I roam carefree. We explore the acres of woods and rolling pastures. My older brother, Gadget, my adopted Aunt, Gigi, and I march single file on the dark, fertile forest soil. Occasionally, the crispy maple leaves *crunch* under our feet. Our uniforms are plain colored shorts, t-shirts, and sneakers. Gigi, who is the same age as my brother and me, is adorned with pink thick-rimmed glasses, and Gadget wears a green felt hat with a full circular brim. It is a bit too large and covers most of his curly blond hair.

We stop to inspect a rotten tree that has fallen. In our imaginary world, the crumbly white bark pieces become chicken. I use my jackknife to cut it into pieces. We all pretend to munch on it.

Gigi, says, "Ummm ... yummy chicken!" Suddenly, a stick cracks behind us. We all peer quickly in that direction. We scatter and run over the incline.

I shout playfully, "We are being chased by a wolf!"

Gigi laughs while running and yells, "No, it is a bear!"

Gadget runs by, saying, "It is a mountain lion." We stop to catch our breath beside a brook.

Gigi says, "We are lucky to have escaped."

I ask, "Did you see how big it was?"

She replies, "Yes, kind of. It had dark fur."

I say, "Let's send a message on a boat to warn others." Gigi plucks up a fern. Gadget finds a piece of birch bark. Gigi writes an invisible message on it, speaking aloud as she writes. "We heard a wolf in the woods. It could look like a bear or a mountain lion. Be careful!" I poke a hole in the birch bark and insert the fern to create a sail. As it floats slowly downstream, we watch until it disappears.

We rock-hop up the brook until we meet the trail where the tractor crosses the brook between fields. One pasture is covered with corn about my height. It will grow two or three times as high. Then it will be like one giant corn maze: a great place to play hide-and-seek. But not today.

Today, we follow a cow path that skirts the cornfield. We are heading to our favorite apple tree, which overlooks the surrounding pastures. We climb up and sit on low branches the size of elephants' trunks. From here we can spy the white farmhouse, the old red barn, and the towering silo. The wind gently blows the cotton-candy clouds across the blue summer sky.

There are about forty black and white Holstein cows grazing in the back pasture. Each cow has a numbered tag hanging from a chain around its neck. Late in the afternoon, cows will be herded past us, across the road, and into the barn for milking. I notice that cow number 46 has milk leaking from its teats.

I tell my tree-mates a story: "Grandpa used to milk by hand. Sometimes Mom and her brothers would come up to him with a wide-open mouth, wanting milk. He would squirt milk in their mouths."

They both laugh, and Gadget asks, "Who told you that?"

I reply, "Mom told me."

Gigi says, "They must have gotten milk all over their faces."

I say, "Imagine my Mom and her brothers with milk all over their faces." We all giggle.

We claim our fortress for another timeless day. The proof rests in a half-moon-shaped tree fungus placed on a moss-covered rock. My Aunt Fuzzy Bear carved it with a sharp stone. It tells everybody that we are The Wormy Apple Gang. We have found the best place around.

ABENAKI HISTORY

There's a spot at the top corner of the pasture where we get a spectacular view of the mountains rising from both sides of Lake Willoughby. The locals just call it "The Gap." This 300-foot deep, icy-cold lake is a great place to swim on a hot summer day. Willoughby Lake was made when a glacier plowed through 10,000 years ago. Native Americans, primarily from the Abenaki tribe, have lived in Vermont since then. This lake has been sacred to the Abenaki people for many generations. According to Vermont Historical Society...

> "It was part of the land Ndakinna where the Western Abenakis lived. Their land included what is now Vermont and New Hampshire. It also included parts of Maine, Massachusetts and Quebec, Canada. Historians estimate that 10,000 Abenakis lived in what is now Vermont.
>
> "Abenaki Indians lived on this land. They hunted in the woods and fished in the rivers. The Abenakis grew crops in fields and built wigwams in villages. After the Europeans came, the Abenakis traded with them. The French and English traders wanted furs to sell in Europe. The Abenakis traded these furs for metal tools and cloth. The Europeans also gave the Abenakis new diseases they had never had before. Many Abenakis got sick or died from diseases like small pox.

"Some of the Europeans came to North America to stay. They started settlements, then towns, and then colonies. The English settlers wanted to own the land where they built their houses and farms. Sometimes the Abenakis and Europeans got along and shared their spaces. Sometimes they fought each other over the land. The Europeans had more guns and more people than the Abenakis. The Abenakis knew the land better than the Europeans.

"The European settlers took most of the land from the Abenakis. Many of the Abenakis moved farther away from the Europeans. Some moved into the forests. Others moved north to the Abenaki villages of Missisquoi and St. Francis. And the Europeans kept coming to what is now Vermont." [1]

But to me, a 10 year old, it looks like someone took a huge ice cream scoop and plopped the chocolate-flavored earth on the west side of the lake to form Mt. Hor. Then they took a few more scoops from deep in the lake and plopped them on the east side to form Mt. Pisgah.

FINDING THE SCRAPING STONE

One Sunday, my mother, The Lamb, joins The Wormy Apple Gang for a picnic at the top corner of the pasture, overlooking The Gap. I am with Gadget, my younger sister, Priceless, Gigi, and my favorite aunt, Fuzzy Bear, who prefers to be barefoot whenever possible.

While exploring a stretch of slate ledges, I find a Native American artifact resting on top of a mound of slate shards. It is shaped similar to an arrowhead but much longer. It's a charcoal black stone that has been chipped a few dozen times along both edges and is about eight inches long and two inches wide.

I treasure it. Years later, I have it examined by an expert from the Fairbanks Museum. He says, "This is not a local stone. Most likely it was traded up the coast from southern states. It was probably used as a scraping tool." I could imagine it being set down many years ago as the Native American owner gathered a variety of slate pieces for weapons or tools. For me to find this rare artifact on our family's farmland makes it even more sacred.

When I am sixteen, The Lamb tells me, "Your grandmother told me years ago that her great grandmother was a full-blooded Indian."

I learn that our family on her side is of Native American descent, most likely from the Abenaki heritage. My maternal grandmother, Lily, was referring to Eunice Jackson. She was a full-blooded Native American. Eunice married Lily's great grandfather, Joshua Dunn, on February 12, 1812, in Jay, Maine. During that time, being of Native American descent was considered a disgrace. It was best kept a secret. Vermont approved a sterilization law on March 31, 1931. It was intended to curtail reproduction for the mentally ill, but often women of Native American descent were targeted and herded into this category. To better ensure their survival, many Abenaki women claimed to be white on their marriage certificates.

In an attempt to find solid evidence that we are Native American, The Lamb contacts one of her cousins, who sends her a photo of Luella Dunn, who is my grandmother's Aunt. Eunice Jackson was her grandmother and my great, great, great grandmother. She certainly appears to be of Native American origin, with her wide face and strong cheekbones.

Luella Dunn (b. 1844)

Finding the scraping tool marks the beginning of a feeling of connection to my Native American heritage. As a child, I often wore leather moccasins and a coonskin cap. I would race through the woods as fast as a deer, pretending to be an Indian. As a teenager, I learned to hunt and track animals. I was always curious about Native American culture. But I did not participate in the Native American traditions, such as the sweat lodge ceremony, until I was in my thirties.

OUR BRICK HOME

I was born and raised in a typical, small Vermont town. There is one gas station that sells used cars, a church with an oversize stained-glass window portraying Jesus, and a one-room schoolhouse with a bell. There is small grocery store that doubles as the post office.

My family three-story home was built in the mid-1850s by a retired colonel. It has a regal quality, and is the only brick construction in this village. A local historian, Mac Ford, said the bricks were hauled by oxen from Boston. There is a stone foundation topped with granite slabs and a double layer of bricks with a one-foot space between the interior and exterior walls. The windowsills and lintels are also granite. Black wooden shutters border each window.

Inside there are nine-foot ceilings and wide, custom-made trim boards. The front stairway leads to the upper hallway, with the railing extending around the opening. Casement windows open onto a small balcony surrounded by a black, ornamental iron railing. Above it, a decorative triangular facade of brick with granite trim rises to meet the gothic-style peaked roof. It is an impressive architectural design adorned with historical significance.

At one time, a trapdoor in the kitchen floor gave access to a completely enclosed crawlspace with a dirt floor. A rug was kept over the trapdoor. Mac Ford believed our home was part of the Underground Railroad: a network of secret routes and safe houses used by slaves to escape to Canada. He thought that a tunnel somewhere in the basement led to the riverbank. As kids we would tap on the walls and search for the tunnel. We never found it.

Down a steep embankment behind our home is the Moose River. We can always hear the water flowing over the rapids. There is a train trestle above them. As a child, I would listen for the train before cautiously stepping across the trestle. There is a ten-inch gap between each timber, and one side extends out three feet. If the train ever comes and I am caught in the middle, then my plan is to crawl out on the extension and hug it. On the other side of the river there are huge foundation stones and the remnants of an old grain mill.

Next door is a dairy farm. They have a red barn the size of an ocean liner. In the spring, the field in front of the barn is filled with yellow dandelions. On a blue sky summer day, the yellow dandelions poke up from the green grass and wave in the wind. With the red barn for a backdrop, it creates a pallet of colors. Farming is like that: a plate full of wholesome living. They raise Jersey cows and sometimes wooly brown and white sheep in a small side shed.

The farmer and his sons chug around on an old John Deere tractor. It is time to hay their pastures. I am not old enough to help yet, but the neighborhood kids that are big enough throw bales of hay onto the open-sided wagon being pulled behind. The hay bales are stacked six layers high and form a pyramid at the top. A rope is carefully tied full length over the top so the tractor can pull the wagon without a spill. Then they go up the front ramp into the big red barn to unload and stack the hay.

One morning at Sunday school, I am asked to memorize Psalm 23, "The Lord is my Shepherd, I shall not want...." At that point in my life, The Lord was not my Shepherd, and I had no need to want. I had everything I needed.

I attend a one-room schoolhouse with about twenty neighborhood kids, all of whom are my friends. Our first grade teacher, Miss O, is well liked by all of the students. She drives a white Saab with rusty fenders. She has a big sheepdog with eyes you can't see; they are hidden somewhere, deep under all its hair.

Miss O leaves our school after my first year. After my second year, the new teacher suggests that I skip the third grade because I am excelling in my studies. My parents give their consent, yet I don't recall being part of the decision process.

Vermont consolidated schools in the late seventies. They closed down and sold most of the one-room schoolhouses, including mine. Now I will be riding a bus to a new school, five miles away. On my first day in the fourth grade, I see a few hundred new kids, but only one girl from my old one-room schoolhouse. All my other friends were sent to different schools. Because my birthday is in October and I skipped a grade, I am at least a year younger than the other kids in my class. I feel awkward and begin to search for a way to find the peace and tranquility I once knew.

My grandmother, Hosanna, lives a few blocks away from my new school. Sometimes I walk to her home after school. She had been a school teacher for many years. She encourages me to tell her about my day and listens with interest. In her presence, I feel comfort and love. We play games, and she teaches me how to play cribbage. When I spend the night, she reads aloud about Ethan Allen. As I listen intently, I visualize him swinging a grain sack over his shoulder and holding it in his teeth. She reads to me about the Revolutionary War, when Ethan Allen led the Green Mountain Boys to capture Fort Ticonderoga on Lake Champlain in 1775.

One day after school, I notice two guys from my class standing behind the school. I ask them, "What are you doing?"

One says, "We are waiting to beat up Jimmy."

Jimmy lives down over the bank, on a street parallel to the school. There is a steep trail that he takes as a shortcut. He lives with his mom. She is usually at work, and his dad no longer lives with them. He is poor compared to the other kids. Jimmy is quick to be mouthy and provoke others. He likes to call himself James West, after the television show. In truth, he needs to be as tough as nails, stay alert, and remain cunning to survive. I don't know many other kids without a dad at home. I wonder how hard it is. I like him and certainly do not want to join in beating him up. They have no real reason.

At recess, I play on the red and yellow merry-go-round. The kids push it hard and fast. It makes my whole world spin. Everything has become a blur of whirling colors. It is symbolic of how I feel inside. Academically I am doing well, but socially, it is difficult to connect. I feel like an outsider. Somehow, I lost my inner compass. Life is not making sense like it once did.

MY FIRST GIRLFRIEND: SARAH LEE

In my hometown, I have a girlfriend: Sarah Lee. She lives in a red house next to the church. The kids are asked to help with the candle lighting during the church service. While we do it, I hold her hand. She likes that. We ride bikes with the other kids in town on the grocery store's paved parking lot in the evening, after they close. When Sarah Lee and I stop to talk, we bump our front tires together. At that age, girls begin to mature faster than boys. I know little about how to kiss except what I had learned from watching others. My parents seldom kissed each other on the lips in front of me.

Sarah Lee and I meet at the end of our long driveway. There is a thick rope hanging down from one of the tall pine trees. Sometimes, my friends and I swing on it for hours. One day, Sarah Lee and I go behind some cedar hedges. That is where we have our first kiss. I can smell her cherry ChapStick. She keeps applying it to her lips and mine. I guess it's meant to keep our lips from wearing out. We certainly *are* kissing a lot.

One day she says, "Let's French kiss." I don't know what that means.

I innocently say, "I don't know how."

She acts surprised. She says, "You don't know how to French kiss?"

"No," I reply.

She explains, "During the kiss, you touch tongues." So, Sarah Lee teaches me how to French kiss. It feels tingly and warm. After that day, we often French kiss. To signify my devotion, I give Sarah Lee a silver ring that goes around in spirals. It is huge and only fits her thumb, but she is glad to have it.

In the winter, we go sledding in a nearby field. One day, her knee pops out. She tells me it has done that a few times before. I place her on my sled and pull her back home. She is grateful that I rescued her. On Valentine's Day, I want to buy her something special, but all I have is change in a jar. At our home, I find a heart-shaped chocolate box. I go to the little store and buy a bunch of cherry chocolates. They are sold in packs of three, for a quarter. I fill the box with them and wrap it up for her.

In the parking lot, I proudly give her the box of chocolates. She opens it and says, "Chocolates. I love chocolates!" Then she bites into one.

Upset, she says, "Oh no! This one is a cherry chocolate. I don't like cherry chocolates. Are they all cherry chocolates?" I feel foolish for a moment. But being kids, we say what we feel and quickly get over it.

JULIA

Sarah Lee is still my girlfriend in the seventh grade, but we go to different schools. In my class there is a cute girl named

Julia. She is silly at times. She will talk into a person's ear when somebody is on the other side. She pretends their head is hollow. Julia has beautiful light brown eyes. We both have a few warts near the ends of our fingers on our right hands. For what it's worth, we have something embarrassing in common. During science class, we are sitting at our desks and our eyes meet from across the room. We hold a spellbound gaze. My heart begins to race. I can't stop looking at her.

She sends a note through a friend telling me that she will be at the winter carnival dance during the weekend. To attend, I will need to climb out of my protective shell. She is worth it. There are already different cliques forming. I feel like I am not part of that crowd. But this could be my chance to break through the social barriers. In a way, I want to be friends with some of them.

The real problem is that I am having my first dilemma with two girls. I consider Sarah Lee my girlfriend, but I have a real crush on Julia. It would be a great time to seek advice. I don't feel comfortable talking to The Lion (my father) about my girlfriend situation. I never recall him discussing things with The Lamb (my mother). He just makes all the major decisions. Usually, he is too busy to be bothered with his kids' minor problems. I decide not to go to the dance. I want to be loyal to Sarah Lee. Afterward, I am shy about it. I never tell Julia the reason why I didn't go to the dance. I assume she was looking for me and felt let down. She must think I am not interested in her. I am crazy about her. I just never had the chance to tell her.

It's not so much about what did happen; it's about what *didn't* happen. I keep my emotions inside. The idea of talking to Sarah Lee about how I feel towards Julia is foreign. Men I have grown up with don't do that. I didn't know how to open up my heart and take the appropriate steps to talk with Julia. I regret it now. If I had gone to the dance, there would have been a decisive moment when I could have shown my courage.

It would not have been easy, but I would have asked Julia to dance. I missed the perfect opportunity. I felt disappointed, but I learned a lesson. The next time I feel a crush on a girl, I will be loyal to my heart. I will not hold back. I will tell her how I feel.

MY MARTIAL ARTS INSTRUCTOR: MR. R.I.P.

In the seventh grade, for no reason, some older bullies threaten me in the bathroom, just as my friends did with James West. They punch me in the gut a few times and demand that I steal them some merchandise from our family business. My response is to attend a martial arts class. The black belt instructor, Mr. R.I.P., introduces a new sense of character and discipline into my life. I start to feel more confident. He is an emotional man from nearby Canada who will burst out singing a phrase from an old rock song, "Jeremiah was a bullfrog..." and then wait for his students to finish the line. He encourages his students to persevere. We race each other across the lawn, do pushups in the brook, and loudly assert a *kiai* as we throw punches by the roadside. The sound echoes back from the green mountains. It reassures each student that he is a worthy opponent for life's battles.

One day, there is a commotion in the back parking lot. Mr. R.I.P. is there in a flash, ready to defend the underdog. He isn't trying to be a hero; it is natural for him to uphold justice. Once, while sparring with him, I get cocky and throw a few fancy kicks. With three solid side kicks, he catapults me across the room. I never knew what hit me. He put me in my place. Over the next ten years, he gains my admiration and becomes a secondary father figure.

As a 12 year old, life is a dream. I begin high school. I often hang out with my older brother, Gadget, and friends from our little hometown. I especially admire two of Gadget's older friends: Judas Priest and Cheap Trick. We create our own tribe: the outsiders. Our weekends are spent in the great outdoors. We like to ride mountain bikes, drive around in jeeps, and go camping in the woods. We fish for trout in the remote ponds and brooks. Most of us can shoot a partridge on the fly.

The townies that live closer to the high school are a different breed. They participate in sports and afterschool extra-curricular activities. They're on the football team, act in plays, or play in the school band. We really are not that different, but we create a barrier based on where we live, what we do, and who we hang out with.

Judas Priest reassures me by saying, "If anybody in high school messes with you, I'll beat 'em up."

Cheap Trick could be a stand-up comedian. He finds a way to make nonsense out of everything. He has given a handful of friends, including me, the ridiculous nickname of Fluffy. He yells it out from afar with much exuberance. I feel safe around Judas Priest and Cheap Trick. Gadget lets me hang out with his gang most of the time. We cruise around in a Chevy Nova with fur on the dash and fuzzy dice hanging from the mirror.

We go to the roller rink on the weekends, the arcade after school, and occasionally to the movies. On Fridays before school, we all go to Anthony's Diner for a logger's breakfast: two eggs made to order; home fries smothered in ketchup; your choice of bacon, ham or sausage; and two eight-inch pancakes with melting scoops of butter floating on a pool of pure Vermont maple syrup. Delicious!

Sometimes in the evenings, we gather in a side room to play pool. Judas Priest rocks out on his drum set with a strobe light and fog machine. I am part of their tribe. They accept me for who I am. But who am I? I have not yet found myself. I have not yet found a passion for anything in particular. At this age, what I really want is to hang out with the rest of the gang. These two older guys are cool! They have their own cars, play jamming rock music, have jobs, and are dating girls. I want to be like them.

CHAPTER 2

THE LION AND THE LAMB

The Lion attended the same high school twenty-four years ago, that my brother and I now attend. He was a natural leader who commanded respect. He was the football quarterback, on the all-star baseball team, played every instrument in the band, and was president of the student council. As a father, he wants me to be just like him, which is a big order to follow. It makes it difficult to figure out who I am and what I want. I had been taught early on not to express my feelings. I tucked it all inside. When The Lion is at home, I know, as he often says, "Children are to be seen, but not heard."

The Lion insists that Gadget, Priceless, and I take piano lessons. It feels like medieval torture on a sunny afternoon when all the other kids are outside riding their bikes. After a few years, I buy a drum set. The Lion says I can stop the piano lessons if I learn to play the drums. Before I get set up with a superb drum teacher, I learn to play the drums from Judas Priest. He shows me the really important thing: how to twirl the sticks like a rock star.

In line with his vision, The Lion made me play football with a bunch of other boys I didn't know when I was in the fifth grade. Imagine a small boy who knows nothing about football, standing alone on the field holding a pigskin, as eight huge guys wearing pads and helmets charge toward him. The other boys were full of testosterone and aggression, yelling their war cry before coming in for the kill.

In my senior year, with The Lion's urging, I participate in wrestling and track. I am paired up in my weight class with one of the toughest wrestlers in the school. He is a weight lifter and built like a Marine tank. I am like a rag doll, floundering as he tosses me around on the mat. Although I bond with a few friends on the sports teams, after the wrestling season, I feel like a survivor in a P.O.W. camp. I am stronger because I made it out alive.

THE LION

The Lion was born with a broken leg. The accident probably occurred when my pregnant Grandmother, Hosanna, slipped on the front steps of her home during winter. The Lion came into this world in pain. His broken leg was not growing at a normal rate. When he was twelve years old, doctors at the clinic placed staples in his opposite leg to slow down the growth so he would have close to equal length in both legs. He remained in the hospital after the operation for a month due to infection. As a last ditch effort, they used penicillin. If it hadn't worked, they would have had to remove his good leg. There is no question he is a fighter and a survivor.

He was either born with, or acquired, the ability to endlessly taunt his younger brother. As a child, he chased him around with the vacuum cleaner telling him he was going to suck him up inside it. Another time, he dug a hole and claimed it was to bury him. He is commonly sarcastic, frequently spouts off quirky quotes, and will retell a story until my brother and I hold up fingers to indicate how many times we've heard it. It's best that I use some humor when writing about The Lion, as a way to swallow the bitter medicine with a spoonful of honey.

The Lion was driven and became a millionaire by the age of twenty-two. Perhaps the root of his mixed-up priorities is that he became rich at a young age. Money can overinflate a person's pride. The Lion has a meticulous memory for numbers, compulsively counts things, and constantly jingles the coins in his pocket. Being rich and affluent means driving a new Lincoln Continental, owning a colossal home, and having employees, power, and success. His goal is to create an empire. His first priority is to make money; next in line come friends. They keep him well connected. Family often gets worse treatment than friends. But, in reality, family can be trusted more than employees. They are willing to work harder and receive less pay.

There is no question that The Lion provides well for his family financially. Actually, we are envied by other kids and their parents. We have a swimming pool, mini-bikes, snowmobiles, a pool table, modern kitchen appliances, and new clothes every school year. We are showered with gifts for Christmas and on our birthdays. We were each given a safari suit after The Lion returned from a vacation in Florida. We have all the material comforts, but The Lion didn't model the proper moral conduct. What sticks with me is his joking around and saying, "A child is no good until he is old enough to go get me something!"

THE LAMB

I understand why The Lion and The Lamb were drawn together and married. They went to different high schools but were considered the "cream of the crop" in their own ways. The Lamb had wavy, dark brown hair, prominent cheek bones and hazel eyes. She was a beautiful farm girl. She helped raise her five younger siblings and was groomed to be a responsible mother. She was a talented artist who repeatedly won art achievement awards in high school. She was a member of the National Honor Society, which acknowledges students who are exemplary in scholarship, leadership, service, and character. Her beauty is the rare kind that comes from the inside. She is naturally elegant and would complement any man, be he rich or poor, because she is dedicated and completely honest.

During my teenage years, The Lion comes to visit my brother and me as we are painting the Burklyn Mansion. I am asked to sit with him in his car, and I comply. This is where many of our serious conversations took place. He says, "I will be moving out of the house. I have found a new roommate." I guess it is difficult for him to just come out and say what is really happening. What his statement means is that he has a girlfriend, with three kids, and will soon move in with her. It doesn't work out. Later on, he moves back into our home, I believe primarily to be there for my younger sister, Priceless, until she graduates from high school. She is his adorable daughter. She is that cute little blonde with blue eyes dressed up like a zebra for her dance recital.

My brother, Gadget, at nine years old, knew The Lion had other girlfriends. He was awkwardly trained to practice repeating The Lion's lies in case The Lamb ever inquired. He would say, "I was at the cabin all night. Now you say it."

Back in the brick house, on his way to work in the morning, The Lamb would want some affection, a simple kiss or a hug, when he would leave and return home. As a child, I see his reluctance to giving her a quick peck on the cheek. Somewhere inside, a part of me began to question if The Lion loved me.

When I come back from college, I find The Lamb alone in the kitchen leaning against the counter, crying. She is holding her heart and just can't stop sobbing. The Lion told her he was leaving her again, but this time she knew that he would not return. Priceless graduated from high school on June 6th, and he left on June 9th. I am eighteen but feel like I am eight years old again, completely helpless. I don't know how to comfort my mother. All I can do is be with her.

It's difficult to explain the deeper ramifications of The Lion's leaving on these occasions. In an article entitled *Children*

Deeply Shaped by Divorce, which is provided by Marriage Missions International, the author writes,

> "Most studies show that children of divorce are two to three times more likely to end up with lasting social and emotional problems — things like addiction, mental illness, an arrest record, or a teen pregnancy — but the majority are not scarred in this way.

> "But in a first-ever national study of grown children of divorce, which I conducted with professor Norval Glenn at the University of Texas-Austin, these young people told us that, even if they were not forever damaged by their parents' divorce, they were still deeply shaped by it in ways that should make parents think yet again before divorcing.

> "It turns out that any kind of divorce, whether or not it's amicable, gives children an entirely new and burdensome job. After a divorce, the parents no longer have to confront their different worlds — their different values, beliefs and lifestyles. In fact, their inability to handle that challenge may have led to the divorce. But the big job of making sense of the parents' two different worlds does not go away once the divorce papers are signed. Instead, this job gets handed to the child alone.

> "Many grown children of divorce told us they had to grow up negotiating two wholly separate worlds. They rose to the challenge by becoming a different person with each of their parents. They had a mom-self and a dad-self inside them and pulled out the one they needed, depending on where they were that day. They had to grow up fast and often felt much less emotionally safe than their peers with married parents, even compared with some whose parents were unhappily married." [2]

As a child, divorce was the only reality I knew. I felt hurt, confused, and abandoned, but not as deeply betrayed as The Lamb. I am told he loves me, but as a child one always asks, "Why does our family need to break apart?" As a young man, The Lion set a broader example that marriage is not meant to last forever; it lasts only as long as the man is content.

SEXUAL INTEGRITY

I have begun to scratch the surface in relation to three topics: relationships, my tribe, and my spiritual journey. The fourth topic is more difficult to approach, but necessary: the realm of sexual integrity. I weave these four topics throughout my story. As they evolve, I mature, and vice versa. I feel reluctant to disclose the truth about my previous sexual addiction, but it's as integral to my story as the other three topics I've shared.

I don't realize I have a problem with sexual addiction for many years. By my late 30s, I am in way over my head. I can't look at an attractive woman without creating a sexual fantasy. I have no idea it is a problem until the day someone points at me and says, "There is the beast!" I have since acknowledged my sex-related issues, but continue to feel reluctant about having them exposed in writing. The beast of this addiction is so hideous that I must first wrap it up in chains before it's safe to slowly drag it out into the light.

T.C. Ryan, in an article called *Where Lust Leads*, explains,

> *"But the nature of addiction is that the chemicals released in the brain during addictive behavior reinforce the patterns of the addictive cycle. The chemically nurtured, feeling part of the brain is repeatedly strengthened and quickly develops the ability to overrule the reasoning part of the brain. Sexual addiction is a person's use of sex to alter moods that progresses to the point where they are unable to control their use of*

*sex, suffer consequences, and are behaving contrary to
their will and desire. It becomes a substitute for healthy
relating; it takes over a person's will, and it's patholog-
ical — that is, it's destructive."* [3]

I learn about sexual addiction and sexual integrity after
years of misusing sex. When writing about my sexual addiction, I feel that I am placing myself on a sacrificial slab. Having
experienced what I have to reconcile these issues, I feel this
transparency is worthwhile if other men and women can find
their own healing or a better understanding about this taboo
subject. I also write about it to free myself further from the
chains it once had around me.

SEXUAL ADDICTION

I slowly open the door to this dark, basement room with
compassion. There are spiral stairs, which lead me down, step-
by-step, into becoming trapped by sexually-addictive behaviors. I must face my darker side with compassion. I have made
a commitment to move forward and, if it's possible, to never
return. Just as there is a spiral staircase leading down into these
problems, I now know there is also a step-by-step process for
lifting your head up and leaving this place, with self-respect,
healthy thoughts, and sexual healing.

The beast is first exposed as sexual addiction when I attend
a men's sexual-integrity group at a Christian church associated
with Liberty University in Virginia. In these support groups, we
often tell the story of our own sexual-addiction history when
someone new joins. It captures my attention when a man who
has been attending the group for several months says, "I was
addicted to heroin, and it was easier to kick that habit than to
recover from my sexual addiction."

I usually start my story by saying, "I was spoon-fed porno
at a very young age." Then I tally off the porn magazines, strip

clubs, and sexual fantasies. It progressively became worse as I grew from a teenager to a young man. Initially, it is embarrassing to uncover and reveal my hidden, darker side. The other guys' faces hold a sober gaze with an occasional nod. They have heard the same story many times over. It takes a truly deviant confession to phase these guys.

LEARNING TO LUST

As a child, I drew a picture of myself with a briefcase. I said, "When I grow up I want to be a business man, like my dad." I wanted to be like The Lion in every way. I wanted to walk like him, talk like him, and grow up to be him. I looked up to him, as an idol. As a child, I never questioned my father's actions. It is regrettable that when I was at an early age, he displayed an example of how to treat women: without respect.

I don't want to point the finger solely at The Lion because I've been told that my Grandfather, Buck, would occasionally party late into the night with other women while Hosanna was at home with their two boys. This attitude toward women was a generational curse of sorts that was passed down from man to man. Pornography was commonly left on coffee tables at our family's camp, wives were cheated on, and women were thought of as sexual objects, merely for play. These are the men that hand-delivered the beast in a cage to the basement of my psyche and let it go.

I am blessed, for in my life there has always been an opposing force of protection and love to add some balance, usually in the form of a woman. In this case, it's my Grandmother, Hosanna, who is a devout Christian. One day at camp, she grabs up all of the pornographic magazines and sputters in an emotional outburst directed toward Buck and their two adult sons, saying, *You should all know better!* The men look at each other with eyebrows lifted and smirk. She looks her husband and sons in the eyes with disgust as she lets out

24

her disapproval with a cry that sounds like a wounded rabbit. She walks briskly with the armful of magazines, which she throws into the flames of the box stove. Over time, the magazines reappear at the camp. When lust is ignited in the heart of a man, it's not easy to extinguish. More often, it burns and spreads to other men like wildfire.

Most of what I learned about sex came from my friends and what I saw in magazines, but one can't learn to care and be intimate with a woman from a Playboy centerfold. Photographs only churn up illusions in the form of lust. Love is really what I want, but I start to believe that sex is the equivalent of love. While at one of our forts, my teenage friends and I decorate a Christmas tree by cutting out two-dozen photos of naked women from an issue of Playboy. As we attach them to the tree, it seems as though we are expressing what we want: to be loved by a beautiful, sexy woman.

THE BIRDS AND THE BEES

Soon after this, while at our hunting camp, The Lion takes my 12-year-old brother, Gadget, on a twenty-minute jeep ride to give him advice about women, condoms, and sex. The Lion's explanation of sex is another fearful moment. I am told to wait at camp, but I sense the importance of this rite of passage. It is happening today. Gadget is having a man-to-man talk in the jeep. When they return, The Lion is on his way towards becoming drunk. His drinking buddy is a large friend who is called Dancing Bear. They debate for a moment whether I am too young to handle a discussion about sex, but after one more drink, The Lion is ready.

He stands up and starts in with a loud, hysterical, frightening laugh. "A woman has two melons ... no, two grapefruits..." as he cups his hands on either side of his chest. Neither of the men can contain themselves, and they both let out sinister laughs.

Dancing Bear's laugh is combined with hissing, which makes it even worse. I am a frightened and confused ten year old boy standing with my back against the door. My shoulders are shrugged forward, and I have limp, claw-like arms held up in front of my chest. I try in vain to protect myself from an invisible opponent.

The Forevermore Factor

As a 22 year old, life is a dream. I am a young man in college. I first met Forevermore on the beach at Lake Bomoseen, which is in the western edge of central Vermont. She strikes me right away as a woman with confidence. I need to complete one summer course, trigonometry, at nearby Castleton State College in order to graduate within four years. During the day, I stain a few horse stalls for family friends in this area. Forevermore, by happy chance, lives next door. She comes over to shovel the manure out of the horse stalls. This may not seem romantic, but she is a stunning farm girl, fresh and alive, galloping around on her horse. She is unlike any woman I have known.

We go on walks in the fields together. During the summer nights, I park my 1966 Mustang in her driveway. We sit inside and listen to music and chat. We usually stay up too late, and the next day I fall asleep in my 8 a.m. trigonometry class. Matters are made worse because I don't find the subject interesting and the professor has a boring monotone voice. Forevermore captures my heart. She is intelligent and passionate, simple and carefree. Besides, she is drop-dead gorgeous.

During one of our walks, we come back holding hands. I spontaneously tell her, "I love you." I don't say those words lightly. Her eyes are sparkling. When you are young and in love, every breath tastes like wine.

A few years later, I am attending Saint Michael's College in Winooski, Vermont for a master's degree in business management. I desire more adventure and want to travel. I plan to go for a semester abroad to study Australian culture at Melbourne University. Forevermore moves to nearby Burlington and rents her own apartment. We have been dating steadily for a few years. I am contemplating proposing to her. Being apart in Australia will give me time to decide. I want to sow some wild oats before settling down.

In Australia, I find an affinity for photography. I enjoy taking photos of our group in nature or interacting with animals. This semester is an expedient learning adventure. Our group of 17 students visits an animal reserve with dingoes and the duckbilled platypus. We go down in a coal mine, watch sheep dogs at work, and attend a concert by the Melbourne Symphony Orchestra in the Sydney Opera House.

On one outing I scale a giant rock the size of a ship, which I later found out was the well-known Cave of Hands. I was skeptical of aboriginal sovereignty at these sacred sites. But a fifth sense told me I was a lawbreaker. I stand halfway up on a twenty-foot ledge that leads to a thin catwalk around the bend. Here I spot and begin to photograph two shaggy big-horned goats. I realize my vulnerability when one raises its head and begins to charge at full speed. I am being chased and soon cling to the edge with a prayer: *Let me live!* I give birth to a new respect for these sacred aboriginal spots with their guardian protectors.

I have some of my photos published in a few magazines and brochures to promote The Experiment in International Living. It's a big boost. It confirms my talent as a photographer and launches my career in photography.

THE MARRIAGE PROPOSAL

Upon my return from a semester abroad in Australia, I am ready to commit to Forevermore. I love her. I need not search anymore. I propose to Forevermore in a hot air balloon over

28

Lake Seymour during the fall foliage season. I decide to ask her by surprise. We spend the night in a cabin near the hot air balloons launch site. The next morning, under the premise of photographing the hot air balloons, we watch them launch. I take photos of the giant flamethrower filling the floppy fabric, which inflates to become a balloon. It must be held down by sandbags. Somehow, I misplace my lens cap and make a big fuss looking for it. I prearrange to have one balloon for the two of us, but there is another larger balloon that holds eight people launching at the same time.

The woman who will take us up is wearing a leather pilot's jacket. She craftily says, "I am going up all alone." Then she asks, "Would you two like to go up with me?" Of course we accept. I am taking photos of the peak foliage and the other balloon. It is all quite breathtaking.

Once the wind pushes us out over the lake, I look at Forevermore and say, "I have a surprise for you." She jokingly replies, "What! You found your lens cap."

I say, "No, that's not it. I have something for you." I hold out a black velvet box with a diamond ring in it. Then I ask her, "Will you marry me?" She becomes tearful. She looks me in the eyes and says, "Yes! I will."

A few minutes later they yell over from the other balloon, "What did she say?" I am confused at first. Then I figured it out. They all knew I was proposing to her. The pilot and I yell back, "She said yes!"

THE WEDDING CEREMONY

Forevermore and I are married a year later. It is during the peak of the foliage season, under two rows of maple trees in a small picturesque park in Lunenburg, Vermont. Prior to the ceremony, the guests exchange handshakes and hugs, smiles, and small talk.

While I am standing in the paved parking lot, The Lion

shares some unwanted advice. He says, "I spoke to my friend, who is Forevermore's neighbor. She said you would be better off marrying her sister." His rude statement takes me off guard. I feel furious inside. How could he say such a thing on my wedding day! I am marrying this woman because I love her, not her sister. I am afraid to express my emotions, otherwise I would ask him to leave my wedding (or punch him in the gut). Instead, I revert to my childhood reaction. I say nothing and do nothing. I pack my feelings somewhere inside.

We chose to have a wedding during fall foliage because it's my favorite season in Vermont. The sun shines on the maple leaves, which turn a vibrant collage of reds, yellows, and oranges. The air is refreshingly crisp and cool. To take a deep breath awakens my soul; it invokes a connection with nature and with the many generations of my ancestors that rest beneath these rolling green hills.

The wedding guests are seated on several rows of dark brown benches borrowed from the church across the street. I stand patiently awaiting my bride. I feel love and support pouring down, like thick honey, from my cherished neighbors, my old school mates, and my uncles and aunts. Of course, my Aunt Fuzzy Bear, Gadget, Priceless, Hosanna, and The Lamb are all present.

The justice of the peace is a woman named Joy. She and her husband, Joe, own one of the last large tracts of farmland in central Vermont. He is one of the old-time Vermont farmers that refuse to stop farming and for whom selling out is not an option. For the last two decades, Forevermore grew up across the road from Joe in an old white house that was built for the farmhand. Joe and Joy treated Forevermore and her sister, Spoony, like they were their grandchildren. They are given full access to roam on the farmland. They gallop across the fields on their horse named Buddy. Her family sketched out a map and made up a label for each knoll, ridge, and brook. This way they could describe in detail the location where they had spotted a deer or a flock of wild turkeys.

Joe walks bowlegged, and his knees cause him great pain after fifty years of farming, but there is always a sparkle in his eyes whenever he sees his girls. Joe is as solid as the land itself. His smile and the look in his eyes are enough to bless our marriage. It need not be spoken aloud. We both feel it. For him, marriage is a deeply-dug well that is meant to be drawn upon forevermore.

Our marriage ceremony is one of those timeless moments. Forevermore wears a custom-made, spandex, knee-length wedding dress. It is fire-engine red to match the leaves and her fiery Italian passion. Her hair is done up exquisitely. The bridesmaids wear casual knee-length dresses of white and yellow. My best man and I have on dapper, black, tailed tuxes. Mine has a fiery red cummerbund that matches the bride's dress.

I can hear the crackling of leaves as the bridesmaids, and then Forevermore, meander in their snazzy high heels down the two rows of maple trees. I am bedazzled and filled with loving thoughts about our future together. Forevermore radiates with sensational beauty and confidence. She comes to stand by my side. We peer into each other's eyes. Our wedding ceremony begins.

The justice of the peace asks, "Is there any reason these two should not be married?"

All of our friends and family are silent. It is a perfectly crisp, sunny day with only one small cloud in the otherwise pristine blue sky. To our surprise, in this moment of quietness, gentle thunder rolls out from behind that one little cloud and for just an instant, a few sprinkles fall from the sky. I stare up in the sky and wonder if God is offering us some sort of ominous warning. We are not sure how to react, so Forevermore and I smile at each other, and then say our vows.

We start our life journey together with a year-long honeymoon. We travel out west to live for a few months in Seattle, Washington, with her sister, Spoony. While in Seattle, Forevermore enrolls in a program for a career as a dog groomer. I am unable to find decent work in Seattle. I become desperate. I am willing to take any job. I water down my resume to get hired in a convenience store.

For a month, I get a gig photographing children and babies in people's homes. It requires a lot of driving and shaking a silly puppet to make them smile. Then I get hired as a guide in Ketchikan, Alaska. By accepting this job, I will be away from Forevermore for a few months. I hop on a ferry with my mountain bike and a backpack. Forevermore will drive our Chevy minivan to Alaska once her dog-grooming training is complete.

As a guide, I use my paddle as a rudder to steer an ocean-going canoe as twenty tourists from the cruise ships paddle around a mountain lake. We pull ashore and I point out the banana slugs and the carnivorous sundew plant. After this job, I am hired to photograph the Native American Tlingit Tribe, which makes totem poles, does intricate bead work, and performs their traditional drumming and dancing. They are content people, and the children are always playing and laughing.

Joyce, who is about thirty, arrives for our photo shoot in her traditional red felt dress, carrying a woven basket. She pauses during our photo shoot to pick and eat a few orange salmon berries. Then we move down beside the sea. She tells me that soon she will be married in a traditional wedding. Her groom will arrive by sea in a canoe.

I make friends among the Tlingits during my two weeks of photographing. I tell some of them that I will make copies of some of the photographs to give them. Later, I am disheartened to find out that the non-native corporation that hired me to take these promotional photographs will not allow the Tlingits to have any of the photos. The corporation owns the legal rights to all of the photos. They tell me they might try to sell them. I am told one such photo showed up on the side of a bus. I apologize to the Tlingit tribe for my false promise. I arrange a photo presentation so they can at least enjoy viewing them. I feel the tension between the Tlingit tribe and the non-native corporation that gained the right to control them, for better or worse, as a profitable business. I am rudely awakened to their current reality. In order for the White man to market them, they had to give up certain rights. It feels like the indigenous people are still getting the short end of the stick.

Once reunited, Forevermore and I travel to explore the interior of Alaska. The last frontier is a wildlife photographer's dream. There are herds of caribou, and the snow-covered caps of Mount Denali in the background are spectacular. While we are there, a large wolf chases a large caribou down the river. He takes it down singlehandedly. As he is feeding, a grizzly bear comes along and wants an easy meal. The grizzly bear chases off the lone wolf and gorges itself. It literally sleeps on the carcass for three days. The wolf came back with two others from the pack. They venture in close to try and grab some meat. The bear swats at one with a huge claw. It runs away yelping like a puppy.

We hike 33 miles along the Chilkoot Trail. The Chilkoot Trail was the most famous route taken by prospectors who made their way to the Klondike Gold Rush. Chilkoot Pass was an aboriginal trail that had been used for years by the First Nations people who lived in this region. The steep mountains and the harsh weather make this trip extremely grueling. We had to traipse through deep snow to get over the pass in the middle of July. During the gold rush era there was a law stating that all who entered Canada had to bring one ton of food and supplies.

Forevermore and I create strong memories while hiking and

camping. We are happy tramping around in the rain or snow. In part, being together is what matters the most. After a year, we return back to Vermont. In northern Vermont regions, I give a public photo presentation called "Alaska: Natives, Nature, and Nonsense."

FOR BETTER OR WORSE

Back in Vermont, I begin to work in the family business, and to photograph weddings. We rent a home, and Forevermore opens a dog-grooming salon. She doesn't want to settle down in the vicinity of her new father-in-law, The Lion. She despises how he mistreats women. The Lion is not just my father; he is also my boss. It makes the whole scenario complex and frustrating at times.

Forevermore is a strong advocate for the fair treatment of animals, women's rights, and the environment. She never holds back from speaking her mind. Some people improperly label her as a snob, because she has ravishing beauty and speaks so directly. She is a beautiful and intelligent woman with stunning brown eyes and long dark hair, which I enjoy watching her comb through each evening. Her hair always smells fresh and clean. We lack the skills to communicate effectively when conflicts arise, and we begin to argue over little things that aren't important. I am guilty of not always listening to her. Perhaps, I am caught up in focusing on my own needs.

I continually push myself to live, work, and play hard. My world changes after I herniate a disk in my lower back. The injury limits my ability to sit for long without pain. Our marriage begins to lose the romantic spark. I do not feel like going out to the movies or having dinner with friends. I can no longer share in doing chores like washing the dishes, taking out the trash, or hauling firewood, which was part of my role as a man and her husband.

I can no longer enjoy fun activities like downhill skiing,

mountain biking, or hiking, as we once did together. Instead, my daily routine includes physical therapy exercises and a walk each day to keep my body limber and my mind sane.

After months of living with chronic pain, emotional trauma and anger begins to creep in. Often, my back muscles tear for little or no reason. I can open the car door and it drops me to my knees. One afternoon, Forevermore returns from work and I am lying on the carpet watching a movie. She greets me by asking, "How are you feeling?" I explode, "How the hell do you think I'm feeling?" Afterwards, I apologize. She was being kind. I should have shared how I felt.

Just for the record, I was feeling a lot of pain that day. Pain that limits my normal ability makes me feel helpless, and if it is prolonged, it progresses to become hopeless. It can get really frustrating. One morning, my back pulls while I am walking alone on a dirt road. I have to crawl back home on my hands and knees. Underneath, I am asking myself, "Why has this happened to me?"

I follow the example The Lion set for me in terms of how to cope with stress and survive. His methods are to take a pill, have a drink, or take it out on somebody weaker. Unfortunately, some of the bad seeds he planted years ago begin to sprout. For a while, I drink alcohol, but I realize it's only making me depressed.

I begin to watch a few movies each day, rationalizing that watching movies is a healthier way to relieve my stress and pain than drugs or alcohol. Slowly I begin to focus on movies with sexual content. It's not my nature to rent X-rated videos. That would be sinking too low. Yet, I experience an adrenalin rush when I watch R-rated movies, and eventually get hooked on the visual stimulation of the sex and action-packed Hollywood films. There is a melding of the sexy women in the movies within my reality. I start to have sexual fantasies of other women, even when I am with Forevermore. During love-making, I am certain she feels it when I drift away to my fantasy world instead of being in my heart with her, my beautiful wife.

Joe Zychik, the author of *How I Overcame Sexual Addiction and How Anyone Can*, explains,

> "A person begins addiction by using a substance or activity to escape dealing with the difficulties of life. The escape fails because escape never works - and it always worsens life's problems. Then - and this is the big mistake - the person decides to flee further into addiction rather than face the problem." [4]

DIVORCE

My decision to buy a local home in nearby Danville and remain an employee in our family business causes a division between Forevermore and me. Instead of moving into the house I just purchased, she chooses to live nearby with her sister, Spoony, in the house we were all renting together. It's clear in hindsight that we, as a married couple, should have been in agreement about buying a home or any major decision.

Forevermore longs to travel the world. I sense that the physical limitations of my back injury are dampening her freedom. She goes with her sister to spend a month biking in Europe. I go to the local video store and pick out a few more flicks. I naively believed that we would always be happily married. For a variety of reasons, I begin to wonder whether our lives would be better if we were apart.

WHAT DOES THE BIBLE SAY ABOUT AN UNHAPPY MARRIAGE?

> "One thing we know for sure: being in an unhappy marriage is not biblical grounds for divorce. In Mark 10:11–12 Jesus said, "A man who divorces his wife so

he can marry someone else commits adultery against her. And a woman who divorces her husband so she can marry someone else commits adultery." Based on the Bible, we see that people don't have the right to dissolve an unhappy marriage. God intended that marriage be for a lifetime.

"Ephesians 5 presents marriage as a picture of the relationship God has with us. This is one reason why God has such an interest in keeping marriages intact. He is the One who established the concept of "until death do us part." He established this for our own good. Failed marriages and broken homes are devastating to the husband and wife, not to mention the children involved. Financial ruin is only one of the unhappy results of divorce. The family unit is the basic building block of any society, and rampant divorce has a tragic impact on all of the culture.

"This is not to say that God wants to force us to remain forever in an unhappy marriage. He doesn't ask us to just grit our teeth and suffer through it. When God approaches marital problems, He does so from the perspective of how to fix them, not how to dissolve the marriage. For example, the Lord speaks of demonic impact in marriages (1 Corinthians 7:5). He states that the couple should be active in the sexual relationship so that Satan cannot tempt them. He encourages husbands to treat their wives with understanding so their prayers will not be hindered (1 Peter 3:7). From these passages we can see that marriage is a spiritual battlefield. It takes work to fight for the relationship, not to fight in the relationship.

"God encourages us toward reconciliation. Matthew 18:15–16 demands open, honest communication that deals with hurts and frustrations caused by sin. It even encourages us to get help to resolve problems.

God also calls us to find our joy in Him (Philippians 4). Joy is a superior experience to happiness. Happiness is temporal and temporary, but joy rises above all circumstances and lasts for eternity. Joy is something you can have regardless of conditions. In all of God's guidelines for experiencing joy, none of them require a spouse to cooperate. A spouse does not control our capacity to have joy or peace. James 1:3–4 tells us that deep, abiding joy comes as we persevere through trials, with God's help, and as our faith matures and strengthens. Mere happiness tends to be fleeting and depends upon temporal factors like circumstances or other people. Joy, on the other hand, is true contentment that comes from internal factors like our faith in the Lord. True joy is everlasting and not dependent upon circumstances." [5]

THE FOREVERMORE FACTOR

During this stage of my life, I did not seek the Bible for guidance. I ask Forevermore, "Do you want a divorce?"

She says, "Yes!" without any hesitation.

There is never any further discussion. In her mind, after she signs the divorce papers, we are all over. Before I know it, she is with another man, one that is galloping beside her on horseback, even before I drag myself alone into court to make our divorce legal.

When it sinks into my heart that we are actually divorced, I am devastated, teetering on the verge of a breakdown. Our marriage lasted four years, but it continues in my mind for the next decade. My heart has a tender spot where all our memories are engraved.

Perhaps it's understandable why I now become sad during the autumn. I call it "The Forevermore Factor." When I see all the beauty in the vibrant red, orange, and yellow leaves, it only reminds me of our beautiful wedding day. Now I feel all alone and depressed. All my pain is buried under the layers of colorful leaves. Now I am glad to watch them drop to the ground. Each winter the snow temporarily covers my dream of being happily married and living together with her.

I remove all of Forevermore's photos and all the items that remind me of her from my home. As a wedding gift, The Lamb and Fuzzy Bear sewed us a handmade queen-size quilt. It has an intricate design with a mesmerizing storm-at-sea pattern, consisting of shades of dark and light blues interspersed with white. When seen from different angles, this combination of triangles, squares, and diamonds gives the effect of the motion of multiple waves converging during a chaotic storm at sea. We cherished it, but there are too many emotions wrapped inside it to consider sleeping under it without her. Yet there is so much love and beauty embedded in that quilt that I cannot bring myself to part with it. Our marriage began as beautiful, then it ironically became the storm at sea. Now, the confusion, the helplessness, the loss, the anger, the loneliness, and the fear of that storm rage on inside.

SAILING

As a 31 year old, life is a dream. I am a supervisor overseeing and purchasing items for a trendy department in several stores that our family business operates with success. A few years after my divorce, I impulsively purchase a 24-foot McGregor sailboat. It's a way to conjure up fun and put adventure back into my life. There is an overnight cabin, and it can sleep four people. It's great for a weekend on northern Vermont's lakes. I sail with friends and family, primarily on Lake Memphremagog.

My friend, Cleopatra, and I often go sailing on long weekends. When there is not enough wind to sail, we chill out in the sun, read, or dive off the side for a swim. My favorite time to be on the sailboat is during sunset. We often have a barbeque dinner as the lake becomes still. At night, we lie out flat on the deck and look up at the stars. One day we dock to explore Province Island, which divides the international border. On this foreign soil, we spot dozens of pheasants, and there are even wild boars. We thought we had found Fantasy Island.

With some hesitation, I accept an invitation by Cleopatra to move in with her. She is from a Jewish family, born and raised in Queens, New York. She fell in love with Vermont and moved here after she saw fresh snow sparkling in a field like diamonds rolling in the sun. Cleopatra is part of the generation that went to Woodstock and never really came back home. We have jubilant experiences together; going out dancing with her undoubtedly means staying until the club closes down for the night.

I become certified for bareboat chartering at the School of International Sailing, located on Mallets Bay on the northern part of Lake Champlain. I consider purchasing a larger sailboat to explore islands in the Caribbean. Cleopatra, another female friend, and I charter Ragamuffin, a fifty-foot sailboat, with a captain and his wife, to sail for a week around the British Virgin Islands. My two sail mates spend the bulk of their time sunbathing as I rig the sails. I decide that being a captain of a sailboat in the Caribbean is not for me. Yet it is nice to kick off our shoes to watch the porpoises and turtles and whales that swim alongside our sailboat.

SALINE ISLAND

We travel to various Caribbean Islands, including Aruba, with long sandy beaches, and Bonaire, renowned for its snorkeling in the coral. Cleopatra considers these her tropical vacations, but I am searching for a place to establish a spiritual retreat center. On our last two trips, we fly into Grenada, then hop on a ferry which brings us to Carriacou Island. I am negotiating to lease 52 acres, called Saline Island. Nine siblings inherited this island from their father, George John, who purchased it decades ago. It's a secluded paradise with sandy, white beaches surrounded by lush mangrove forests and swaying coconut trees. There are towering black volcanic caps where wild goats roam, a salt pond where they harvest salt, and a beautiful cove for snorkeling with the angel, zebra, and trumpet fish among the coral reef.

It's my dream to start a spiritual retreat center in the Caribbean, perhaps on this island. We meet at their cottage on the island, and I present a business plan. We plan to meet again in Grenada to negotiate a price for leasing the island. We have both consulted with our lawyers, and I have high hopes that our next meeting will conclude our negotiations.

Outside, it's the height of Carnival celebrations. Carnival is a festive occasion; the streets are filled with people in glittery costumes, elaborately painted faces, and parties that go on for days. Island music blares through refrigerator-size speakers or dark-skinned men pound on homemade oil-pan drums late into the night.

Amidst the chaos of this celebration, the siblings can't come to an agreement among themselves about what they want to do with their island. A few local siblings want to continue to use the camp as a place to spear fish, relax, and drink beer. We then receive word that their lawyer has been hit by a car. He has suffered a broken leg and must go to the hospital, so they will not be attending our negotiations. It's not going to happen. We end our negotiations. I return to Vermont rather disappointed.

AN INTIMACY AND ATTACHMENT DISORDER

Cleopatra desires to be in a long-term relationship with a man. I am not in love with her. I introduce her as my friend, not my girlfriend, which makes her mad, but it better represents my feelings. After living with Cleopatra for a few years, I begin to search for other women to date. Now with hindsight, I should have moved out. After Cleopatra discovered my quest, she gave me the boot, without any hesitation.

Single again, I realize I never processed my divorce with Forevermore. Cleopatra was a pleasant distraction, but I need to face and feel the pain. In an attempt to erase all the beautiful and painful memories, I cut out all but one of her photos from our wedding album. The one I left is a dark silhouette of our bodies in an embrace in a hallway. Now she is more like a shadow or a ghost. I have been repressing my feelings surrounding my divorce, and they built up like a dam that is ready to overflow. When the dam finally breaks, it takes down the walls. I am filled with a torrent of anxiety and depression.

It hurts my heart to let go of Forevermore. I have spells of what is called *saudade*, which is a Portuguese word that means: feelings of intense longing for a person you once loved. At times, it is an obsession. After our divorce, I idolize our perfect moments for the next decade. I wipe the slate clean of all our petty arguments and any harsh feelings.

Now, I just feel lonely. Being legally divorced does not feel any different from being married. There were moments when I desired a divorce, but underneath, what I really wanted was to find a way to stay connected. Unbeknownst to myself, our relationship needed deep emotional intimacy to survive. This meant expressing my emotions and *really* feeling empathy for hers.

Sexual addiction, to a large degree, is an intimacy and attachment disorder. I had not yet learned how to be emotionally intimate. I rarely communicate my emotions effectively and I block off the circuits that feel empathy and compassion for others. I found it impossible to detach because "letting go" meant I was losing whatever little scraps of love, (which were merely an illusion) I had left. Somehow, I came to falsely believe that I would feel less pain if I held on tightly.

FRENZY, THE ACUPUNCTURIST

To cope with my depression and anxiety attacks, I receive regular acupuncture sessions from a woman named Frenzy. She has it together. She has wild, straggly, blond hair. I find out later, when she means business, she conveys it in a frenzy of swearing. She's a flower child from the sixties who lived in various spiritual communities.

Frenzy's office has an Oriental charm, with bamboo decorations and the smell of burning mugwort and simmering tea. It's difficult to gauge how much the acupuncture improves my depression, but I do feel slightly better for a few days after each treatment. Frenzy genuinely cares for my situation.

She lends me a book called *Acu-Yoga* by Michael Reed Gach. She says, "Start each day with ten deep breaths." This simple breathing exercise allows me to become grounded, stay calm, and start each day on a positive note. I begin to practice yoga a few hours each day. After I practice yoga, my feeling of depression is replaced with a sense of peace. For the first time, I start to turn within myself and face my pain.

VERONICA VOGUE: CROSSING THE BORDER

One afternoon, I am at Lake Memphremagog tending to my sailboat. I meet a slightly older woman named Veronica Vogue, who has journeyed down on the ferry from Magog, Canada. I invite her to go sailing. She joyfully accepts. Being the captain of my own sailboat carries certain responsibilities and rewards. At this point, I am seeking a romantic interlude. Let's put it bluntly: I am craving sex, which in my confused mind is the equivalent to being loved.

It's a gorgeous afternoon for sailing. We have a little wine and cheese, and it's fun to be out on the water. At one point, she leans her back against me in the sailboat. Her touch is flirtatiously appealing.

I drive her back up to Magog in my S.U.V. At the Canadian border crossing, they ask, "What is the purpose of your trip?"

I answer, "Strictly pleasure."

We have dinner together in the quaint city of Magog, overlooking the water. Veronica, like most Canadians, dresses in a vogue fashion, with a blouse made of netted material. We have a stimulating conversation. She is foreign and somewhat bored with her life, but she seems rather exotic and alluring to me. Veronica is taking a getaway from her husband. She smokes a cigarette while telling me that her marriage is shaky, but she does not want to share the details. This time is reserved for her to get away from him.

We walk along a paved path by the beach. I am giving her my full attention, and she is responding. We have a long hug near the water.

She says, "It's time for me to return to my hotel room." She is hinting that it's time for me to go.

I say, "I don't want to leave. Can I spend the night with you?" She pauses to check in with herself.

She asks, "What is it that you want?"

I say, "Sex would be nice."

She takes a few deep breaths, contemplating all the implications.

Her response comes with a slight tag of reluctance. "Sex is what you want? Here is my hotel key. I will get another one at the front desk. Meet me in room number 44 in ten minutes."

I go to my S.U.V and get my shaving kit. Anticipating a lascivious sexual affair, I pull out a condom and place it in my pocket.

Her hotel is right by the water. I walk down the wide, red-carpeted hallways past rows of white doors with gold numbers until I reach room number 44. I knock on the door. She comes out of the bathroom. While standing, we embrace and kiss. She has just been smoking a cigarette. It's true, to kiss a smoker is like licking an ashtray, but what comes to my mind is even worse. It's one of The Lion's comments about anything of disgust: "It's like kissing your sister on the lips."

I barely make it through her kiss without gagging.

Veronica says, "My husband must never know about this."

I agree not to tell him. She picks up the phone and calls down to reception. A few minutes later, a bellboy arrives at the door holding out a small silver tray with a condom on it. She pays him, along with a three-dollar tip. Obviously, we are both anticipating the need for a condom.

This is all building up to a crescendo. I am preparing for

the big performance. We have most of the essential ingredients, but one is lacking: love. We roll on the sheets, moan and groan, and claw to take each other's clothes off. Underneath her clothes, she has on sexy, black, thong underwear and a lacy bra. There is a problem. I have a desire for sex, but one essential body part is not cooperating. I try to find ways to stall. It's starting to get embarrassing. I have never had this sort of dysfunction with a woman.

I dare not repeat her exact words. Let's just say at this moment, Veronica Vogue tells me exactly what she wants, and she is *extremely* clear about when she wants it — *right now!* Well, it's not going to happen that way. How am I going to explain this to Mrs. Veronica Vogue?

It turns out there will be *no* big performance tonight. By now, it's no big secret. She deals with it gracefully enough. As we lie in bed, she smokes another cigarette.

We say goodbye and I drive across the border, back to where I belong. I did not love this woman. I did not even enjoy kissing her. My body let me know it. My heart did not want to lend itself to a married woman, regardless of how sensual and exotic she appeared. My mind and its lusty thoughts had a plan, but thankfully my heart trumped over my body. If I can stop judging my body's performance, then I can listen to what it really needs. Sex with Mrs. Veronica Vogue is not what my body needs.

> *"The one who commits adultery with a woman is lacking sense; he who would destroy himself does it, wounds and disgrace he will find, and his reproach will not be blotted out. For jealousy enrages a man, and he will not spare in the day of vengeance. He will not accept any ransom, nor will he be satisfied though you give many gifts."*
>
> *(Proverbs 6:32-35 NASB)*

CHAPTER 5

SOFT RAIN

Imagine a series of soft rain showers, and each time it rains, a few pieces of a puzzle fall to the earth. I innocently pick them up as I find them. I don't think it odd to find a puzzle piece or two; somebody might have dropped them. I gather the random pieces in a wooden box. As time goes by, I fit some of the pieces together. I believe that I am starting to figure out my puzzling life.

I have been praying ardently for a yoga teacher or guru to enter my life. In my prayers, I request … *the wisdom to help others, regardless of how much suffering I must endure.* God hears my persistent prayers, and they manifest, but certainly not as I expected….

September fourteenth starts like any other normal day. I wake up and splash water on my face. I cook some home fries and scrambled eggs for breakfast. I sit down to eat, as usual, on my porch. My cat, Safire, nuzzles my leg. Then it begins to rain softly. I notice a few puzzle pieces on the ground by my doorstep. How bizarre! It is like they fell from the sky.

DOWSING

After my endeavors for a retreat on Saline Island failed, I set a new course. I become a dowsing fanatic. It's relatively easy to do, with the National Dowsing Headquarters located in my hometown of Danville, Vermont. At first, I am simply curious. I am my own teacher. I dowse to find out about dowsing. Soon, I discover a way to immerse myself by escaping into an exciting and unknown spiritual world that is providing me with answers normally hidden from view.

Dowsing is an ancient form of divination used to seek information. It utilizes handheld tools such as L-rods, pendulums, and even the body rocking forward and backward to provide answers in a kinesthetic way with either a yes or no, numbers, or by pin-pointing a location. Dowsing is most commonly known in association with searching for underground water, but it can also find ley lines and be used to gauge energy levels. Dowsing can be applied to search for artifacts, missing persons, substances, and entities.

Perhaps I am not properly educated or protected for dealing with the spirits I am calling forth. Initially, I start by dowsing for water and energy lines and then dowse rocks, plants, and animals. I set up energy grids around my home with rocks I haul from a nearby brook. Dowsing is generally related to forms of earth energy, which leads me to my favorite topic: healing. I begin to use dowsing to find ways to heal my family, my friends, and myself.

Dowsing begins to encompass all facets of my life. Dowsing guides me about what to eat, whom to meet, and where to go. I am having fun! But sometimes, when I am not specific about a question, or when I am tired, my answers come in riddles. I begin to wonder what spirits guide dowsing and if those spirits are always looking out for my best interests. I convince myself that little harm can come from two L-shaped metal rods as a gauge for a spirit to answer yes or no.

"Let no one be found among you who sacrifices their son or daughter in the fire, who practices divination or sorcery, interprets omens, engages in witchcraft, or casts spells, or who is a medium or spiritist or who consults the dead. Anyone who does these things is detestable to the Lord; because of these same detestable

practices the Lord your God will drive out those nations before you."

(Deuteronomy 18:10-12 NIV)

It turns out that today is anything but normal. Through dowsing, I am sent a code of ethics concerning communication with spirits, which I write down in my laptop. In addition, I am given a warning that I should not share this code of ethics or I will pay a hefty price. I promise to never reveal it or allow anybody access to it. Dowsing informs me that I will receive the final instruction after I sit in lotus position for fifteen minutes. This is not an easy task. After my back injury, I have had extremely tight thighs and hip muscles. I could probably get into lotus position for a few minutes, but fifteen minutes would be excruciatingly painful.

THE FINAL INSTRUCTION

I take a deep breath and sit down in lotus posture, determined to meditate for fifteen minutes. I want to receive that final instruction. I have experienced a lot of physical pain; when it will not go away, it engulfs my whole world. Pain is like an annoying, drunken friend. I can tolerate it, but I wish it would just go somewhere else. Over time I have learned to adapt and accept pain as my reality. The pain is easier to handle when I have the ability to stop it. I am curious about that final instruction, so I don't. While in the posture, I rub my palms together rapidly until they are burning hot. I take a few deep breaths and blow into my hands. Next, I do a series of short breaths through my nose, called "the breath of fire." Now my mind is clear. I focus on my third eye.

After I complete fifteen minutes in lotus posture, I lie flat on my back to relax. Suddenly, my legs start to tremble in short rapid movements. It works its way up through my legs, up my back, down my arms, and across my face. It feels like something is trying to crawl inside my body. My legs twist tightly around each other like a pretzel. With my legs still squeezing tightly, I go up in a shoulder stand. My breath is shallow. While inverted, I perform the breath of fire in short bursts to contract my abdomen. Suddenly, a swirling smoke enters my heart. I feel movement under my skin near my heart. It's like space is shifting and adjusting. It's not uncomfortable. I don't feel afraid. Next, there is a mild tingling as my spirit and that of another merge to share the same space.

As the author, I feel inclined to place a disclaimer at this point. If any reader is foolish enough to try these same silly steps, I need to warn you about one tiny side effect: your nervous system gets fried!

What just unfolded feels natural, yet I know it's an uncommon occurrence. I admit, I am not sure how it all fully transpired. Let me just say, I am not alone anymore. I am fully awake and aware of experiencing some new sensations. There are no instruction manuals about this sort of thing. This is how I can best describe it: a doorway to my spiritual perception opens up. I am suspended in time and space somewhere in the universe. For a lack of words, I will call it the cosmic consciousness. There is not just one spirit, but simultaneously many spirits coexist in this space.

When you open the door to a house and walk inside, light and air also come through that doorway. They are not invited. They are not good or bad. They just always enter when the door is open. It felt that same way with the spirits. I am not afraid. Once the door leading to the cosmic consciousness is open, it does not just slam shut. It remains open a while. In a way, the whole universe is in there. Either I enter it or it enters me. Then we merge together. Maybe this universe was inside of me all along. I just never knew how to access it.

Regardless, there is one spirit present that predominates. It seemed to have the power to enter my body. This spirit will hereafter be called "The Guru." The Guru opened the doorway. According to the Bible, a spirit, be it good or evil, must be invited in order to enter a body. I took that step, somewhat unintentionally. I also believe my actions, the proper breathing technique, and the yoga postures were essential.

SWAMI SRI YUKTESWAR

I lie flat on my back and stretch my arms up above my head. I let out a 300-year-old yawn. Then I sit up and watch a car pass by on the road. The Guru looks through my eyes at the car. In my mind, The Guru says, "That is a car!" Perhaps his way of adjusting is to focus on the first moving object that comes into view.

A deep, gentle voice whispers, "I am Swami Sri Yukteswar." The Guru's voice is distinct, and his thoughts are separate from mine. It's clear that we are sharing the same body. We are sharing the same senses, and mine feel slightly enhanced. He is aware of my emotions and my thoughts. We communicate in my mind, but it sounds like we are speaking, as in a regular conversation. Our conversations have no limits or boundaries. He responds to my questions in a polite manner with the utmost patience.

This guru has composure. I acknowledge that I have merged with somebody who has great power and understanding. My posture changes. I hold myself more like a king, with my sternum and side body lifted up. My head faces forward, no longer looking down. When I assume this subtle shift in posture, I feel his inner peace and confidence surface.

The Guru explains he is from a lineage called Kriya yoga. He has entered 30 bodies prior to mine. He is able to retain the knowledge from each mind. He learned the technique of how to enter a body through Kriya yoga, as instructed by his guru, Lahiri Mahasaya. I have a copy of *The Autobiography of a Yogi*, by his disciple, Paramahansa Yogananda, and begin to read the parts about Swami Sri Yukteswar. Overall, there is a sense of timelessness. There is no urgency. I don't rush. I am living in the present moment.

I did pray for a guru. Somebody upstairs was listening. Perhaps next time I need to be more specific and pray, "I want a guru to enter my life — *not* my body." Anyhow, I am thankful and feel our student and teacher connection is based on a mutual desire, even though I can't fully grasp all that is unfolding. Yoga philosophy says that gurus and disciples come together when the time is right. Swami Sri Yukteswar explains that he is a guru of wisdom, which was part of my prayer request. Perhaps we are destined to be together.

THE FIRST FEW DAYS WITH THE GURU

The Guru and I go through some cosmetic changes. We no longer wear any metal because it affects the energy flow. I rip the zippers and metal buttons off a few pairs of loose-fitting pants. The texture of the clothing against my skin becomes important. I only sleep a few hours each night. My typical meal is simple grains with a steamed green vegetable and a piece of fruit for dessert or a snack. I drink a few quarts of mega-green spirulina the first few days. Then I call the local health food store and order a case of it. My sense is that this assists in the transformation on a cellular level; plus it boosts my energy.

I ask The Guru to talk about the past bodies he has entered. He is reluctant, but makes a few remarks. He has entered the bodies of both men and women in various parts of the world. Once, he entered the body of a doctor, which I conclude was a positive experience. He prefers to speak of his life as a guru in India and speaks fondly about his disciple, Paramahansa Yogananda. He tells me about taking long walks with him along the river, the fragrance of the blooming trees, and the smells of spring in India. These are the memories that he cherishes. Being raised in a home next to a river, I can relate to the tranquil sound of the flowing water.

During the first night, The Guru guides my hands to do manipulations on my body while I am in a semi-sleeping state. The Guru is definitely in charge here and takes over to use my hands to self-massage or press key trigger points. I hold stretches in strange positions, which bring relief to the muscles in my legs, back, neck, and shoulders. They have been tense for years. The Guru has a heightened sense of body awareness, superior to my comprehension. After the first night, I am given step-by-step instructions to learn the most important stretches to benefit my body.

The Guru sternly says, "You need to pay attention." It normally takes a few repetitions for me to retain a new routine.

I am shown a wonderful stretch where I grab my left toe and pull it behind my head. The Guru is a patient teacher and extends compassion for the condition of my aching body.

For ten years, I failed to acknowledge my limits or listen to my body's warning signs, like mild pain. Eventually, it became a habit to push myself without taking breaks or stopping, even when my body needed to relax. I sense The Guru did not know how tight or restricted different muscles and body parts were until he got inside. Even a guru can't choose a body and take it for a test run. He must work with the body he has chosen. He explains that it is not an easy process to enter a body; my understanding is that the soft spot on the top of a baby's head, known as the fontanel, is the portal where a spirit enters. I assume many factors must line up and that one gets chosen partially by destiny or grace of the Guru.

Leaving a body is a different story. He says, "It's painless to leave a body after it dies."

I hope there are other options!

During the day we practice focusing on an object for ten minutes. The real transformations will take place in my mind. I am instructed to find a small object with a glimmer, then stare at that spot. It is best if I don't blink … just focus. I make a joke during this exercise. The Guru sternly brings me back to focus on the object. During this practice, he is serious. If my gaze is broken, then my attention is lacking. He tells me that communication can occur simply through thoughts between a disciple and their guru, but the disciple must develop the ability to focus.

During this time, I notice that I can locate select people, objects, and driving directions through what I call my spiritual radar. A few days after The Guru enters the scene, my laptop is stolen from my home. I left it on the desk in my house, open to the page with the code of ethics concerning communicating with spirits, that I promised to never leave accessible. (Oops!) I assume the thief is a drug addict friend of my lower level tenant, Lizzy. I don't try to find the laptop or the thief. What I really need is to find a coworker who has a backup for an important work project that was on the stolen laptop.

My coworker is not at his home, so I drive away from his house and start to think about him. About a half-mile away, I pull over. I walk across the road, jump over a guard rail, trudge through some tall grass, and cross over a small brook. It opens up into a field where there are two high school soccer games in progress. Somehow, I know this is where he will be. I walk straight up to him.

TRACING MY NATIVE HERITAGE

I sit late one afternoon on a grassy hill to meditate. I go deep inside to hear the birds and feel the wind. The sun begins to set as I stare up toward the pink, wispy clouds. I see a wild vision in the clouds. It starts with four Indian chiefs looking down upon the earth. Then I see a pregnant woman with braided hair, reclining on her back with a look of discontent on her face. She leans forward slightly, and a fountain of debris is released from deep within her belly. Afterwards, she leans back, now with a relaxed, contented look. She is Mother Earth spitting up the pollution, the poison in society, and the wrongs done to this planet. The Native Americans and indigenous cultures around the world have generally been ransacked and left displaced. But they know how to live in harmony with nature. They know that their actions affect the next seven generations. Perhaps we can humble ourselves enough to learn from them.

This brings us back to the Native scraping tool I found at my uncle's farm when I was ten years old. I use dowsing to register the aura or energy field around it. An average person will register an aura at 10-20 feet. The flatter top and bottom edge of the scraping tool emits an aura 550 feet, the rear extends 450 feet. The sharpened side edges register 798 feet, and the spear point registers out a whopping 1600 feet. Dowsing informs me that it originated in Mississippi with one tribe, passed hands to another tribe, then was in Abenaki hands for 38 years. Each tribe blessed the stone in their own way. I can feel it emanating a healing power when I hold it.

Early one morning, I take the Native scraping tool and begin a ceremony. I am in bed in my underwear under the blankets. I firmly press the sharp point to trace a line starting on the inside of my right instep, up across my hip, along my shoulder, and down my right arm to my wrist. I pause at major points in my hip, shoulder, and wrist. Some sort of healing is starting to be activated by the Native scraping tool. I sense it would be better if I am lying flat on the earth.

There is dew on the grass and it's about forty degrees. The sun is starting to rise. I lie down, shivering, and retrace the lines over the same points. My mind focuses intently on the Native scraping tool and the connection it has with the ancient people that first carved it. The Guru and I are heading into uncharted spiritual territory. The Guru is keenly interested in revealing any knowledge from the Native scraping tools prior ancestral owners. My sense is that being of Abenaki descent provided the key to access this gateway.

I feel like the lines that I trace on my body with the stone have opened a portal door. I am in a dream state. I watch my Native lineage, tracing back through my Native ancestors, generation by generation. It's being stacked up in a pyramid of blue, glowing human silhouettes. Suddenly, it stops like a spinning slot machine. I am at a point in time when a primitive ancestor is massively upset. Tears begin to flow from my own eyes. I can feel our connection through my flesh and my spirit. My ancient ancestor is horrendously angry because some of our ancestors lost "The Gift." It's one of the most treasured gifts in the ancient culture: the ability to communicate with animals.

Then we begin to merge. I temporarily embody this ancient being. Next, I jump up and stand with my legs spread wide. I hold the rock with both hands over my head and yell out in his ancient language. It has not been spoken for dozens of generations. My voice echoes off the surrounding green mountains. In my vision, I see the energy from the Native scraping tool shoot upward in a blue, laser light beam that radiates up and circles the earth. I sense that we are attempting to communicate the ancient wisdom from his extinct culture to our modern generation.

In my underwear, I walk through the woods to a pond behind my home. I am still embodying the spirit of my ancient ancestor. I begin to speak in chatters and grunts, beckoning the wild animals to come closer. There is no response. I have never heard these noises coming from my lips before. I call out in hawk squawks, deer grunts, coyote yelps, fox barks, and rabbit squeaks. Sometimes, it's a high-pitched sound made by sucking my breath in. Animals like to gather near the pond. I realize that if the trust between animals and humans has dissolved, it will take days or weeks of living in the woods with the wild animals to reestablish our friendship.

I walk back down by my house. I go to a wire-mesh fenced in area where I am raising ten white turkeys. I've been struggling to find enough fresh green grass for the turkeys. I rip down the wire enclosure and let them all run free. In a high-pitched language, I tell them to stay away from the road and that there are foxes and coyotes around. I let them know they can go up to the pond for water if they want, but I will place food and water inside their shelter. I speak loudly into the woods and inform the coyotes and foxes that the turkeys are loose. They may take one or two, but we need to share and live in harmony. The turkeys stay near the barn and live much happier, healthier lives.

SPEAKING IN NATIVE TONGUES

After I experience the merging in spirit with this ancient Native ancestor, I gain the knowledge to speak different Native American languages. I examine a chart of all the Native American tribes in North America and identify fifty languages that I can speak. The Guru is most interested in this phenomenon. Even today, if I speak out to pray in what one might call "tongues," it comes out in a Native language. It is a gift. It's a hard one for most Christians to understand. I use these Native languages to pray or sing when guided. There is a feeling of gratitude in the air when I sing a song or pray in a language that has not been spoken for eons. Native American ancestors smile down when they hear a language that they cherished and once spoke being rekindled.

Do I know for certain that I am speaking fluent Native American languages and not a bunch of gibberish? No, but what is more important to me is that when I pray or sing in these languages, it's from my heart. I don't always feel comfortable singing them around strangers. When anyone speaks in a foreign language, they get some funny looks. On rare occasions, I command unwanted spirits to leave a body or request healing by utilizing the Native American languages and songs.

I don't understand these mysteries well enough to explain it, but these Native languages are filled with power. Those who are the recipients of my prayers or songs feel positive shifts, in the form of healing.

The primal feeling that I experienced with that ancient spirit can be felt by all people. It doesn't really matter if your ancestors are Native American or not. We all have the ability to connect with nature: the earth, the trees, the water, the stars, the animals, and ourselves. There is no clutter attached to this feeling. It will remain eternally pure and accessible for all people.

LESSONS ON THE TRUTH

y life has been intense since The Guru entered it. Changes continue to take place in my body, emotions, and mind. Sometimes, different spirits that I know are not The Guru communicate with me. On these occasions, I start to learn how to discern between different spirits.

For a spell, I begin having delusions in all five senses. It happens one by one. My hunch is that The Guru has control over my senses. He starts to alter my sense perception. One morning, the scrambled eggs at The Lamb's house have that pungent smell of rotten eggs and they taste like chalk. I spit them out and gather all the eggs cartons from the fridge and hide them in the woodshed. I look at a picture of my sister's family on the mantel. Half have red eyes. I am sure the devil is living in that half and the rest are angels. I begin to question all that I know, because I no longer know what is real. My senses are all screwy. Some of my friends and family are starting to think I have lost my mind.

The Lamb probably thought she would find some relief when I say, "I am going to tell you why I am being so weird."

I tell her with all sincerity, "Extraterrestrial beings have come to take over the earth. They have chosen me as an initial test dummy. I can feel where they inserted a computer chip in my skull. It gives them the power to control my actions." I can feel where the chips were inserted, so it must be real. When I talk to my mother in this way, she is filled with concern.

She begins to think, *Ahhhh, my poor son really has lost all his marbles.*

Perhaps, I am a puppet and The Guru is playing games by pulling strings to control my senses. If that is not the case, there is a chemical imbalance in my mind. Regardless, I learn from these experiences that I cannot always trust my own senses. It's contrary to what I normally accept as the truth. I am experiencing some exceptions to the rules. If I am battling some unknown spirit, I can't always believe what I see, smell, feel, taste, or touch. The delusions in my five senses bring my awareness to a new level. I need to operate from a deeper place where the truth resides.

LUSTY THOUGHTS

The Guru states he is not without flaws. Each person has issues. They either work through them in their past lives or they come up again. The Guru tactfully explains that he has a problem with lustful thoughts. He tells me, "Now it's our problem. You need to get it under control." Great! I have a lusty guru. Maybe this is The Guru's way of saying I need to face my own lusty thoughts. If somebody tells me not to think about sex, then it instantly causes a sexual image to pop into my head. Remember, I have had a circus of pornographic fantasies floating in front of my eyes since I was eight.

The Guru commands, "Stop thinking of sexual fantasies!" It makes me anxious and fills me with fear. I try to focus on something else and clear my mind. But then another sexual fantasy pops in. We try a few different strategies with no success.

The Guru says, "I am open to your suggestions."

My suggestion is sprinting down the road. Often hard physical exercise distracts my mind.

He says, "If you think a sexual thought, you will be struck dead, so you had better run fast."

The Guru has a sense of humor.

Luckily, it's not an instant death, but when I have lusty thoughts, I feel my stomach acid gnawing at my insides. This gives more relevance to the notion that if I am not able to focus on something other than a sexual fantasy, The Guru could leave my body and then I really will drop dead. I decide that I better run fast ... more fear ... lustier thoughts ... *don't do it again* ... more anxiety ... and more fear ... and more sexual fantasies. Oh no! Pain in the stomach! *I will die soon ... better run faster ... am I scared? Yes! I am scared! I can't run any faster and I am out of breath!*

What I am attempting to do, without success, is repress my thoughts. Joe Zychik, in his book *The Most Personal Addiction: How I Overcame Sexual Addiction and How Anyone Can*, explains his revelation regarding repression,

> "*I knew I had discovered something so important, it could change my life and the lives of millions of addicted people. But getting that message out took another 25 years. So let me share with you what I have observed since 1975 about repression and how addiction is successfully overcome.*
>
> "*I define repression as: an attempt to consistently exclude from consciousness a thought or feeling you decide is threatening. If you conclude that a thought or feeling is not good for you, that it is bad, that it is a threat, your first reaction will be an attempt to consistently keep it out of your conscious mind. The attempt to continuously keep it out is repression. Repression occurs two ways: 1. You consciously try to drive the desire out of your mind, and/or 2. Your subconscious automatically keeps it out. The most common form of repression is subconscious.*
>
> "*The symptom of subconscious repression is: At the beginning of the attempt to stop, the desire seems to have gone away or lost most of its power. If you*

ever attempted to overcome addiction and failed, you probably went through a phase in which you truly felt like the addictive desire had left you or had lost most of its power. Although you sincerely believed you had triumphed over your addiction, what you were experiencing was subconscious repression.

"To protect itself from distortion, the mind sends out pain signals when it encounters repression. The pain of repression can be greater than the pain of acting addictively. To relieve the pain of repression, you return to the addiction.

"A client of Joe Zychik exclaims, 'You mean I don't have to push the thoughts out of my mind?' I told him, 'Your attempt to push them out makes it impossible for you to face them. The mind needs to experience its own emotions so that they can be coped with.' He dropped his Twelve Step meeting and his conventional, licensed therapist. I taught him how to experience an addictive desire fully and completely. Then I taught him how to choose whether or not to act on it. Every step of the way he told me, 'This is the exact opposite of everything I was told.'" [6]

THE TRUTH

One of Swami Sri Yukteswar's biggest lessons is to understand what is meant by "truth." It really has an impact. The truth has many faces and is relative to the circumstances. What I have been told or tell myself and believe for years does not make it true. In the past, I chose to live an illusion because I did not want to accept the truth about some aspects of myself. If I can let go of the security of my past mixed-up beliefs, I can dare to doubt everything. Now, I can start fresh. Slowly, I investigate each situation, question my own knowledge, discover from the facts, not preconceived notions. When I hit a wall,

I rely on God's wisdom or "my heart" to discern the deeper mysteries. God wants me to know the truth.

When the truth is told, it resounds with divine purity.

One day, The Guru says, "You cannot accept anything I say as true." Just my luck. I get a lusty guru that lies … or maybe not. Now it's up to me to figure out what is true and what is not! After I think about it, I realize this teaching about the truth is an incredibly real gift.

> *"You are of your father the devil, and you want to do the desires of your father. He was a murderer from the beginning, and does not stand in the truth because there is no truth in him. Whenever he speaks a lie, he speaks from his own nature, for he is a liar and the father of lies."*
>
> *(John 8:44 NASB)*

The devil always uses lies to deceive. I cannot assume people are always telling me the truth. People lie all the time, but the worst offense is the lies we tell ourselves. The truth can be laced with lies. And if you know something is a lie, then the truth can be deduced from it. Actually, the truth may change over time. What is true for me may not be true for you. Why would I expect The Guru to be an exception?

MY PARENTS TELL LIES

During my teen years, The Lion made a promise that if I could go through high school without drinking alcohol, he would buy me a car. It was an incentive that worked. I took his promise seriously. After graduation, I passed by a black 1937 Pontiac with suicide doors parked at a garage in Plainfield, Vermont. On a cardboard sign in the window, it was marked $800. I told The Lion, "I have found the car I want." He said, "I don't believe you made it through high school without drinking."

In his way, he taught me that I should never trust anybody, not even my own parents, especially if it had to do with money. I put up a fuss. He couldn't prove I was drinking and reluctantly agreed to fork over half the money.

My brother, Gadget, is a natural mechanic, inventor, and collector. When he was nine years old, he made a cart with wooden wheels, a car steering wheel, a back bed for hauling, and a brake handle. Gadget got a worse deal; The Lion never offered him a car. He bought his first car and had a few Volkswagen Beetles that he was fixing up in the yard. The Lion said to him, "If you don't remove those pieces of crap out of the yard within one week, they will all be hauled to the junkyard."

When my sister, Priceless, graduated, there was no deal to be met. As a teenager, she had her own private phone line in her bedroom, and a pony. He surprised her by secretly purchasing her a gift: a 1977 240D Mercedes Benz. It was parked on the lawn, all washed and waxed, with a big pink ribbon on top.

It's up to me to figure out with The Lion and The Guru what is the truth in each situation. But I sense that when the Guru says, "You can't accept anything I say as true," that it comes from a place of caring about me. When The Lion makes a promise or says he wants to help me out as an adult regarding money, it can come from a place of taking care of himself first.

It's not always convenient for The Lion to honor his word. I notice that his story is sometimes altered or parts are left out depending upon the receiver. One of the quotes he repeats is, "What you perceive is what you believe." Sometimes, he persuades others to perceive what *he* wants them to believe. In this case, the truth is twisted, it somehow became insignificant to him.

Truth is defined in Merriam Webster dictionary as "sincerity in action, character, and utterance".

At the other extreme lives The Lamb. I know many sons believe that their mom is a saint, but after The Lamb sewed over two dozen quilts to donate to AIDS babies, I seriously wondered about her.

One day while driving along, I asked her, "Have you ever lied?"

She said, "Yes, I lied once."

I said, "As a teenager I lied to you many times. There must have been times you told me little lies?"

She replied, "No, I only lied once in my life."

I said, "Okay, tell me about it."

She was slightly embarrassed, but shared her story, "When I was a girl on the farm, your grandfather would often punish my older brother for little or no reason. He was searching for him with the belt and he asked me if I knew where my brother was. I knew where he was hiding, but I said, 'no'."

I said, "Mom, that does not even count as a lie."

There are times when a lie resounds with truth because it comes from a place of love. In her case, telling the truth would not have protected her brother. The Lamb lives in that place of love. Even when she told what she considered to be a lie, it resounded with the truth.

While in this spiritually-altered state, I am flying high. It's all one big adventure. I am living, at times in a delusional state, with moments of fear or ecstatic bliss. The Guru goes along for the ride and sometimes encourages me to go further into these wild illusions until they explode into nothingness. Once I understand the truth, it seems ridiculous. It's usually all in my mind. That's how I make progress. If The Guru were to point out my flaws, it would be less effective. Until the truth reveals itself, I am haunted by these dragon-size shadows on the wall that turn out to be tiny moths innocently flying around a candle flame. Fear is the reality that we are fed, create, or cling to when unable to discern the truth. Ignorance is a veil. The role of a guru is to guide the student to lift the veil for themselves.

The Holy Scriptures are meant to guide us toward that truth. The spiritual teachers who wrote them had a strong connection to God. They listened to His soft voice. It's natural when one understands the truth to want to share it with others. But Jesus took it beyond the bounds, when He said,

"I am the way and the truth and the life. No one comes to the Father except through me."

(John 14:6 NIV)

Jesus is in union with God. He did not just come to convey the truth. Jesus *is* the truth and the life. This is mind-boggling! These are qualities that we normally associate with God. Jesus is distinct from God. But He offers a way to get to God. That's probably worth checking out.

One day, The Guru says rather nonchalantly, "You are going to read 32 spiritual books. The Holy Bible will be the first one."

THE TRUTH IS IN YOUR HEART

The truth cannot be debated if it comes from that sacred place inside your heart. When we come to this conclusion on our own, it's more powerful and meaningful; plus we retain it. Let's wander off the track and do a short exercise to try it!

Sit comfortably, close your eyes, and enter the space in your heart. Just be there for five deep breaths. Really relax your legs and arms, shoulders, and jaw muscles. Breathe in love with a soft smile on your face. When you exhale, breathe out any tension. Now, bring to mind a person or animal that you love dearly. See their face and feel your love for them. Be with them for a few moments and enjoy it. Nice!

Now imagine that a spiritual teacher comes along and taps you on the shoulder.

She says, "You do *not* really love this person or animal."

Do you believe this spiritual teacher? Is there any doubt in your heart about your love? If you have any doubt, return to your heart to find the truth. Once you feel and know the truth from your heart, then speak your response back to this spiritual teacher out loud. Explain to the spiritual teacher how you know the truth about your love for this person or animal. Can you feel how powerful it is to own an undisputable truth from your heart? ■

CLAN OF THE HAWK

I am at a convenience store reading a historical paper about an Abenaki exhibit in Newport, Vermont. This article, like other occurrences, seems planted, waiting for me to come along during this preordained moment. I call and make arrangements with Bea Nelson to have her examine my Native scraping tool, and to visit the Abenaki exhibit.

I am wearing black sport pants cut off jagged under the knee when I removed the zippers, leather moccasins, and a Mexican wool blanket. It's fashioned into a poncho with a huge Aztec head on the center of the back. I carry a rabbit-fur pouch with the Native scraping tool in it. I am later told that during this altered state, I have pinpoint black pupils that indent my eyes further into my high cheek bones. I walk with confidence and often stare off with a profound look when I converse with my guru.

The Lamb has an interest in our family genealogy. She joins me during my visit to Bea Nelson, who enthusiastically shows us the local Abenaki arrowheads and tools found along the shores of Lake Memphremagog. I have a sense of urgency and ask her targeted questions about the local artifacts. I say, "There is nothing remotely similar to my Native scraping tool."

We go to a table displaying a map. Bea says, "Show me on the map where your Native artifact was found. If you want, it can be established as a sacred Native American site."

She mentions the local Abenaki tribe called Clan of the

Hawk and suggests that I go meet Chief Spirit Water. Her proposal sets off an alarm. We must go visit him ... today! Time becomes tediously slow as Bea continues to ask questions and search the map. I become impatient and insist that we must leave. I rudely clap my hands loudly. I say, "I must leave now." Bea is taken aback by the loud clapping. I apologize and we depart to visit Chief Spirit Water.

SHAKING UP CHIEF SPIRIT WATER

We arrive at Evansville Trading Post, which Chief Spirit Water owns and operates. It's a central gathering point in town for groceries, gifts, hunting and fishing supplies, and everything you could imagine to sustain a Vermont village during the harsh winters. I ask my mother to wait as I inquire inside for the whereabouts of Chief Spirit Water. I am told he will return in one hour, so I walk down the road across a bridge and sit beside the road to meditate and gather my thoughts. A neighbor drives into his yard in an old pickup truck, eyeballing me. A huge maple tree has recently been struck by lightning and has fallen on his lawn. The sound of chimes ring out gently in the flow of the wind. The man walks gingerly by the stacks of canning jars on his front porch.

I call out, "That tree being hit is a sign that change will come."

He says, "Something is in the air."

I sit on a rock in the sun and speak with my guru, reciting the facts that I will relay. Chief Spirit Water returns. I meet him in the gravel parking lot.

I introduce myself by saying, "I am a yogic monk from the Kriya order with a message of great importance."

Chief Spirit Water is a grandfather of sorts, gentle and calm. He has white hair down around his shoulders, covering the back of his head. His round eyes sparkle and smile in the corners. He tells me that he is on a tight schedule today.

I explain, "We need you to be the father of a new nation for a new order."

I am not getting through to him. I explain the situation in Abenaki. He attempts to walk away.

He says, "I want no part as a father of a new nation."

I grab him by the shoulders to force him to stop so he will listen. He brushes me off, slightly shaken and visibly upset as he continues to walk away. I know grabbing him was rude, probably an insult, especially when he is the chief. After the incident, I feel sorry that I used force to get his attention.

CEREMONIAL GATHERING GROUND

The Lamb and I stop at the Clan of the Hawk's ceremonial gathering ground as part of our Native heritage exploration. The grounds are peaceful and surrounded by tall pine trees. We walk around in the sunny, golden fields of grass. I am in a dreamy state, viewing my surroundings as if the village were in a glass snow globe. There is a Christian church with a small steeple, which strikes me initially as being out of place on these Native grounds. Inside there are wooden benches. On the wall there is a poster showing the territories where all the Native American tribes lived in North America. There are books on the table explaining tracking and wilderness survival skills. This must be the place where the younger ones gather to learn from Chief Spirit Water and the other elders.

Next to the church there is a small, barn-board building; a hand-painted sign proclaims it to be the Native American Museum. There is no lock on the door. I enter to find rows of glass cases filled with bones and arrowheads. There are dozens of stuffed animals and birds, and furs limply hanging off the benches, from the ceiling, and in any open space remaining. The museum feels like it's cage-cleaning day at the zoo and all the animals are squeezed into one tiny room and forgotten.

Beside the museum is a small rustic cabin, with an old

wooden chair shedding red paint resting alone on the porch. The door is wide open, revealing a small wood stove with a scorched cooking pot perched on top. Behind the two buildings weaves a wide stream surrounded and filled with boulders of assorted sizes and colors. I notice gray clay seeping down from the far side of the stream bank into the water. Willoughby Brook flows through these sacred grounds, like a gigantic, glittering snake that slides back and forth from the deeper cold waters of Lake Willoughby. The whole place makes me feel like I am being welcomed back home after a long journey. I feel the warmth, like slipping my hands back into woolen mittens on a frigid winter day.

In the center of the horseshoe of buildings, there is a fire pit encircled by a wooden fence. A few car seats and wooden benches are scattered randomly around the outside of the fence, facing toward the circle. There is a small tin roof over one area, which must be where a small group gathers to play drums and chant Native songs. I imagine a few men from the Clan of the Hawk tribe, decked out in their traditional leather with fringes and feathers, dancing around the fire during their powwow. But times have changed; maybe nowadays most of the men wear blue jeans and t-shirts.

There is a labyrinth made out of pointed stones in a far field with tall, uncut grass clumps poking up close to the rocks. I walk over to the labyrinth with The Lamb. I brought a small drum and begin to play a steady beat as The Lamb enters the maze. I strike the drum to the beat of her slow, mindful steps. I sing a song in Abenaki. It is a beautiful language. I sing about the connection between Mother Earth and the sun. The Lamb usually has a natural smile on her face, but I notice her smile expresses additional pleasure because today she is embracing her heritage. When she reaches the center, I stop playing the drum and send her loving thoughts.

A tall man in denim overall jeans walks toward us. He has long, stringy hair and a week-old scruff that has not yet grown in enough to hide his rock-solid chin, jaw, and cheekbones. His facial structure, by no coincidence, resembles the rocks in the labyrinth. He is Stone Tree, maker of medicine wheels and divine dowser of the rock nation. He introduces himself and escorts us over to the other side of the field to show us two medicine wheels that he has formed. These are fairly small medicine wheels, each eight feet in diameter. He explains that some rocks are buried under the ground. Then a pattern of rocks is overlaid, and the pointed rocks sticking up around the outside are set in place last.

He says, "It creatz good medicine."

I tell him briefly of the vision of the new order. He stops to roll a cigarette and starts to rock back and forth. He gives a confirming nod of agreement about what is to come. I learn that Stone Tree communicates with each rock to receive specific instructions through body dowsing before finding its new home. Many rocks came from the river over a mile away. He will stop his old beat-up pickup truck whenever a rock calls out, regardless of its size. Then he will find a way to pry, push, carry, or pull each rock onto his rusty truck bed in order to bring it back to his gathering spot under the pine trees.

Stone Tree walks us by Willoughby Brook and talks about the spirits he has seen rushing by.

With a slow drawl in his voice and wide eyes, he says, "Some of themz spiritz are the size of buffalos, with wings."

He insists that I meet the Clan Mother. We walk toward the pine trees. When I get my first glimpse of his Smithsonian-size collection of rocks stacked along the road edge and under the pine trees, I am flabbergasted. There are hundreds and hundreds of rocks. They are everywhere. One black, prickly stone is the shape of a whale fin; another looks like the mouth of an alligator; and a row of long, black stalactites sits on a mound of pine needles. A crystal temple sits on a clump of moss. I am told that fairies frolic around this stone. He has also seen them gathering the crystal dust to spread about the forest.

The rocks are eerie projections of Native spirit animals. Each called out to him through its prehistoric fossilized stone shield. Every rock holds a tale, and Stone Tree is the curator of this mammoth-size exhibit. It becomes clear that Stone Tree is capable of telling his rock tales as long as somebody is willing to stay and listen. There is no official closing hour. Besides, some stones, such as the panoptic panther and the planetary asteroids, are more active during the night.

CLAN MOTHER, LARGER THAN LIFE

The outer walls of Clan Mother and Stone Tree's home are made from blue tarps laced together with yellow rope. It extends out and is tied around several living pine trees. Clan Mother swings open a blue tarp that forms the door of their home. She has the exuberance of the opening act on stage at the county fair. She is 300 pounds and larger than life, with uncombed, jet-black hair and tobacco-stained teeth. She has tree-trunk-size legs that she quickly explains are radiating with pain.

The sun strikes Clan Mother's clear eyes. The Guru, Swami Sri Yukteswar, instantly recognizes Clan Mother. She is his favorite revered disciple: Paramahansa Yogananda. Our gaze becomes that of two long-lost lovers being reunited. I sit cross-legged on the ground and she in a chair. We face each other. I hold her hands. Tears of joy stream from her eyes.

Clan Mother chokes back the tears to say, "I knew you were coming to visit me. I have been waiting for you. I saw it in my dreams."

We speak for a few minutes and then settle side-by-side into a silent, meditative, heavenly state. When at last I arise to depart, Stone Tree hands me a gift. It's a large bowling-ball-size, white rock. It captures the shape and grandness of Clan Mother.

I depart, saying, "I will be back tomorrow."

MAKING THE MEDICINE WHEEL

I return the next day by myself. Stone Tree and I search to find a location to make a new medicine wheel. Its purpose will be to connect the ancient indigenous ways with the modern-day generation. Once in the woods, Stone Tree shows me a spot where he has marked out a thirty-foot medicine wheel using yellow corn kernels. The lines make a pentagram star. The corn pieces intersect and cross each other, forming various-sized triangles. We agree this will be the perfect location for our new medicine wheel.

We draw a circle in the center the size of a manhole and extend the five-arms of the star around it. Then four lines extend out from the end of each of the five star points. We move slowly and remain completely silent. He painstakingly dowses each location and locates the right stone from his collection. It is placed on the ground to mark its ordained destination. Each stone is partially buried according to his precise calibrations. He is like an architect following the blueprint for laying the foundation of a skyscraper.

I see through my spiritual eye a snake, as thick as a fifty-five-gallon drum and as long as a New York City block, slithering toward us. Covering its body are red, black, and yellow interwoven triangles. During my time spent in the outback of Australia, I was told the dreamtime stories about this snake.

THE RAINBOW SERPENT STORY

"Far off in Dreamtime, there were only people, no animals or birds, no trees or bushes, no hills or mountains.

"*The country was flat. Goorialla, the great Rainbow Serpent, stirred and set off to look for his own tribe. He travelled across Australia from South to North. He reached Cape York where he stopped and made a big red mountain called Naralullgan. He listened to the wind and heard only voices speaking strange languages.*

"*This is not my country, the people here speak a different tongue. I must look for my own people. Goorialla left Naralullgan and his huge body made a deep gorge where he came down. He travelled North for many days and his tracks made the creeks and rivers as he journeyed North. Goorialla made two more mountains, one of the Naradunga was long made of granite, the other had sharp peaks and five caves and was called, Minalinha. One day Goorialla heard singing and said, "Those are my people, they are holding a big Bora." At the meeting place of the two rivers, Goorialla found his own people singing and dancing. He watched for a long time, then he came out and was welcomed by his people. He showed the men how to dress properly and taught them to dance. A big storm was gathering, so all the people built humpies for shelter.*

"*Two young men, the bil-bil or Rainbow Lorikeet brothers came looking for shelter but no one had any room. They asked their grandmother, the Star Woman but she had too many dogs and couldn't help them. the Bil-bil brothers went to Goorialla who was snoring in his humpy but he had no room. The rain got heavier and the boys went back to Goorialla and called out that the rain was heavy. Goorialla said, "All right come in now." The Bil-bil bothers ran into Goorialla's mouth and he swallowed them. Then he began to worry about what the people would say when they found the boys missing. He decided to travel North to Bora-bunaru, the only great natural mountain in the land. Next morning the people found that the boys were gone and saw the tracks of Goorialla and knew that he had swallowed them.*

"You may never see these lakes or mountains, but after the rain you will see his spirit in the sky, which is the rainbow. This is the reason why he is called Goorialla the Rainbow Serpent." (7)

The pictures they drew and carved resembled the design on the snake that is slithering around our medicine wheel. I don't feel threatened, but I would not be surprised if this dreamtime snake gobbled down another man. The snake winds its way up to the medicine wheel and silently slides down the center hole, going down, down, down toward the core of the earth.

THE NATIVE SCRAPING TOOL CEREMONY
WITH CLAN MOTHER

Clan Mother invites me inside her earthen home. Behind the blue-tarp walls, there are two bedrooms. Hanging from the walls are furs and woven baskets. The floor of their upper level is dirt. I am led down steps to another level, which is dug into the earth. It all resembles an archeological dig site. On the lower level, there is a wood-burning stove with a few chairs around it. She pours herself some coffee and makes me a cup of tea. We sit down near the wood stove. I give her a copy of *The Autobiography of a Yogi.* I explain, "Reading this book may explain more about the supernatural connection we both feel."

The Guru and disciple both feel an incredibly strong bond of devotion, trust, and respect, far beyond what is normally felt between a father and son or a wife and husband.

I suggest that perhaps Clan Mother can experience some form of healing with the Native scraping tool. She is in favor of anything that could ease the pain in her legs. Her prophetic dream about my arrival adds a certain level of anticipation. We choose a location near a small sweat lodge site by the edge of Willoughby Brook. I carry over a thin futon for her to lie upon. Prior to starting our ceremony, she swallows a good-sized portion of spirulina powder mixed with juice. She happened to have some in her earth home.

The brook is immensely peaceful. I explain how I traced the Native scraping tool up the sides of my body. We take a knife and slit her sweatpants so the rock can trace a line up her legs. I begin chanting in an ancient tongue. In this Native language, I ask Mother Earth to come down and bless our ceremony. I sense that Clan Mother needs to touch the earth; she agrees. I pull her off the futon to rest on the nurturing soil of the earth. I use the point of the healing stone to trace the lines, starting on the inside of her right instep, up across her hip, along her shoulder, and down her right arm to her wrist. I continue to chant by her side for the next ten minutes.

I wonder what she is experiencing.

She is silent and staring wide-eyed up into the sky like she is caught up in a trance. I am waiting for an ancient relative from another generation to pour into her soul.

I ask in a calm voice, "What is happening, Clan Mother?"

Her eyes open as wide as quarters and she replies loudly, "The leaves and the trees above me are moving and alive!"

She raises her arms up toward the sky and vigorously wiggles her fingers. This is not quite what I expected! Of course, her experience is valid, just different from mine. Later on, she mentions that her legs feel slightly better. She is grateful for the ceremony.

LITTLE FOX AND MOON SHADOW

I go over by the church and sit to meditate. I sense that Chief Spirit Water will arrive soon. I want to apologize for shaking him. A dog comes running up to me with the skull of a fox in its mouth. I think it peculiar, but it's the beginning of my learning how the Native spirit can speak through animals or their bones. The skull is an introduction to the arrival of Little Fox.

Little Fox has white hair in a ponytail sticking out from under his rimmed cap and wears mirror shades. His clean-shaven jaw stands out. His female companion, Moon Shadow, is thin, with a dark complexion. She wears a large sun hat. They arrive on foot and both are casually dressed in jeans. My first thought is that they wear these clothes to allow themselves to fit into a crowd unnoticed. Perhaps they are a cosmic couple from another spiritual realm, visiting in disguise. Chief Spirit Water's pickup truck comes rumbling down the dirt road. He has come to join us.

I introduce myself to the group as a yogic monk from the Kriya order. I keep composure and utmost respect. I apologize for grabbing Chief Spirit Water. After a few minutes of conversation, Chief Spirit Water gets back in his pickup truck and heads back to the Trading Post.

Little Fox asks The Guru, "Who is your guru?"

I say, "It's Lahiri Mahasaya."

Little Fox pours out his heart to explain how one should react if given a message from the Spirit. He says, "You hint and let facts unfold through others and yourself. It's not the way to go around forcing things to happen. Grabbing the chief was wrong, and it's better to let things take their natural course." He continues to explain, "There are many spirits in all of us."

He begins to talk in a Native American language. To stress his point, he takes off his mirror glasses and stares me straight in the eyes. I stare back and realize that he is Lahiri Mahasaya, the guru of my guru. I immediately give a deep-kneeling bow in the dirt. He keeps on talking, even though I am bowing at his feet, like it's nothing unusual. The features, the look, the eyes, the wisdom, the walk, all seem familiar.

Lahiri Mahasaya had some remarkable metaphysical powers. In the book, *The Autobiography of a Yogi*, Paramahansa Yogananda wrote the story told to him by Kali Kumar Roy:

"It appears that the master had an aversion to being photographed. Over his protest, a group picture was once taken of him and a cluster of devotees, including Kali Kumar Roy. It was an amazed photographer who discovered that the plate which had clear images of all the disciples, revealed nothing more than a blank space in the center where he had reasonably expected to find the outlines of Lahiri Mahasaya. The phenomenon was widely discussed.

"A certain student and expert photographer, Ganga Dhar Babu, boasted that the fugitive figure would not escape him. The next morning, as the guru sat in lotus posture on a wooden bench with a screen behind him, Ganga Dhar Babu arrived with his equipment. Taking every precaution for success, he greedily exposed twelve plates. On each one he soon found the imprint of the wooden bench and screen, but once again the master's form was missing.

"With tears and shattered pride, Ganga Dhar Babu sought out his guru. It was many hours before Lahiri Mahasaya broke his silence with a pregnant comment:

'I am Spirit. Can your camera reflect the omnipresent Invisible?'

'I see it cannot! But, Holy Sir, I lovingly desire a picture of the bodily temple where alone, to my narrow vision, that Spirit appears fully to dwell.'

'Come, then, tomorrow morning. I will pose for you.'

"Again the photographer focused his camera. This time the sacred figure, not cloaked with mysterious imperceptibility, was sharp on the plate." [8]

After they walk away, I sit and meditate. For The Guru and me to find his favorite disciple, Paramahansa Yogananda, and now his past guru, Lahiri Mahasaya, is a bit uncanny. If the yogis in the Kriya lineage have superhuman powers, like entering my body and not appearing on film, perhaps they can also send dreams, words, or thoughts to another person's mind. I pause to consider it all. I believe through God and the grace of The Guru, anything is possible. ▪

CHAPTER 8

THE CALL OF THE RHONDU

I drive back to my home. I have a talk with my guru about the evil that surrounds us.

I ask, "Is one person or place more evil than another?"

I let my imagination roam and figure certain roads to my house are safer than others. Some roads suddenly become evil and should be avoided. I recently met a neighbor, who is a well-known international dowser, and he told me he was going to the dragon gathering weekend. I don't know what happens at a dragon gathering, but I surmise that he and his dragon followers are evil. Now, he is clearing ground to build a structure up the road from my home. I decide I better avoid him. But he knows I am here. My guru is getting concerned — very concerned.

I say to The Guru, "We must keep an eye out because if evil forces know I am in this stumbling new form, then I can easily be eliminated. I am like a fawn lost in the woods."

I peer out my window into the darkness. It's 2:30 am. That is when I hear the most blood-curdling wild call of evil I have ever heard. It's coming from down in the woods across from the road in front of my property. I visualize a shaggy, dark, moose-shaped figure with razor-sharp teeth. I name it the Rhondu. It no doubt has the intention to smell me out, grab me, and devour me. Fear starts racing through every cell in my body. My heart is pumping fast. I decide it's time to get away fast. I run toward the door and grab the Native scraping tool on the way. I jump in my old Ford Taurus. It feels risky to drive down my driveway past where I heard the deathly call of the Rhondu. I take the corner out of my driveway and punch the gas pedal to the floor. I hit speeds of 60 mph on the dirt road. Dust is flying up when I skid around the corners. The Guru leaves my body and floats above to check on the status.

He says, "The chase is on!"

I feel my life is at stake. It's exhilarating! I know if the Rhondu or any evil spirits catch me, it's all over. I imagine they will hit me with a blunt force that will splatter my body like a fly on a wall. I am giving it my best damned effort to elude them.

The Guru asks, "Do you know any friends along the way where we can stop and hide?"

I reply, "It's too late. They are not nearby."

We pull on to I-91 north and floor it. The Guru periodically leaves to check the status from above. At those times, I am alone in my body. If I yell he comes back, but it takes a moment. I realize I miss him when he is gone.

Just for fun, I yell out his name, "Guru, where are you!"

He replies, "What is it?"

I say, "Oh nothing."

He says, "Stop playing games; we are being chased by evil spirits."

The Clan of the Hawk is my chosen destination for safety. A few miles before the exit, I feel the spirits are fast closing in.

My guru calmly says, "This will be the end. There is no way you can escape now."

I am preparing for the blow of an evil spirit. Suddenly, a thought surfaces about the Native scraping tool. If I throw it out the window, it may distract the evil spirits, or maybe it's what they are after. I wait for a mile marker so I can return to find it. Then I toss it out the window.

The Guru exclaims excitedly, "They are looking at it!"

I start off the Orleans exit going fifty mph and lose control of the car. I spin around and skid off backwards, sliding on the grass. No real damage is sustained, but the car is definitely not moving.

The Guru yells, "You better get your ass out and run!"

I run a mile toward downtown Orleans village. There is pain in my shins and no air left to breathe. I am sweating profusely. I have a flashback to the time we ran sprints to remove lustful thoughts. But this feels more like a marathon. When you think your life is about to end, you push past the pain. Once, I feel a bad spirit thrust near. It's a miracle I am still alive.

I run past a convenience store. It's 3:30 am. I am eight miles away from Clan of the Hawk. I decide to knock on a neighbor's home and ask for a ride. After a few minutes, a man, half asleep, opens the door in his underwear.

I explain, "My car has been wrecked. I need to be part of a ceremony that starts at 5:30 am at the Clan of the Hawk. It's extremely important that I get there. Can you bring me?"

Half asleep he responds, "Ahhhh ohhhh yeahhh, sure."

I wait in his shed. He gets dressed.

The Guru tells me, "You are safe."

It's working out. We make small talk on the way. I am never as happy as when we drive through the gate into the Clan of the Hawk.

OPENING THE MEDICINE WHEEL PORTALS

I immediately go to Stone Tree at his earth-chamber home. While he is getting up, I bathe in the brook. The bright orange sun starts to rise. I pause to meditate, and sense that the giant, dreamtime snake is nearby. I gingerly commence looking around for it. Sitting on a stump in front of the new medicine wheel, I begin to drum and chant. Then a notion comes over me. I must get up high above the medicine wheel to activate it. I start to climb up a sixty-foot pine tree, until I am very near to the top. I can look over and see the church steeple. There is only another eight feet of tree above me. While swaying in the wind, The Guru questions my sanity. I am getting annoyed with him, mostly due to my lack of sleep.

I start to yell out and then chant in an ancient language for ten minutes. The medicine wheel activates. It spreads a message through a beam of bright blue light. I sense that medicine wheels are portals that were used to communicate between former tribes. The message I deliver from the ancient people explains how we can all live in harmony with the animals, the trees, the plants, and the sea creatures and treat this earth as a sacred home. We all need to share this planet.

My message explains how we can live simply and be sustainable. It means growing our own food and using what the natural environment provides for power sources, utilizing the sun, water, and wind. It calls for making relationships our primary focus and being an active participant in community. Last of all, we need to live from the heart and let love guide our actions.

As I come down from the treetop, The Guru is moaning about how dangerous that was. If I had fallen from that height, it probably would have killed me. I ignore his nagging.

I ask Stone Tree, "Did you feel the activation of the medicine wheel and the transmitting of a message?"

He closes his eyes for a moment.

He says, "Somethin' happen, thingz are feelin' different."

LIZZY AND THE BIRTHDAY PARTY

Leaving Clan of the Hawk, I flag down a car on the road. I offer them $60 to drive me back to my hometown. This leaves me short of cash, but I still go to buy some organic veggies and a few more bottles of spirulina at the health food store. It turns into a small fiasco because I don't have enough to pay for it, so I call The Lamb. She comes and writes out a check. Then she drives me back to my home.

During the afternoon, there is a big birthday party for my

neighbor Lizzy's two-year-old daughter in my yard. She sent me a cute homemade invitation, but I forgot it was happening today. Lizzy lives in my lower duplex apartment and started following the Grateful Dead when she was twelve. We have become friends. She is street smart, but not always truthful. She's very likable and an expert at finagling people to get what she wants.

Lizzy is in a recovery program for heroin addicts. She is being paid a weekly stipend and must get a drug test regularly. At first, I was surprised to find out that the program pays her even if she drinks alcohol, smoke cigarettes, or does what are considered lesser drugs, like marijuana. I come to realize that heroin is a deadly drug. The first step is to get free from it. Nothing else really matters if you can't do that. She and a group of her teenage friends all got hooked. It started when a drug dealer came into the small town of Hardwick and offered them some milder drugs before stepping them up to something they thought would be even better. Now, she counts off her friends who have died from an overdose.

I can see that Lizzy genuinely wants to improve her life. She is struggling to gain back the custody of her daughter. I admire that. I want to support her recovery. Plus, she is rather smooth and cool in her own way. The real challenge has been when her old heroin-addicted party friends stop by. They can show up at any hour, but it's usually in the middle of the night. Most heroin addicts will do or say whatever it takes to get their next fix.

Regardless, Lizzy has made a big deal about promising her daughter a pony to ride on her birthday. She hires a local guy, who delivers a pony in a truck. Her daughter and the other young kids ride it around the yard. They are having a blast with the pony.

I am shocked to find out that Lizzy is now attending a local Christian church. I guess it's her way of finding new friends and living a cleaner lifestyle. Today, she has invited her whole new church family to be a part of her daughter's birthday celebration. I am hanging out with Lizzy and her church friends on the lawn, eating a burger from the grill. I know a few of her church friends, but frankly I don't have a clue what it means to live as a Christian.

I want to liven up the party, so I point two 200-watt speakers from my house towards the party and blast my stereo. I play a few songs like "Light My Fire" and "Riders on the Storm" by Jim Morrison and the Doors. My choice of music is not well received.

To my surprise, Lizzy is attending a Christian church established by Mr. R.I.P. He was a monumental figure in my life as my martial arts instructor. It's hard to fathom him as a pastor. Meeting a few Christians is one thing, but when somebody I greatly respect like Mr. R.I.P. decides to follow Jesus, it makes me wonder, "Why did he turn to Jesus?"

I am told by a friend from my martial arts class who is at the party, that he was suicidal and had been hospitalized at a facility in Pennsylvania. They shared what sounded like a rumor about his having an affair with one of his younger female martial arts students. I don't want to spread a rumor or speculate in my book, but this is rather juicy stuff.

TESTIMONY FROM PASTOR R.I.P.

I really want to know what radical change led Mr. R.I.P, martial arts instructor, to become Pastor R.I.P.? I asked Pastor R.I.P. to write about what happened. I want it to be in his own words to set the record straight. It's in his heart (and mine) to share it with you:

"I WILL RESTORE…"

"How did I ever get here?" That is exactly the question I had to ask myself when I spent 17 days in a hospital in the hills just north of Pittsburgh, Pennsylvania. I was there locked in a ward with over 20 other people who were there for life controlling issues. For some it was addiction to things such as drugs, alcohol, pornography, or work; for others like myself, the issues were of a different sort. They had to do with the sense of hopelessness, depression, and dealing with wanting to end it all with no other options in sight.

Here I was at 33 years old in a New Life Clinic being treated for near suicidal depression; but why? I was at the top of my game, at least in some people's eyes. I had a successful career in sales, I was married to a brilliant, hardworking, and beautiful woman, and I was the instructor of a successful martial arts school with over 100 students. I seemed to be so alive and motivated, yet inside my heart and soul I was suffering from a terminal condition that resulted from years of struggling with abandonment issues, sexual immorality, and alcohol and drug usage, fueled by a passion for winning and success.

After over a decade of teaching taekwondo, becoming a national-level competitor and coach and international level referee, I had built my own empire and was what most people would call a self-made man. As I continued to train young athletes and help them become national champions, taekwondo became my life's passion, and I began to spend more and more time at the gym and less time tending with my own wife and her son.

When I was 32 years old, I really lost my moral bearings and began to have an eye for one of my younger students, who was a national champion and had dreams of being in the Olympics. I began to personally train her and cultivate our relationship, which I wanted to see evolve into something other than an instructor and student one. After pursuing this young woman, she eventually rejected my affections and stopped coming to train. When she did, she told her parents and my wife, and reality hit the fan.

For several months, the shame and guilt of what I had allowed myself to become began to follow me around like a very dark cloud. The cloud became thicker and blacker, and I began to drink more heavily and found myself wanting to smoke more and more dope, to numb the pain. The emotional erosion took its toll. I had messed up my own life and that of others so badly. As a result, I spent several months preparing to take my own life. I had written farewell letters to my wife, my parents, and others, and was making definite plans to exit my miserable life. Things spiraled downward so fast and hard that my wife arranged an intervention with one of my best friends, who was able to remove me peacefully from our home.

After spending a few days with him and his wife, my wife arranged a one-way trip to Pennsylvania for me to get some counseling. When I checked myself into that hospital and began to undergo the barrage of questions and tests, it all seemed like a foggy, bad dream. I was asked to write at least three pages of an autobiography of my life as part of the intake procedure. As I did, I found myself recognizing the reality of my abandonment issues, the insecurity of being a fatherless child, grown into adulthood. The years of looking for love in all the wrong places, and the substance abuse all seemed to hit home. There I was, locked up and away from my friends and family, with a bunch of people who were as out of control as I was.

In the days that followed, I found myself surrounded by Christian people who were able to look beyond my sin and dysfunctionality and extend the love of Christ in ways I had never experienced. There were daily Bible studies and quiet times, role playing encounters, and one-on-one counseling. The interaction with loving, mature believers began to penetrate my martial arts and self-made man armor plating. The program used a Christian twelve-step program that involved surrendering your life to Jesus Christ ... which sounded okay, but I had no idea what that meant; I was about to learn!

One day I met with my case worker, who said I needed to talk to the chaplain, a pastor who was on duty. That day the

Spirit of God tore the scales off my eyes and the light of the gospel came blazing into my heart and life. Pastor James led me in a simple sinner's prayer, and I threw myself at the foot of the cross where the love, grace, and mercy of God overtook my life.

For the first time in my life, on that special day, May 13, 1993, I heard the voice of God. "It's going to be alright," was all I can remember, and at that lowest point of my life, that was all I needed to hear. Little did I know that my precious wife had also been born again some three months earlier and had been praying for me. That is how this process began, and now I have been ministering for seventeen years.

I am reminded of a couple of key scripture verses that have impacted my life. The first is found in Joel 2: 25-27, which begins with these words; "So I will restore the years..." Yes, we can stand and testify that our God is indeed a restoring God. He has restored our marriage, our relationship, our family, our love for one another, our minds, and our lives.

AN EXERCISE IN EXORCISMS

I leave the Birthday party and go to visit my friend, Cleopatra. I am exhausted after my wild ride in the middle of the night and from sharing my body with a guru for the last five days. It's pretty obvious to her by my new clothes, bizarre actions, and the way I introduce myself as a yogic monk, that I am not the same old guy. Cleopatra is concerned and frightened, and does not know what to do. She rushes to find Helen Keller.

HELEN KELLER TO THE RESCUE

There are other people who are concerned, but only one person is able to grasp the situation and take action. This is my friend, Helen Keller. She is a tall redhead with thick bones and green eyes, somewhat resembling a Celtic witch. She has the ability to retain plant knowledge, which probably comes in handy when she brews up herbal potions in her pot.

I call her Helen Keller because she can be overwhelmed by stimulation though her sight and hearing. She compensates with a powerful sense of touch and feeling. She feels her way through life, trusting her intuition in both the physical world and in the spiritual realm. She has an eccentric connection with animals. Her method of coping with any situation is divergent from the norm. She finds out the facts and assesses the situation. She will turn to others when she does not know the answers. She is more concerned about the quality of the outcome than how long it takes to get it done. She is persistent in finding a solution to fit the circumstance in front of her. She is a woodworker who specializes in repairing antique furniture. In her trade, she faces unique problems and must figure out the logical steps to restore wood back to its original weathered and aged appearance.

Helen is eating in the church with her boyfriend, Moon Dog. They are at an appreciation lunch for those who had booths during a craft fair at the local Fairbank's Museum. She had an exhibit showing how to cane antique chairs. Cleopatra bustles up to their table. She says, "You need to come quick. Something has happened to Randy." She looks unusually concerned. They both leave the remainder of their meal to follow her outside. She fills them in with what little she knows.

I meet up with Helen Keller on Main Street. She can tell right away that something strange has happened to me. I walk more upright and rigid. I tell her, "There is a guru in my body. I want to tell you about it."

Helen can sense something foreign in my energy field. It's the presence of what I call "The Guru." She says, "I need to go pick up my stuff at the museum. Can you stop by my house later?"

"Sure, I can stop by in about an hour," I reply

While I am walking through a parking lot in town closer to Helen's home, I pass by my acupuncturist, Frenzy.

She takes a glance in my eyes and says, "You have an entity living in you. This is serious. We need to get it out!"

She schedules an acupuncture appointment on the spot for later that afternoon.

I sit down with Helen Keller at her home. We have a cup of tea. I describe what has happened during the last five days. She notes that my pupils are pinpoints and my behavior is anything but normal.

She says, "Spirits can raise havoc!"

After she starts to get a better sense of what is happening, she insists that I take some precautionary measures.

She says, "I don't want you to stay alone in your home. You need to be under the surveillance of a family member at all times."

Helen's next step is to call upon a dowser experienced with spiritual interventions to perform an exorcism. The guy she calls is named John Wayne. She surmises that the spirit entered into me through dowsing, so it can depart in the same manner.

I am sitting at Helen's house on the porch while she is on the phone

The Guru asks, "Do you want me out of your body?"

I realize I am tired, but the truth and wisdom that has been revealed to me in the last five days is earth-shattering.

I ask Helen, "Would you like to have The Guru in your body?"

She replies, "No way!"

At times I feel overwhelmed, but I don't want this grand adventure to end.

After taking some time to decide, I tell The Guru, "No, I want you to stay in my body."

Cleopatra's son stops by. He is learning Japanese. I am in the shower when he passes on his way down the stairs to leave. To his surprise, I yell out, "Sayonara," which means goodbye in Japanese.

Meanwhile, I have forgotten all about my appointment with Frenzy. I speak to her on the phone that evening. She is outraged, but I apologize and reschedule another appointment with her for the next day. I say, "I will be there this time."

NO BIG DEAL

In my quest to find out more about what it really means to have a guru in my body, I visit a local yoga teacher to discuss the situation. I want to get his opinion. He has an upstairs office next to his studio. I say to him, "A guru has entered my body. I have some questions. I thought you could help."

He says, "I cannot speak to you right now. It's time for my personal yoga practice. I will be done in an hour."

I hang outside in the lobby. He goes in a side room and shuts the door. Clearly, he does not want to be disturbed. There is a poster on the wall showing 100 different yoga poses. Some of these postures are highly advanced. While waiting, I do the most advanced poses, many of them for the first time in my life. When he returns, we speak for a few minutes. He concludes by saying, "Come back to one of my regular scheduled hatha classes." It seems a guru living in my body is no big deal to him.

I return home to grab some clothes and get my cat; I plan to leave her with Helen. Oh damn, I completely forget about appointment number two with Frenzy. I call her. She is normally calm and polite mannered in her office, but now she is yelling out a storm of profanities, "You need to set your intention and get this f...ing entity out of your body!"

Frenzy is serious. Her plan is to utilize acupuncture to perform an exorcism to energetically blast The Guru out of me.

She says, "This cannot wait until Monday. This entity is working to make you avoid the appointments. I will make a special appointment for you on Sunday morning at ten."

I tell her, "I am taking it seriously. I will be there."

I GOT A MESSAGE FOR YOU

At Helen's advice, I go to our family brick home to stay with The Lamb. Don't ask me why, but I do 258 long, deep bows. Perhaps these bows were a way to repent for the three phone calls I was about to make. I leave a message each time, which I assume shook up the intended receivers. I reach out from an emotional place to express some rather hostile feelings in a provocative way.

The first call is to The Lion.

In a gristly warrior voice, I leave a message saying, "YOU

ARE GOING DOWN! YOU ARE GOING DOWN! YOU ARE GOING DOWN!"

When he hears the message, he is terrified. He imagines I am physically coming after him. He knows I have studied martial arts for ten years. He thinks his life is threatened. He starts toting a loaded pistol on his hip in case I show up. I guess somewhere inside I feel angry about the damage he has inflicted.

When I said, "You are going down," I was speaking prophetically or symbolically. I didn't mean it as a physical threat. For him, "going down" means losing what is most precious to him: money and his powerful status as a business owner. A few years later, his empire crumbles. He sells off 14 retail stores, four apartment blocks, and a several rental homes.

The second call is to an old girlfriend I call Sex Kitten. We were dating for about a year. During our time together, lust reached a new level. I was not comfortable with everything we did, but I went along. I did not want to upset her. I lacked the assertion to say, "Okay, let's stop doing this!"

I call her and let her know, "THERE IS A SPIRIT OF LUST IN YOU!"

The third phone call is to a female yoga teacher whom I met a day after The Guru entered my body. When I attended her yoga class, I felt that she was another past student of Swami Sri Yukteswar. After class, I invited her to come visit me at my home. When she arrived, I told her she was a student of mine in a past life. She was open to the possibility. We talked about yoga, and she gave me a CD with beautiful Himalayan music. The Guru likes it more than I do.

I attempt to call her and leave several phone messages. I feel she can somehow help with my precarious situation. Her husband does not appreciate some guy calling himself her guru leaving weird messages. She never returns the calls.

I don't know why, but that night I am struck with a passion for Jesus. Perhaps The Guru knew that I needed Him. I am sleeping in my sister's bedroom, the one with the vinyl wallpaper covered with red roses a foot in length. In a storybook fashion, I get down on my knees and pray with tear-filled eyes. I make a simple and personal request. I ask Jesus to enter my life. I do not know much about Jesus, but I begin to seek him.

That evening at 10:30 p.m., I call Pastor R.I.P.

I ask, "Can I attend your church on Sunday and get baptized?"

He says, "I am glad you want more of Jesus. You are welcome to attend the Sunday morning service. It starts at ten."

Pastor R.I.P. assembles a husky team of deacons ready to give me what they think I need. You can probably guess what they want to do.... Yes! It's another exorcism! This one is planned to take place in front of the altar, directly after the regular church service.

Now I have three different healers all ready and eager to perform an exorcism to remove The Guru, which I do *not* even want gone. It's crazy! A guru is a teacher and an instrument of God. They seek to serve others in a compassionate, loving manner. When one finds such a source, it's like a cool pool in the desert. A guru can perform miracles on God's behalf; often their actions make no sense, but they get great results. A devotee will trust and follow the advice of their guru, even when it's not obviously logical. Clearly, a guru can be in the flesh or in the spirit.

My appointment with the acupuncturist is the same time as the church service. Frenzy is going to be more peeved than ever before! I put on a blue pinstriped suit and go to church. I think I am going to be baptized. I had not attended our small hometown church except for Easter or Christmas for the past twenty years. Since then there has been a Jesus culture revolution. I sit in the front row next to Pastor R.I.P. I notice that after he gave up teaching and practicing martial arts, he gained a little weight around the waist.

There is rock-style praise and worship band. Everybody is standing up and clapping hands to the beat. I have a Bible and start slapping it hard with one hand to the rhythm. Yeah! Then, I look around and realize nobody else is beating up their Bible. Oops!

After the sermon, Pastor R.I.P. calls people to come up to the front altar for prayers. I am excited! Soon I will be baptized. It's my turn. Four large deacons gather around me. The pastor places olive oil on my forehead.

I say, "Hey! Where is the water?"

Pastor R.I.P. starts praying, "Remove this evil spirit..."

Then they all start speaking and praying in tongues.

I am thinking, "What is going on?"

The Guru is sitting back, smiling at it all. The pastor must want me to fall over backward because he keeps pushing my forehead straight back. I can only bend backward so far. The husky deacons catch my body and lower me to the floor.

Then Pastor R.I.P. crouches down beside me to whisper loudly, "What is the name of the evil spirit living in you?"

I never considered The Guru to be an evil spirit. I assume the pastor wants some form of the devil to be in me.

I say, "Beezelbub."

I am trying to say the name "Beelzebub," but it came out wrong.

He says, "AHHHHH. The God of Bees, now bees be gone!"

The Guru says, "Looks like I am not going anywhere."

Eventually, they finish praying and let me up. I am given a few hugs and they proclaim this day as my spiritual birth. The Guru thinks it was all great fun. It was an exorcism by surprise attack. I didn't have much choice once they surrounded me. Their exorcism may have removed a few dark entities, but it surely didn't remove The Guru.

On the positive side, I am given a NKJV Bible with the words of Jesus highlighted in red. On the negative side, I have a very upset acupuncturist. I go home with a desire to read the Bible from cover to cover.

The Lamb is hosting a family reunion at her house. I don't want to make a scene. I grab my new Bible, a backpack, and a fleece and head out the door. I walk to visit a friend but nobody is at home. They have an assortment of fresh garden produce lying out on towels. I take a few veggies to eat: a clove of garlic, a pepper, a cucumber, and a tomato. I find a quiet spot in an abandoned camp in a back field and settle in to start reading.

During the sermon, Pastor R.I.P. had said, "The Word is alive."

I begin to read and look at the Bible with fresh eyes. Could it reveal some answers to questions relevant to my life? I feel guidance is present in the Word, but it also resides in the spaces of silence between the words. Well, it says on the seventh day God rested, so after I finish reading Genesis, I lie down and take a nap; then I return home at dusk.

The Guru has been in my body for ten days. I wake up early and go for a jog. Yes! I am able to run again. I can't believe it. I am amazingly grateful. I jog out to a spot on a dirt road where I used to practice martial arts before my back injury. I believe that the prayers at the church took hold during the night. My back really feels better today. I watch the beams of sunlight shining through the clouds. It's like I can peek up into heaven or somebody is watching down. Could it be God's grace? I feel all fresh and alive again.

CHAPTER 10

Ten Minutes

Two police cruisers slip silently down the middle of the long dirt driveway toward my family's three-story brick home. Pine trees, 100-feet tall, are staggered along either side of the driveway as if javelins were thrown down from heaven, just missing these intruders. I peer out to see them through a small side window beside our white front door.

I run upstairs, out of breath, and enter my sister's bedroom. Vinyl wallpaper covered with foot-long red roses surrounds me on all sides, but this situation does not smell sweet. Panicked, I open the second story window that faces the river.

In the distance, under a cluster of pine trees, is a granite platform covered with pine needles. A prior owner in the late 1800s built it for his throne. I imagine him sitting like a dignified statue gazing down upon the waterfall while he contemplated life's intricate ways.

If I could jump out far enough, I could grab a branch of the giant pine tree near the house. I squat like a bird on the window ledge, pausing to ask myself, *"Is this the right moment to allow The Guru to have full control of my body?"* It seems like a reasonable solution and an easy way to escape this predicament, but deep down my soul suspects that to surrender itself to another spirit is breaking some sacred spiritual ethic. But then again, why not?

Ten minutes earlier, I was sitting in the lotus position on top of a four-foot-long, gold-framed antique mirror that I had taken down from the bathroom wall and positioned on the edges of the tub. It felt as though The Guru sharing my body for the past ten days was ready to blast out of my third eye. I had positioned the Waterpik shower-massager to direct a strong half-inch beam of water toward my third eye, which I was intently focusing upon. I became distracted by anticipating a jolt as The Guru departed, and I was suddenly overcome by fear. I envisioned a sudden blow of pain that might throw me into the shower wall with tremendous force. I found myself beginning to scream as long and loudly as is humanly possible in one breath. Although this eased my fears of imminent bodily harm, it didn't occur to me that my screaming would raise the concern of my mother, who immediately called the police.

Perching on the windowsill with my heart beating rapidly, I make my plea. "Guru, take over complete control and get me out of this situation!"

What happens next is hard to explain. It's as though I am looking through a periscope. I can't see anything to the left or right unless I turn and face that direction. Jumping to the tree branch seems more challenging now, but begins to look more realistic when it comes into focus through my tunnel vision. I leap from the window ledge and catch hold of the branch.

Life is looking better, I fantasize about taking a nice easy float down to the soft, pine-needle bedding ... but before this happens, I hear a *crack!* and a *snap!* My descent suddenly turns into a crash landing. My ankles feel slightly sprained, but they still function. Deciding to run, I discover it's not that easy with tunnel vision. I see a foot here, a branch there ... *look out for that tree!* I make a quick left turn. There's a steep, fifty-foot descent to the river. I find myself airborne, somewhere near the granite platform, floating or flying, a big rock heading my way. I feel the impact, hard against my skull. Blood trickles down my cheek. I feel numb, sick, and woozy.

Time passes: ten minutes ... ten days ... or ten years? As if in a dream, I stand up and wade through the waist-high ferns. I feel like a cornered warrior, forced to retaliate.

I come back to something resembling reality when a tranquilizer is injected into my hip. This wakes me up from one dream and puts me into another. I first notice the smell of hot vinyl seats. Then I realize that I am locked in the back of a police car and have pepper spray in my eyes and a black mesh sack over my head. I feel blood on my face and hands, and my ribs feel cracked or broken. It's painful to breathe. My right shoulder has a bloody scrape where I was dragged on the ground. I feel chains on my lap that lead to a set of handcuffs around my wrists and a pair of ankle cuffs below. I have been captured like a prisoner.

I have no memory of what happened after the impact. It's all a mystery. My memory completely blocked out what happened for about ten minutes. Perhaps it was due to the impact or it was so traumatic that my mind chose to erase it. I was told I put up a fight and went down hard. The Lamb is not willing to share the details of what actually happened. Her only comment is, "That day was a Mother's worst nightmare!"

GOD'S GRACE IN THE HOSPITAL

A medical unit arrives and the police explain the situation to them. The ambulance crew is reluctant to transport me to the hospital. They feel I could be dangerous. The police are being cautious, with just cause, after my difficult apprehension. They know I am in some sort of altered state, but it's not drugs, as they presume. It's an urgent situation because I have some life threatening injuries. Finally, one police officer volunteers to deliver me to the hospital in his police cruiser. I awake in the local hospital, handcuffed to a metal bed. The Lion and The Lamb stay by my side for most of the night. I am told that one police officer kept me under surveillance, for security reasons, all night long.

The next day, Gadget and Priceless come to visit me. Soon afterwards, I am transferred to a larger hospital in Burlington, Vt. The doctors make a puncture to insert a hose to drain the fluid in my lung, and the damaged ribs heal rather rapidly. I receive reconstructive surgery to install three titanium plates with screws to repair the fractured bones under my left eye. To complete the operation, they lift up the whole left side of my face and reattach it under the gums in my mouth and under my left eyelid. I have an excellent surgeon. There are no noticeable scars. I can feel the screw heads under my skin if I rub them. On occasion, I feel slight numbness from nerve damage on the left side of my nose to the corner of my lip.

I barely feel any physical pain or discomfort throughout the whole recovery process. I am kept under surveillance in a level-two psychiatric ward for the next 25 days. It is designated for those with minor mental disturbances. It all went smoothly. I know without any doubt that God's grace was present before, during, and after the injury to my head.

Since The Guru entered my body, I am speaking Spanish and German better than I could before. Perhaps my memory is better able to recall foreign words that I had learned, or maybe with the acquisition of The Guru I have tapped into a universal language bank. The hospital performs various tests, including having me speak in German to a person who is fluent. Their conclusion is that I am not fully fluent but know some words. This is pretty remarkable because I never had any exposure to the German language. A physiatrist diagnoses me as having bipolar disorder. This means I have oscillating moods of depression and mania.

They say I have a classic case of bipolar disorder. They even ask me to tell a group of visiting medical students about my experience. They don't believe a guru entered my body or that there were any spiritual forces implicated. Basically, their theory is that the chemicals in my mind malfunctioned to create the whole scenario. Their medical explanation is that I had a

10-day manic episode. I was elated during the ten days, but their methods don't test spiritual components. The bipolar-disorder theory lacks an explanation of how I acquired a whole array of new spiritual gifts. I believe it was a spiritual intervention by The Guru, Swami Sri Yukteswar. I don't doubt he has the capability to enter a body. I have more reasons to believe it was him than to believe it was not him, but I can't say that I am absolutely positive.

SCORES OF VISITORS

All this commotion happens in a small Vermont town. People here don't like to go to the hospital unless it's something serious. I can imagine the word traveled fast, with something as bizarre as me jumping out of a second-story window to elude four police officers. I have scores of family and old friends that call or visit me in the hospital. When people call or come to visit, it shows that they care. It's a small part of their day, but a big deal for me when I am alone in the hospital.

The Lion visits me, and this action alone shows he is concerned about my welfare.

He asks, "Is there is anything you want?"

I say, "I would like a gold cross. Not the chain, I have one. Just the cross."

During his next visit, he brings me a gold cross. I am thankful and wear it for years. The Lion gives me the cross along with his remark, "The price paid for this cross was way too much!"

He is trying to tell me this gift was too expensive. But I can sense that he feels glad I am still alive. I know it's not what he meant, but in his words there is another kind of truth, if you relate it to Jesus.

Pastor R.I.P. and his pastor, The Bishop, come to share a word of wisdom and pray with me. Pastor R.I.P. says, "There are 31 days in the month and 31 Proverbs. Read one a day.

Proverbs will allow you to understand man and the world better; Psalms will allow you to understand and be closer to God." I take his advice to heart.

I find inspiration from reading the Bible. I make a collage out of magazine clippings in the art room. It shows God and all of creation. It symbolizes how the Bible has taken a more significant role in my life.

INTERGALACTIC DETECTIVE

After the whole Guru incident, I feel like I had been asleep in a time capsule for 25 years. It's more than a mere "What happened?". I go through a process of trying to unravel what happened during those ten days and the ten minutes after the impact. Some reference points and knowledge of the facts shared by my family and friends have been revealing and reassuring, but the momentary lapse of memory after the impact remains.

Questions come up after ten days of being in an altered spiritual state. Did The Guru really enter my body? Why did dowsing give me that final instruction? Did I make a big mistake by asking The Guru to take over my spirit? Why did I get tunnel vision after I asked The Guru to take over my spirit? If I was under the safeguard of The Guru, why did I receive such a life-threatening impact? Did all these events happen for a reason? It brings up more questions than answers.

Sometimes it's better to have somebody from outside of the box look in at the situation. In order to make sense of this incident, let's broaden our perspective and investigate what happened in a fun and different way. I am going to call upon a fictional character, Miss Clarity I.D. She is an intergalactic detective who has a reputation for solving tough spiritual mysteries throughout the Universe.

I find Miss Clarity at an intergalactic lounge called Saturn's Turn. I spot her peering nonchalantly out toward Saturn's rings. She is wearing a tight red dress that looks like it's made of petroleum jelly. Miss Clarity is not from planet earth. She is similar in size to a human, but her body is much longer with greenish-amber scales like a snake. Her huge eyes are green and yellow like other reptiles. She uncoils, after being comfortably spiraled up on a black furry loveseat in the sun. Her forked tongue extends to take a sip of a blue frosty cocktail from a tall glass. She motions to me by patting her long tail on the seat next to her. I walk over and introduce myself before sitting down. She hisses loudly and the bartender sends over an orange terra ductile with a cherry. It arrives on some sort of neon floating Frisbee, which zips back once I snag the drink. It's quite tasty.

I start the conversation, "I would like you to investigate an incident on planet Earth. It's a lush planet bustling with various life forms."

She responds with a smile, "I know plenty about it, silly earthling. I was not hatched last week. What can I do for you?"

I ask, "What do you know about a guru being able to enter a human body?"

She replies, "They are an advanced life form, disciplined yoga practitioners, originally from India. Some of these master teachers were or are enlightened beings. They are capable of transferring their conscious energy or spirit while alive, or after death, to inhabit the physical body of other humans."

I explain, "I had what I believe is a guru living in my body. I was warned in the initial communication with spirits through dowsing not to allow any spirit to take control of my spirit. It seemed like good advice, but I did not follow it."

Clarity casually retorts, "Typical human; most earthlings don't follow my advice either. I bet it became crowded in there?"

I continue, "Yes it did. After ten days I asked The Guru to take over my spirit."

She draws out an electronic cigarette that was tucked in her belt and takes a few puffs, "What sort of physical changes took place?"

I reply, "I instantly had tunnel vision. Maybe I was given worthy and warranted advice through the dowsing."

She interjects, "Let me point out, I have not yet established whether we can trust this dowsing spirit's advice. What else did you notice?"

I say, "It seems that The Guru could control my senses. At one point, I experienced delusions in each of my five senses, but that was before I asked The Guru to take over my spirit."

She says, "If The Guru had the capability to enter your body and could control your senses, it's reasonable to expect he could be capable of taking over your spirit upon request. If, in fact, he took over your spirit I would expect you perceived some changes."

I nod and reply, "If there were spiritual shifts, they were very subtle. But my vision was like peeking through an empty toilet paper roll."

Clarity says, "It's most probable that shifts would occur spiritually, but it's very serious to surrender your spirit to another."

She takes a breath and sighs, "It seems that the natural instinct of humans is to keep control of their own body and spirit. I find it interesting that you asked The Guru to take over your spirit."

I explain, "I was under a bit of stress that day. Four police officers were chasing me around the house. I trusted The Guru and felt he was better suited to handle the situation."

Clarity's eyebrows lift and she interjects, "It's impossible for me to determine if your request was for the better or worse."

I say rather shyly, "Well, sixty seconds after my request to The Guru, I experienced what most humans consider a severe traumatic injury to my head that could have easily caused my death."

Clarity says, "Oh my! I am assuming that you did not die. That injury seems like an important detail."

I chuckle and say, "Yes it is. Anyhow, I am wondering if The Guru is still in my body."

She responds, "Well, you need to figure that out for yourself. Were there any changes that you noticed after the impact?"

I pause to think and then reply, "Other than getting all bloody and having a sick, numb, woozy feeling. I can't recall much of what happened after the impact."

Clarity says, "Really! On my planet we call it a "mind warp." Did your tunnel vision ever cease and come back to normal?"

I say, "Well yes! It came back just after the impact. I never thought about it, but I never had the tunnel vision again."

She asks, "Could it be possible that The Guru left your body and spirit at the time of the impact?"

I answer, "Anything is possible. I could not always believe The Guru, but he said, 'It's painless to leave a body after it dies.'"

Clarity's eyes light up, "There are few human beings in this universe that don't lie. But you can always trust a unicorn. Perhaps, once you were unconscious, The Guru departed your body?"

I say, "Yes, that makes sense. I never considered it. I seldom heard The Guru's voice after the impact."

Clarity scans over some information from a computerized hand-held device before she continues, "I find that a guru, by the definition found in earth's history, can work in one's life in ways I don't understand. It's possible that The Guru guided your body to receive a blow to the head in the most compassionate way known to him. It allowed The Guru to depart and you, silly human, to continue on your journey slightly altered."

I say excitedly, "You mean The Guru could have planned my injury as a way for him to leave my body; for the proper conditions, I had to be momentarily unconscious. It's better than the second alternative, which is to be dead. If what you say is true, it's incredible!"

Clarity replies, "If that is the case, then The Guru really

cared about your well-being. You did say you trusted him. From my observations, you silly humans are rather stubborn when it comes to changing behaviors. My hunch is that he came to assist you."

I respond, "What you're saying is I needed a big God slap to wake me up and to change my ways?"

Clarity, in a dignified manner, says, "Yes, that is one way to say it. Do you have any more questions?"

I reply, "No more questions. Thanks for the clarity, Clarity."

She lets out a hissy guffaw and says, "Very amusing! Call on me when you need clarity. Our case is complete. You will get my bill electronically in three minutes."

We say goodbye. Once I stand up, she coils back into a spiral on the black furry loveseat. I stare out for a moment at Saturn's rings, until my bill arrives. Saturn's rings really are magnificent.

Perhaps a better approach is to examine my spiritual transformation over the next ten years. There is no doubt, I have been touched by God's grace, and it left me with an insatiable hunger to know and understand God, the Truth, and Love.

"As the deer pants for streams of water, so my soul pants for God."

(Psalm 42:1 NIV)

God's Grace

This is a self-portrait that I entitle "A Scream for Help." I had no intention of killing myself. As a photographer, I aim to take pictures with impact. It was, in part, an assignment from my psychiatrist and also my way of expressing how I was disgusted with the western medical system.

A Scream for Help

After my release from a level-two psychiatric ward at the hospital, the typical western medicine prescription and diagnosis occurs. I am disheartened to hear the medical doctors say that I need to take prescription medication for the rest of my life to keep bipolar disorder under control. The doctors, or the medical system, consider my body, mind, emotions, and spirit to be disconnected. They want each sector to be individually diagnosed and medicated. It feels distant from the true wholeness and harmony known as healing.

If I listen and comply with all of the doctors' advice for medications and accept that I have all the diseases on their extended lists, then I am already doomed. It feels like my doctors are collaborating like a terrorist network to take another patient hostage in the system. Some doctors have laid claims on my body, but the psychiatrists are holding out for my mind. It probably brings a higher price. As part of my ransom, they are requesting that I hand over my sanity. No deal!

In the end, the terms of the negotiations for my release from the hospital include that I must agree to take prescribed medications and continue to have appointments with a local psychiatrist. I am not keen on taking the prescribed medications, but I do it for several months to appease the doctors. I am discharged to the care of a local psychiatrist named Debbie Goldfinger.

She seems to be the first professional who shows genuine kindness. She really cares about my situation. She tells me to call her during the middle of the night, if necessary. She is empathetic about my not wanting to take prescribed medications. We find some holistic alternatives. During a normal session, I share what is going on, and Debbie suggests ways I can be more social or express my feelings. I admit my attitude needs some adjusting.

During one session, she is attempting to find a new way to get me to express what I feel. She asks, "Can you find an artistic way to express yourself?"

I am fervid about photography, so I take a self-portrait with my mouth wide open in a scream. I am holding two pistols. One is a 38 special and the other a 9 millimeter. They are each held up and pointed at either side of my forehead. I enlarge it along with a few other photos to 8x10s and bring them to my next session. Debbie looks at each photo and finds a way to compliment how I am expressing myself. It feels like we are playing a game. When she comes to the photo with the pistols pointed at my forehead, her eyes open wide and she gasps. She attempts to hide the fact that she is shocked.

She exclaims, "Oh my! It looks like you are expressing some anger here."

I respond, "Yes! This is my self-portrait. I call it 'A Scream for Help.'"

Once the full impact of this demented photo strikes home, her energy shifts. She keeps staring at the photo. Her face becomes puckered and wrinkled. I assume the worst possible nightmare for a psychiatrist is to have a client commit suicide.

She asks in a concerned tone, "Those guns are not really loaded?"

I reply, "I wouldn't kill myself. I am expressing my frustration with the medical system."

She suggests, "I am making a request. Can you keep your guns with a family member for the next several months?"

I reply, "Sure, I can do that."

An unhealthy process starts when I and others began to constantly focus on my pains and wounds. When a friend says, "How is your back today? I hear you are in pain."

I say, "Yes, my back hurts today."

In my mind, like a skipping record, I repeat, "I am never going to heal. I am always going to be in pain. I am not going to be able to work. I am not going to be able to have any fun."

My emotional sick-boy stew is simmering with anxiety, depression, mania, irritability, mental fatigue, unwarranted fears, panic disorders, suppressed anger, grief, loneliness, and trust issues. It's no surprise that once insomnia visits, my soul seeks to numb out or escape through television, alcohol, drugs, sex, and the occasional thought of suicide. All that matters when I feel as sick as a leper rolling in the agony of my pain, is to find a way out. The last thing my soul wants to do is a make friends with my pain, feel it in my heart, and have some quality time together. There is one person who has been treating me worse than anybody else: myself. *Boy, I am pathetic, somebody please stop this jerk!*

Well, maybe it took a guru to open my eyes. It is hard to change long-existing habitual patterns. They feel normal. My positive and negative thoughts are powerful. My negative thoughts have the ability to attract more illness. They actually reinforce my illness and give my cells permission to become as I believe. This is not the path to healing; it's the path toward prolonged suffering.

Thankfully, after The Guru, my attitude begins to change. With the assistance of a steady yoga practice and the Bible, I began to develop the power to control and purify my thoughts. Until my thoughts become more purified, it's best to avoid the environments, behaviors, and people that stimulated those negative thoughts. One of the root causes of my chronic conditions was stress. Because I was not adequately prepared or permitted to express my feelings in a healthy way, I stored pain in my body.

The greatest disharmony for me as a child included the fear of men, being socially challenged at school, and my parent's divorce. As an adult, I had a high level of stress at work, especially with The Lion being my boss. Of course finances were a concern, but I was able to cope with it all until after the emotional turmoil from my divorce. That was the big one!

INTERNAL RHYTHM

The love I felt from my wife brought me peace and harmony. Once it was gone, I lost my internal rhythm. According to Hazrat Inayat Khan,

> *"When a child's rhythm and tone are disordered, the healing that a mother can give, often unconsciously, the physicians cannot give in a thousand years. The song she sings, however insignificant, comes from the profound depths of her being and brings with it the healing power. It cures the child in a moment. The caressing, the patting of the mother does more good to the child than any medicine when its rhythm is disturbed and its tone is not good. The mother, even without knowing it distinctly, feels like patting the child when it is out of rhythm, singing to the child when it is out of tune."* [9]

My divorce disrupted my natural rhythm. My loss of love eventually even affected my breathing pattern. I believe the implications of divorce in this regard can be more severe for a man than a woman. A man will calibrate his rhythm to that of his wife. In this manner, she replaces his mother. A woman has her rhythm intact naturally with her monthly menstruation. It connects her to the cycles of the moon and the earth. Of course, men can find ways to connect to the earth and the moon, but it feels natural to make that connection through a woman.

It was natural for me to seek a relationship with another woman soon after my divorce; perhaps it was to keep my internal rhythm in synchronicity. I spent much of my time with Cleopatra. I give her credit, for she knew how to rebuild my self-esteem. It did not take much, but a few well-placed words of encouragement made a world of difference.

HOSPITAL VOLUNTEER

As a 33 year old, life is a dream. I am eager to serve. A few months after I return to my home, at the suggestion of my psychiatrist, Debbie Goldfinger, I volunteer at a local hospital. I make beds, file charts, deliver urine samples, and read poetry to the patients. My tasks are simple and humble. I observe the nurses, who show incredible compassion for their patients. They exhibit kindness, often more from how they say it than from the words. When a nurse says, "How are you feeling today, Martha?" her tone gives Martha permission to express her feelings and be heard.

On occasion, a patient will die and the nurses on the floor become very quiet. They have to cope with death regularly. Often they come to know a patient as a friend. I don't know what they are feeling inside; sometimes I notice a tear flowing down a cheek. The nurses compassionately express their emotions among themselves. I suspect that some detach from feeling the pain, but the real heroes in the group embrace life and accept death. One's individual form of faith is personal. I once heard a nurse standing in the corridor whisper prayers softly. Her eyes were gently closed. I am not sure she noticed me. This type of heartfelt prayer must have the power to heal and comfort both the giver and the receiver.

I start off my yoga career with a Korean style of healing and meditation called SunDo. A Korean Master named Hyunmoon Kim established a retreat center near my home in Barnet, Vermont. I am told that this ancient practice was handed down from hermits who lived in the Korean mountains. Because of the direct lineage, the practice has retained much of its original form.

During the 90-minute practice, there are few verbal instructions given. It starts with a series of warm-up exercises and ends with a cool-down. The heart of the practice is holding postures with breathing exercises designed to strengthen and balance internal energy and sooth the internal organs. After each set of postures is done one hundred times, the student can advance to the next level of postures. During the breathing meditation, there is a recording of a traditional Korean chant. I can't understand a word, but it is rather peaceful. Different breathing patterns are learned at different levels and the chant helps guide one to know when to change postures or how long to inhale and exhale.

Students do their set of postures during the forty-minute meditation portion of the class. Over time, the student naturally becomes aware of his or her body, mind, and spirit transforming through the SunDo practice. There is profound beauty when one discovers for themselves a relevant truth in their own practice. It can never be taken away or disputed. These gems cannot be handed out; they crystallize.

Master Hyunmoon Kim is a large, strong, dark-skinned Korean man who speaks with the gentle voice of a monk. He says, "One must practice each day to be effective, like a baker makes bread each day. Better yet, practice in a group and it will lead to more energy, like many sticks on a fire."

I attend the local SunDo classes and practice regularly in my home for the next four years. After a few years of practice, I have a desire to teach, so I attend a retreat with Master Kim in Barnet. During the retreat, he explains, "One must give full concentration during meditation, remain like a statue during a posture, if you want to get in touch with the universe inside."

It's difficult to get the new breathing pattern correct along with the inward spiral visualization within the lower abdomen. His instructions are just not sinking in. I can't get it. I am feeling frustrated. Instead of pushing it any further, Master Kim takes me aside and shows me how to do a full, deep, traditional bow. I start standing with my hands in prayer. Next, I bow down on my knees with my palms flat on the ground. Then I touch my forehead down and push myself back upright with my palms. He does it beside me until I learn it. A deep bow is a humble act; the fact that he takes the time to show me how to do it properly shows he cares.

> *Fun bowing exercise: In order to feel the humbleness of a deep bow by yourself, do several of them. If you want to try it with a friend, then face each other. One person can remain standing as the other bows to them three times. Take turns. For some, it can be harder to receive a bow than to give one.*

KRIYA YOGA

As part of my quest to find out the truth about The Guru, I attend a Kriya yoga class. Swami Sri Yukteswar, the one I call The Guru, lived from May 10, 1855 – May 9, 1936. I desire to find the purest source of his teachings. One of his students, Hari Harinanada, established a Kriya yoga center in New York City. I am disappointed to find out that he recently left his body. But he appointed a young man from India, who is in his late 20s, Super Star Ananda, as his successor. He is renowned for having a brilliant mind and can recapitulate the yogic scriptures by memory. I want to attend a class taught by Super Star Ananda.

I am told that in order to attend any Kriya class, I must take initiation into Kriya yoga, otherwise they will not reveal the teachings. It seems like placing the horse before the cart, but being the only way, I concede. They ask me to bring flowers and a piece of fruit as an offering for the initiation ceremony.

On the appointed day, I take a train to New York City. I stop to purchase a few yellow roses and a coconut before I arrive.

There are a dozen other people who are initiating. In the front of the yoga studio, there is an altar with photos of their Kriya lineage: Hari Harananda, Swami Sri Yukteswar, Lahiri Mahasaya, and Babaji. I feel a strong presence from a large photo of Swami Sri Yukteswar. At times, it feels like he is staring at me. It's a strange feeling, but I feel more comfort than not from his photo. The legend is that Kriya yoga came from Babaji, who lives eternally as a young man in the Himalayan Mountains.

One by one, we go to decorate the altar with our offerings of flowers and fruits. It is a beautiful, colorful display. Super Star Ananda is standing by the altar, waiting to initiate us. He holds his hands on the top of our heads and sometimes touches our spine to transmit the energy from the Kriya lineage.

I feel a slight tingling, but nothing dramatic happens. Afterwards, all the new initiates and a few dozen regular students join in a Kriya yoga practice instructed by Super Star Ananda. It is a nice practice, and during the meditation portion, there is a vibrant, pulsating, blue light in my third eye. When I focus on the light, it becomes brighter and forms the circular shape of the sun. I wonder if this is the tunnel of light that guides people to heaven after they die. It feels like I could dive into it. I dare not, for I might not be able to get back.

After the meditation portion, Super Star Ananda says, "Now lie down on your back and relax."

I ask him, "How do I relax?"

He replies, "You just relax."

His response did not answer my question. I feel that his tone implies that I should know how to relax. I need a more detailed instruction. I really don't know how to relax.

During the lunch break, I chat with other classmates at a street-side cafe about our initiation and our first Kriya yoga class. We stride back through the bustling city traffic wearing sunglasses. The midday sun makes the pavement sizzling hot, yet we are all cool. We just got initiated! Now, we are part of the Kriya yoga lineage, whatever that means.

In the afternoon, we rejoin the others to listen to a discourse by Super Star Ananda about the philosophy of Kriya yoga. I purchased two small bottles of orange juice with the intention of offering one to Super Star Ananda as a refreshment. During a pause in the program, while we are assembling, I lift up one bottle of orange juice and ask Super Star Ananda, "Would you like an orange juice?"

He snaps back, "No! I am the juice."

It brought some laughter, but his joke points out his greatness. Master Hyunmoon Kim is the only other yoga master I have known. He is a humble man. When asked a question, he would pause, listen deeply, and reply with compassion. Super Star Ananda may have had great Kriya powers, but during our day-long encounter, he didn't show me any kindness.

Rhythm of the Breath

YOGA MEANS UNION

At this point, I start to live a nomadic lifestyle. I volunteer in the summer and autumn at various spiritual retreat communities. During the winters, I explore the Caribbean islands and continue my search for a location to start a spiritual community. I am blessed to have the freedom to live this lifestyle.

I am drawn to retreat communities that offer yoga. I know it keeps me sane by allowing my body and mind to relax. Yoga is a healthy way to escape my pain, anxiety, and depression. It's not so much an escape as an entrance to a more peaceful world. I start to get to know myself again, as a friend, and begin to like who I am. Buried under the pain lives that child who enjoyed swinging on rope, eating ice cream, and lying in the grass, lazily gazing up at the puffy clouds. Yoga allows the innocent child within to come out to play again.

The nature of the principal of yoga is unity. We are all on our own journey, but connected. We are here to learn, to be open, and to accept ourselves and others. When my practice is to love myself, then it's not difficult to love and accept others. I become more aware of my connection with other people through the practice of yoga. The people I meet through yoga are a fun, caring, and loving bunch. People attend yoga classes for various reasons, but it seems we all enjoy being together. It feels like we are all one big family.

Yoga is a healthy lifestyle that will forever be part of my spiritual path. It started off as a personal commitment to a daily practice. Over the years, the daily discipline of a yoga practice transformed me. It opened my heart, kept me present, and melted away the stress. Now I consider yoga any action that I do with loving kindness. On the path of yoga there is a huge invisible finger that points towards God. I am told that He lives somewhere on a puffy white cloud in heaven. In the beginning, I don't know how to reach God. He is so far away. Eventually, I figure out that the finger is actually pointing at my own heart. This is where God lives!

GOD REALLY EXISTS

While in Vermont one winter, I press in closer to find God. For thirty days, I do a disciplined routine of prayer, meditation, and silence, and I read the Bible daily. I want to know that God really exists. I read a passage about Isaiah calling out to the Lord.

> *"Then you will call, and the Lord will answer; you will cry for help, and he will say: Here am I."*
>
> *(Isaiah 58:9 NIV)*

That is exactly what I do on the last day. I jump up and down and throw a little temper tantrum like a child.

I yell out, "God, show me yourself!"

I don't stop; I just keep crying out. "I want to see you, GOD! I am not going to let up until you pay attention!"

Surely God will notice my tears during a childish fit. I want God to appear in whatever form He chooses. It could be a vision, an angel visitation, or a bright light. I lie down on my back and close my eyes. At that moment, I receive a vision that I shall never forget.

In it, a ghostly blue spirit rises up out of my body at my waist and peers back at me. It's like I am at a mirror-smooth lake and I am looking up at a reflection of myself from in the water. I see

God for the first time. He is a reflection of myself staring back into my own eyes. I feel like an innocent child.

I say, "This is God? It's me!"

I feel like somebody just swung open the gate and let my spirit out of prison. It's mind blowing. I no longer doubt that God's light and love live in me. It does not answer all my questions about God ... many will remain a mystery ... but if God is in me, then God is in you, and God is in everybody.

THE LOVE BLAST

The first yoga community I visit is at the Himalayan Institute of Yoga Science in Honesdale, Pennsylvania, in the winter of 2003. I attend a month-long self-transformation program. I chop a lot of vegetables, learn how to prepare and cook healthier food, and participate in daily yoga classes.

There is one teacher named Julia who studied with the late founder, Swami Rama. After the end of one of her yoga classes, I sit cross-legged in a row with the other students. She peacefully faces us in silence. She gathers love in her heart with her hands held in a prayer position. Then she sends a burst of love to our hearts. It physically travels like a beam of light. It blows me away. I don't physically move, but I feel reverberations that shake my soul.

Julia teaches restorative yoga. After the love blast, I schedule a private session. After listening to my issues, she places me in a supported child's pose. Bolsters support my chest and my face is turned to the side. All my muscles relax.

Julia says, "Be still in this posture for five minutes." I am always active. I think to myself, *Five minutes is a long time to be still.* During those long five minutes, I feel held and nurtured. I feel my breath returning to find its natural rhythm. I am relaxing, no longer trying to do anything. I am healing!

Forget for the moment all that is in your mind.
Feel the contact with your body and the solid dark earth,
heavy and grounding. Notice your breath.
Feel the rhythm of the earth around you:
the movement of the wind, the seasons,
birth and death, naturally.
The mesmerizing flames from a fire.
A wolf trotting in the woods.
The waves hugging the beach and crawling back,
again and again, powerful with rhythm.
Feel your breath.
Imagine you inhale a flowing stream –
vibrant, filling every cell with vital energy.
The stream flows into a serene pond,
with the calmness of a devoted mother
nurturing a newborn child in her arms.
The pond gently leaves by way of another stream.
The exhale begins –
The rhythm, the cycle is unbroken.
It begins again. Feel the connection, the gentle flow.
In your heart, your essence, your soul.
The heartbeat of the solid dark earth.
And realize…. You are…
The breath of the Earth.

During one of my walks, there is a foot of fresh snow in the field. The wind is blowing and tossing around mini whirling gusts of powder. I run to the top of a knoll and hold my hands up. I cry out to the Creator of this universe. For the first time, I am ready to surrender. I want God's presence in my life. I don't know exactly what it means. It feels different. I let go of a part inside that is no longer serving me. It fills with a desire to know and serve a divine, loving God. When I open up my heart, a light shines into the dark caverns of my soul.

I ask for a private meeting with the new spiritual head, Pandit Rajmani Tigunait. Swami Rama requested that after his death, Pandit Rajmani take over, with one stipulation: he must remain silent for two years and observe the retreat community before making any changes. I respect the wise request. It impresses me that Pandit Rajmani could be silent for two years. I am eager to share with him my guru experience. I want to know his opinion.

I auspiciously find the one book Swami Sri Yukteswar wrote in their bookstore. It's called *The Holy Science*. The theme of his book is to examine the underlying unifying philosophies of Hinduism and Christianity by comparing *The Yoga Sutras* to the *Holy Bible*. I am intrigued and spurred on, after finding the book, to know more about him. At this point, I am not sure if The Guru is still in me. I am still trying to figure out what happened.

I meet with Pandit Rajmani in his office. After some casual conversation, I begin to explain how Swami Sri Yukteswar entered my body. All of a sudden, he jumps up out of his seat and bolts out the door like I just set the room on fire. He has a look of cautious perplexity on his face. No answers about The Guru are coming from him.

THE SACRED SILENCE

I continue my search for a yogi who will have the knowledge to answer my questions. A friend tells me there is one enlightened yogi in the United States named Baba Hari Dass. He was the inspiration for a retreat called Mount Madonna Center. He came to regularly teach and serve in this community, whose interests are unified by the common practice of yoga. It is located on 355 acres of mountain-top redwood forest and grassland overlooking Monterey Bay, between Santa Cruz and Monterey, in northern California.

He took a vow of continued silence in 1952 and lives the highly disciplined and austere life of a yogic monk. He does not encourage people to live as he does, but guides each to live their own life by doing what is best for them in their given situation.

I fly out for a weekend retreat that he is teaching called Disciplines of Peace. He is a kind, gentle, and peaceful man. I can feel the room light up when he enters. He writes on an erasable board and takes the time to answer individual questions, often with humor. I am able to meet with him privately to ask my personal questions. I ask him about being silent and share that I feel my spiritual path could include more silent time.

He writes on paper, "It's good to keep silence some times. Every part of the human body needs rest. Silence can be given to the mind, if one does not contact people."

I tell him I have a burning desire to establish a spiritual retreat. I have been searching for a location in the Caribbean islands during the past few winters.

He writes, "It's a good aim, but first, prepare yourself to take such a big responsibility."

I explain, "I am concerned about my health and have some physical limitations."

He writes, "Yes, your health is your first duty."

I have written down what I identify as my major issues and hand it to him. It explains how I have muscle tension, back issues, and difficulty expressing myself.

I explain, "I was devastated after my divorce and since then have spells of anxiety and depression."

I mention a few things about my parents' character; The Lamb, who acts saintly, and The Lion, who is a controlling businessman with random acts of ruthlessness or generosity.

He writes, "Your physical problems you partly inherited from your parents and the way you grew up. You can't go back, so you need to find ways of freeing your mind and body completely from the old conditioning."

I show him a list of my weekly routine, and he puts check marks next to the items he feels are most beneficial. My routine includes silence, yoga, concentration exercises, selfless service, aerobic activity, and a healthy diet. He suggests that I do regular meditation and Pranayama (breathing exercises) to release the old mental conditioning.

In regards to being silent, he says, "Talk only when necessary."

I ask him "What can I do to better understand God?"

He answers, "Purify your mind. Identify your ego attachments and desires honestly."

I save the big guru question for last, just in case he might try to rush away. I rapidly say, "I believe a guru entered my body. I don't know if The Guru is still in me. I don't understand what really happened. During the experience I gave up control of my spirit. Shortly thereafter, I received a fractured skull, which required reconstructive surgery that included three titanium plates screwed into my forehead. Afterwards, I began a feverous search for God and the truth."

He pauses and then writes slowly, "If you feel The Guru entered inside your body, then trust that guru. If it's only your imagination, then it will fall away."

Afterwards, I return to Mount Madonna a few different times for one-week and two-week segments of a 1000-hour yoga therapy course. Babi Hari Dass becomes a predominant spiritual influence during this time. We write letters back and forth. His humble honesty in the letters often touches my heart.

Once, after answering my questions he writes, "I have written so much today that my fingers hurt. I am unable to write anymore."

Whenever I visit Mount Madonna, I join Baba Hari Dass in the weekly Satsang. During this time, those in attendance can ask him questions. Both times I return to Mount Madonna I become involved in a relationship with a woman in the yoga therapy program, either sexually or romantically. I write a note for Baba Hari Dass for advice around my behavior.

He says, "Get professional treatment."

It is good advice, but I have too much pride to admit that my sexual behavior could be out of control. In my mixed up mind, I say to myself, *I am not that kind of man. I let go of some unwanted habits like drinking alcohol, and sex is how I choose to fill in the gap. Sex is a healthy and natural alternative.* Eventually, I start to realize the importance of time to build an intimate friendship before it becomes a relationship. These sexual encounters or romantic flings that start fast, end suddenly.

THE CHANUPA

I have learned more from the sacred ceremonial pipe, commonly called the *chanupa*, than from any human teacher. I am emotional and in tears as I reminisce. Just before participating in my first sweat lodge ceremony, I have a vision: a chanting medicine man with a long eagle-feather headdress dances and twirls around in circles. He turns into a whirlwind of animal spirits, and a red-tailed hawk soars out of him and flies up into the sky. The hawk's flight turns into an arrow that strikes the side of a buffalo. Next, I see the Native American people giving thanks for the buffalo. They show their respect by utilizing all the meat, bones, and hides.

A woman dressed in white buckskins, whom I later find out is known as the White Buffalo Calf Woman, appears beside the buffalo. She walks towards me and says, "You need to learn how to use the chanupa so your prayers will be heard." Then she turns into a white buffalo, a swan, and a woman again before disappearing. I wonder if the vision is real or created by my imagination.

The White Buffalo Calf Woman brought the first chanupa to the Lakota Nation. She explained the symbolic meaning and showed them how to use the chanupa to pray. It is a fascinating story. I enjoy the version told by John Fire Lame Deer that appears in *American Indian Myths and Legends*, by Erdoes and Alfonso Ortiz.

Soon after, I have an encounter with a real wild swan. It is an unnatural and remarkable experience. I am walking by a river when I spot two wild swans. I slowly go to the waters edge. One swan swims boldly toward me and looks me in the eye. I am actually able to touch its tail feathers, and the White Buffalo Calf Woman lets me know through our encounter that she is not just a fabrication of my mind. She is as real as the wild swan.

Her message is that there is a connection between what I experience in the Spirit World and what happens in the physical world. Both worlds are real. They each have a purpose, and I interact with them differently. Prayer is how I cross the bridge and communicate with the spiritual realm. In return, the Spirit World communicates with me through visions, dreams, responses to my prayers, or through signs in the physical realm.

MY FIRST CHANUPA

Today, there is a thunderstorm in the air and it's raining lightly. It's the perfect time to place the bowl and stem of my first chanupa together. I am standing on a sacred mound of moss in the woods overlooking a stone wall near my tent site in upstate New York. On a nearby tree, there is a big gnarly knot forming a silhouetted Native profile that seems to guard this spot. Hanging six feet high in a nearby oak tree is a deer skull that I found on a mountain top. In the distance, watching my every move through the branches, is a three-foot grey stone statue of an Indian holding a bow and arrow.

When I first begin to get signs to make a chanupa, I ask a friend I call My Native Brother if he will teach me how to make one. After praying about it, he agrees to show me.

My Native Brother shares his knowledge about how to make a chanupa using the traditional ways.

He says, "Make the bowl and the stem by hand, without any power tools. This way your energy will be in it." He explains how to burn a hole through the stem using a red-hot metal rod that has been set in the coals of a fire. He teaches me how to honor the directions, smudge, and handle the chanupa.

Smudging with sage is a powerful purifying technique from the Native American tradition. Smudging calls on the spirits of sacred plants to drive away negative energies, and allows me to better center myself. Smudging can be done with tobacco, sweet grass, sage, or cedar. I burn sage in a turtle shell and use a red-tailed hawk feather to fan it.

My Native Brother explains, "A pipe carrier uses his left hand to hold the bowl and his right hand to hold the stem."

He looks me in the eye and says, "You need to move slowly when you carry or handle the chanupa. It's a sacred item and an extension of your heart. The chanupa will teach, if you listen."

After I located what I felt was the perfect piece of cherry wood, I began to make the stem. It was a lot of work to do it all by hand. When I made it, the burning rod was not long enough to reach through the 14" piece of wood, so I entered from both ends and the holes met haphazardly in the middle. The hole was off center, and the interior burn ended up in the shape of a lightning bolt. For me, this was a sign that lightning energy is in this chanupa. It must enjoy being in thunderstorms. When making a Native American handcrafted item, it's acceptable and expected that there will be one flaw. It lets us know we are not perfect.

After I finished the stem, I decided it was easier to purchase a bowl online, so I ordered a red-pipestone bowl made by the 4th-generation pipe maker, Alan Monroe. From my limited knowledge, it's a good-quality traditional pipe.

I imagine that the first time I insert the stem into the bowl will be dramatic. There will be thunder clapping and lightning in the sky! I am ready. There is excitement in my blood. My Native Brother taught me to move slowly during these sacred moments, so I do. First I smudge myself with sage, and then the bowl and stem. I lift the two pieces up to the level of my chest.

It begins to rain a little harder. In my egocentric mind, I am about to become a sacred pipe carrier. I wait for the thunder. KABOOM! I can feel the power. Now is the moment! I insert the stem into the bowl for the first time and ... and ... and ... it breaks the bowl in half! *What!* The bowl breaks in half. *Ohhhh no!* This is not what I expected. I feel humble and small. Why did this happen?

I sit down to contemplate and look at the two pieces of the bowl. Buying a pipestone bowl seemed a lot easier than carving a stone myself, but now it rests in my hands, broken in half.

I wait in silence and check deep within myself. Then it comes: I need to make the bowl with my own two hands. Yes! There are no shortcuts, no quick and easy ways on this Native American path called the Red Road. I hold the two pieces. At least now, I can better understand how to make a bowl because I can see both the inside and outside. Today is not all in vain. My pipe is speaking to me and *now* I am starting to listen — really listen.

MAKING MY PERSONAL PIPE

My heart merges with the stone and wood as I place my time and energy into making a chanupa. The pipestone I choose for my pipe is black. It comes from Kanori, Canada. I figure my Abenaki ancestors were located closer to this black pipestone than the red pipestone commonly used from Minnesota. The bowl represents the feminine qualities, and the stem represents the masculine aspects. When both pieces are fitted together, it's like a man and woman coming together for a wedding ceremony. Something magical happens; the bride tends to glow. The power of a male stem is dormant until coupled inside the female bowl. Once the two pieces are united, it's activated.

Alone, each piece, as a man or woman, has a purpose, but once together their purpose is no longer just about the individual. It's about becoming a team to serve each other, their family, and the larger community. With the chanupa, I pray for myself, but usually it's for family, friends, or a cause larger than myself. I pray for the tree nations in the rainforests that are being burned, the four-legged animals like the polar bears that are being affected by global warming, and all the creatures in the sea nation affected by pollution like the dolphins, sea horses, and whales.

THE AMERICAN BALD EAGLE

Just as a man and a woman have different needs, the feminine bowl and the masculine stem call for different types of energy. I am currently a volunteer at a rapture center, so I place the bowl in the cage with two American bald eagles for a week before I begin to work on it. The pipe will absorb the energy from living and non-living matter in its surrounding environment, just like us. During our conception and as a youth, we are more susceptible to being molded by our environmental influences. I assume that the bowl, before being conceived, is similar. It's calling out for exactly what it needs. I am listening.

Let's tune in to why this pipe bowl desires American bald eagle energy. Let's consider the symbolic meaning and qualities represented by the American bald eagle. The bald eagle is the emblem of the United States of America. They are the only eagles found exclusively on the North American continent, so they are true Native Americans. Bald eagles typically mate for life, except in the event of their partner's death or impotency. They build large nests and return to them year after year. They are dedicated and loyal to their partners.

In her book, *Native Americans of San Diego County* by Donna Bradley, she says,

"Most all Native American Indian Peoples attach special significance to the Eagle and its feathers. Images of eagles and their feathers are used on many tribal logos as symbols of the Native American Indian. To be given an Eagle feather is the highest honor that can be awarded within indigenous cultures." [10]

The Native Indians saw the Eagle as a symbol for great strength, freedom, courage, leadership, and vision. I note that these are the types of energy that my bowl is requesting and the types of energy I want for myself.

It's easier for me to focus on the bowl, which represents a reflection of myself, to uncover some of my deeper needs. I chose to volunteer at a rapture center because I wanted to be near this type of energy. As an American, the eagle represents honor, respect, and dignity. When I acknowledge this, I feel good about myself. My heart is also called to be near my dogs, the ocean, and in the rainforest.

Pause and reflect upon what energy are you called to be near.

REFLECTING UPON DEVIL'S HILL

In the final sanding phase of the bowl, I work on it at ledges under the full moon at Owl's Nest overlooking Peacham Bog in Vermont. Once a year, usually in the fall foliage season, I hike up to the top of the mountain, which resides on the opposite side of this valley, called Devil's Hill. It's my favorite spot in Vermont. During my visits, I pause to notice the changes in the surrounding environment and myself. There are rock cliffs and caves. As a teenager, I explored them with friends. We would crawl around in the crevices. Sometimes we would explore the lower caves on our bellies with headlamps. From the top of Devil's Hill, there is a spectacular view of the valley, Owl's Nest, Peacham Pond, and the rolling green mountains.

I am usually on Devil's Hill looking over here, so today I am gaining a new perspective. When I sit here and look toward my favorite spot in nature, I get a reflection of myself contemplating on Devil's Hill. I consider myself a steward over that piece of preservation land. It gives more to me than I can ever give back. I feel grounded and peaceful when I sit on these mountain ledges. This is the energy that this chanupa bowl and my soul want to capture.

COMPLETING THE BOWL

I complete the bowl while I am under the great redwood trees at Mt. Madonna Retreat in California. I am sitting on a bench in a manmade cave built into the earth. A waterfall spreads out like a lacey white blanket flowing over the roof. The sound of the waterfall is soothing. Nearby, alone in the field, is a gigantic eight-foot silver Om symbol placed on a cement pedestal. *Om* is said to be the first sound of creation and represents the almighty God. In this case, God is sitting in the field watching people come and go. Like any artist, God adores those who appreciate his creations: the dew on the spider webs in the morning, the patches of neon violet flower petals, and the way the sun rays turn the waist-high grass into a field of gold in the late afternoon.

I am doing my final fine-sanding on this chanupa bowl. On the back wall of the cave rests a weathered gray statue from India. Devotees have left flowers and fruits as an offering at the foot of the statue. It is Vishnu, the Preserver, the second member of the Trimurti, along with Brahma, the Creator, and Shiva, the Destroyer. It makes sense that this is the frosting energy that my pipe bowl desires near completion. These glorious pallets of energy are packed in this one pipe bowl for a purpose, beyond what I can conceive. It takes significant patience and care to complete a bowl, and during that process, it becomes an extension of myself. If I offer my chanupa for another person to hold, I feel like they are holding my heart in their hands.

While carving the wooden stem, I called on forty angels, one-by-one, while listening to devotional chants by Snatam Kaur. Her voice is angelically pure and uplifting. During the process of being created, the female bowl traveled to exotic and beautiful places while the male stem is content to just get'er done at the tent site by the fire.

To honor the White Buffalo Calf Woman, I purchase a fancy and expensive braided bracelet with entwined turquoise and amber stones at an upscale jewelry store in Great Barrington, Massachusetts. I attach the bracelet around the stem closest to the mouthpiece. I have also acquired three white swan feathers that will hang from the opposite end.

PLACING THE CHANUPA TOGETHER

When the chanupa is complete, I go to a sweat lodge gathering with Chief Calvin, who presides over the Native Nations of Manitoba, Canada. I go to his room and offer him some tobacco. I show him my chanupa and ask for his advice.

He says, "For the first full year, smoke the pipe by yourself; get to know it."

The pipe and bowl are wrapped in a dark brown deer hide, which I purchased from a man who goes by the name of Geronimo.

Chief Calvin says, "That deer hide would make a nice pipe bag."

I call this pipe My Personal Pipe. I am the only person to ever smoke and pray with it. I get to know My Personal Pipe and myself better by praying and listening without any distractions.

I invite Feather Maker, a female companion at this Native American gathering, to sit with me on my buffalo robe to examine my chanupa.

As I hold my stem and bowl, it feels complete. I sense that I am being asked, "What is the purpose of the chanupa?"

I reflect upon loving myself, living the truth, sending out prayers, and connecting with my Native American ancestors. I slowly hand the bowl to Feather Maker. She holds the bowl next to her heart.

She says, "I feel energy, like thunder and lightning in my heart."

While she holds the female bowl near her heart, she describes the lightning energy in the masculine stem. Men and women have different needs and ways of expressing themselves, but just like the bowl and stem, we are designed to be together.

I ask Feather Maker to join me in a ceremony to place the new bowl and stem together for the first time. I choose a time when two sweat lodge ceremonies are simultaneously occurring. One is for the men and the other is for the women. She stands close to the women's lodge and I am near the men's lodge. She smudges the bowl and I smudge the stem. There is a straight line between the two lodges, with the fire in the middle. She holds the bowl in front of her at midlevel, and I hold the stem in front of me. We walk slowly toward each other. We meet near the fire and gently insert the pipe stem into the bowl. We can hear soft singing from the women and the deeper voices of the men from their corresponding lodges. I feel in my heart a spiritual bond beyond what we can hear or see. It exists between all men and all women.

I stand firm and hold the chanupa. In my inner vision, there are Native American chiefs sitting around the fire and Native American women creating an outer circle. There is a medicine man with a long, eagle-feather bonnet, dancing wildly around the fire. I honor the four directions as I fill the pipe with kinnikinnick. It's a combination of herbs that includes red willow bark, bear berry, yerba santa, and raspberry leaf.

I visualize the White Buffalo Calf Woman walking out of the woods from the north. I notice she has on her wrist the bracelet that I purchased to honor her. She has accepted the gift. She goes to the chiefs and speaks to them. Then she walks forward and sinks into the fire. The hearts of the Native American chiefs, the pipe carriers, and the women behind them are glowing bright red. I am now listening to the chanupa to honor this beautiful Native American tradition, my ancestors, and myself.

The Native American tradition is tangible and solid. It's like going barefoot to feel the earth, walking slowly and mindfully up to a tree to touch the rough texture of the bark. The blue jay and chipmunk live in the woods, and when somebody walks in their living room, they know it. My Personal Pipe allows me to slow down and reflect upon myself. I ask: *Why is this guy in such a hurry?* When I slow down in this way, my living room expands to include all of nature and the Spirit World.

Here I am smoking my chanupa under a pine tree. When I pray and listen, I become aware of what is going on inside myself. I am a part of nature, and how I treat the earth and all its inhabitants is a reflection of who I am. Spirits dart and move all around this big world, but there is one I should get to know better. It's the spirit that lives inside of me.

I am of Abenaki descent, and the chanupa is a Lakota Sioux tradition. I want to honor and respect them. I feel it's appropriate to include an explanation about the significance of the chanupa from a respected authority like John Lame Deer from the Lakota Sioux Nation. This excerpt is from the book, *Seeker of Visions; The Life of a Sioux Medicine Man* by John Lame Deer and Richard Erdoes.

BLOOD TURNED TO STONE

"I held the pipes. Their bowls were my flesh. The stem stood for all the generations. I felt my blood going into the pipe, I felt it coming back, I felt it circling in my mind like some spirit. I felt the pipes come alive in my hands, felt them move. I felt a power surging from

them into my body, filling all of me. Tears were stream-
ing down my face. And in my mind I got a glimpse of
what that pipe meant.

"That Calf Pipe made me know myself, made me
know the earth around me. It healed the blindness of
my heart and made me see another world beyond the
everyday world of the green frog skin (money). I saw
that the pipe was my church, a little piece of stone and
wood, but I would need nothing more as long as I had
this. I knew that within this pipe were all the powers of
nature, that within this pipe was me. I knew that when
I smoked the pipe I was at the center of all things, giv-
ing myself to the Great Spirit, and that every other In-
dian praying with his pipe would, at one time or other,
feel the same. I knew that releasing the smoke to rise
up to the sky, I also released something of myself that
wanted to be free and that thereby I gladdened all the
plants and animals on earth." (11)

THE HEALING PIPE

I make my second chanupa a few years after My Personal
Pipe. It's in the shape of a disk. I call it The Healing Pipe. I
work on the bowl as I live in a screen tent on top of a mountain. I am a volunteer for The Abode of the Message, a Sufi retreat center in New Lebanon, New York. I need a hand-crank
drill, and a friend, Devin, who spends a lot of time in nature,
appears. He lends me one. That is how it works in the Native
American realm. We are all brothers. We are all related. I work
on the bowl most of that day. Then I lie down to sleep for the
night.

During the night, a black bear comes by to investigate. It
leans against my screen tent to sniff inside. In the morning,
there are bear claw marks in the side. I felt safe enough and
never woke up. It is an honor to have this visitor bring bear

medicine to my chanupa. I have been told that a black bear instinctively knows when it needs to eat plant medicine and where to find it. They are natural healers.

The primary intention I place in this chanupa is to bring healing. Friends and I pray together with it. I invite select friends to join me to smoke and pray with The Healing Pipe in a teepee at the Abode.

One friend, Fascia asks, "Why do you need to use a pipe to pray?"

I say, "Just come and see what happens."

I was taught by others who lead Native gatherings that you need to create a sacred, welcoming space, so we had blankets spread out in front of the fire and pillows to sit on. It is not just about praying with the chanupa; part of a pipe ceremony is learning about the way to listen and respect each other. Fascia prayed with my friends and me, using the chanupa.

Afterwards, she said, "I felt something happen. It is a powerful way to pray."

You don't need a chanupa to pray. One needs to pray from the heart, from a place of authenticity, and then listen — really listen — and be open to receive with faith. My Native Brother shared different ways I can even use the chanupa to set a strong intention without praying. For example, if I am facing a challenging situation, I can load the chanupa and set it aside for a few days or weeks before I actually smoke the kinnikinnick and pray. During this time, the chanupa is "loaded," and my prayers are simmering. Often, the intentions of my prayers will start to address the situation.

For me, having the chanupa creates a sacred space. A pipe carrier has a responsibility to honor the chanupa, even if at times they don't honor themselves. A pipe carrier must prove themselves worthy, just as a Knight of the Round Table had to prove he was chivalrous enough. In the legend, the Knights swore a Code of Chivalry. Meaning they promised to uphold the rules given to them. Those include: to help a woman in need and never harm her. Another was: do not be cruel, and grant mercy unto him who asks for it. My friends who are pipe carriers set a living example and share a code of conduct that is similar. It includes: treat all living creatures with compassion, graciously serve others, and strive to live from the heart.

THE UNIVERSAL PIPE

My third pipe comes about in a rather peculiar manner. I am showing Wise Wolf how to make a chanupa. I send him the two pieces of that first chanupa bowl that broke in half. It's a guide for him to see, inside and out. Wise Wolf takes it upon himself to mend this broken pipe. When I receive it back, I am pleasantly surprised to find the two halves cemented together. I take it as a sign and make a stem. This is my third chanupa. I call it The Universal Pipe. The chanupa and I are broadening to accept God in different forms, religions, and traditions.

When I finish the stem, I tie it to a tree branch on the edge of a field to let it wave in the wind. I had been spotting a black bear grazing on grass in this area. Before I leave the pipe stem in the tree, I check out the area for bear signs. I discover the bear was on top of some ledges. I squat down to identify blueberries in some fresh bear scat. I am embarrassed to say that I lingered near the feces with the chanupa stem in one hand. It was a dumb thing to do, especially at this vulnerable stage of energy absorption.

I question if starting with a broken pipe bowl, even though it's mended, is a wise move. Some things are sacred, and once they crack or break, they lose their value. Years later I receive confirmation through a Lakota expert: "I would not use a broken bowl, even if it was repaired by a trusted source. The energy gets out through the cracks, even when they are mended." My best solution would have been to make a new bowl. But I go forward with the mended chanupa, because I don't know any better. Besides, it has sentimental value after my mentor, Wise Wolf, repaired it.

I let the stem swing on a tree branch for a week. Afterwards, I take my first medicine walk with The Universal Pipe. During the walk, I come across animal scat wherever I turn. I find that of the fox, deer, bear, and moose. There are also animal bones scattered all over. Perhaps it's too late. Have I called in death and an assortment of (excuse the pun) crap into my life? Yes! The Universal Pipe goes on to teach me about the darker side. Let me explain what I mean by the darker side. ■

DEATH AND DESPERATION

My grandmother, Hosanna, was a schoolteacher. After my grandfather, Buck, died, she found comfort in studying the Bible. She did not just read the Bible; she grasped hold of each word and chewed on it and digested it as a teacher. I am her student, and when I visit, we dissect her latest Bible passages. When I leave from a visit with her, I am spiritually filled. Her home is a sanctuary for family and friends. They are always welcomed with a smile, an endearing conversation, and a meal consisting of little bits of leftovers. Her couch is also a comfortable place to take a short nap. She is monumental for me as a teacher. She lives to the best of her ability as instructed through the Bible and as guided by the Holy Spirit.

She prays that her two sons will live in harmony. The Lion borrowed $20,000 from her retirement fund. It took years for her to save that much. After several years, she says, "If you can get along with your brother, I will forgive your debt." Her heart is in the right place, but her attempt to buy harmony between her sons seems to be the wrong approach.

Hosanna has devoted herself to Jesus. She prays constantly for her grandchildren, great grandchildren, and friends. She has one nephew, Firecracker, who is in and out of jail. She has taken him under her wing and writes to him regularly. She is probably his only remaining family member that deeply cares about him.

Hosanna held a sharp mind, even in her nineties. She told me in detail about how the windows shook in her house during a hurricane that happened when she was five years old. She enjoys playing different games. Now that she is in her mid-nineties, she has reverted to being more like a child. On occasion, she cries when she doesn't get what she wants.

THE FINAL DAY

At age 96, she had a stroke, and half of her body became paralyzed. Hosanna could no longer talk as she once did, which was rather constantly. When she tried to communicate, it came out as garbled sounds. It left her and family members frustrated. Soon afterwards, she was taken from the hospital to live out her remaining days at an elderly facility called The Pines. I stop by to visit her and often read from Psalms in the Bible. She listens intently and smiles.

After a few months, her condition deteriorates rapidly. There is a large black cat that lives at The Pines. It will linger for a few days in the room of an elderly man or woman before they die. The nurses all know what it means when the black cat shows up in Hosanna's room. She has decided a week earlier to stop eating. She is ready to move on to the next destination, without her body. In her mid-nineties, she spoke with jubilation about when she will be with Jesus. She said with anticipation, "What a glorious day it will be!"

One afternoon, our family gets a call from a nurse explaining that Hosanna is near the end. When I arrive, she is wrapped up in blankets like a cocoon. The Lion and my uncle are in the room with her. It is one of those awkward moments because in our family men rarely express their emotions. Pastor R.I.P. stops by to read Psalm 23, sing a song, and say a final prayer. It brings all of us some comfort. The Lion and my uncle leave to go home around suppertime.

I want to be there so she is not alone when she dies. Time passes slowly. I intend to read her psalm 91, which is one of her favorite passages. It has 16 verses about the safety of abiding in the presence of God, but somehow I end up reading Psalm 119. It's 176 verses known as *A Meditation on the Excellency of the Word of God.*

In its own way, reading her the deep, longer passage is more appropriate as our last teaching. I am her student and her grandson. She was my first Bible teacher and my grandmother. Now, she is dying.

It's 9:30 p.m. and Hosanna is on morphine and going in and out of consciousness. I place my hand on hers and cradle the back of her head. Her body is starting to shut down. Her skin color is turning purple progressively, from her feet up to her head. Nurses regularly come into the room to check her vital signs. Her breathing is rapid and labored. Her heartbeat goes steadily from 26 to 60 beats per minute.

Her blue eyes stare into mine for what seems like an hour. I am staring into God's light. She is filled with love and radiates the presence of God. When a person is dying, the last sense to go is hearing, so I sit down next to her and keep talking. I speak to her as a life coach might during a last session.

I say, "Don't resist. Be soft; don't be afraid. Be aware of everything that is happening and feel it."

Her staring into my eyes brings up a lot of different feelings. It's her only way to communicate and remain connected. At one point, I stare into her eyes and see the reflection of my own eyes. I wonder if she is able to see God in my eyes the same way I do in hers. I am sure it brings some comfort to gaze into another soul just before death. She has moved beyond acknowledging me as her grandson. We are both united as one Spirit of God. My spirit remains in my body. Hers is preparing to take a journey. Just after midnight on Halloween, the nurses roll her back onto her right side. It's the side she favors. Her last breath is more a sigh of relief. She lets out a soft, *"Huhh-hhhh."* The nurse feels her heartbeat and pulse.

She softly says, "She is gone."

She was ready to leave her body. I actually feel some joy for her departure. The nurses roll her on her back, and a minute later, the most incredible Cheshire-cat smile comes over her face. She is in bliss. I think she has just met up with Jesus.

A nurse confirms it when she says, "Those that know Jesus get a big smile after they die. I have seen it before."

As I drive home, I sense her saying, "Thank you! It was easier with you there."

She is there in the light that I saw in her eyes.

I ask her, "What is it like there?"

She says, "I am free!"

It's more like a celebration than an ending. I have some sadness, but I would not call it grief. I feel blessed for the precious moments we shared during her life, even right up to the very last minute. Besides, she knew Psalm 91 well enough to recite it.

> *"Whoever dwells in the shelter of the Most High will rest in the shadow of the Almighty. I will say of the Lord, "He is my refuge and my fortress, my God, in whom I trust."*
>
> *(Psalm 91:1-2 NIV)*

DESPERATION

Years ago, I turned my home into a duplex rental unit and renovated my guest cottage into a rental home. It provided a decent income, but being a landlord is no fairy tale. At times, it's more like a horror movie. Sometimes, tenants stop paying the rent, punch holes in the doors and walls, move out unexpectedly, and usually leave behind bags filled with foul-smelling garbage. Every job, relationship, or addiction I encounter has a lesson in it. Being a landlord helped purge my anger. A half dozen times a tenant has had the nerve to look me in the eyes and say, "I am not going to pay the rent. I am not moving out!" Then they cross their arms and give me a look that implies, "What are you going to do about it?" I would often explode and do some foolish, violent act that I would later regret.

After years of facing difficult rental situations, I realize that getting angry is not the best approach. Getting angry often causes the other to react immediately. Sometimes, I get the desired results, but it never resolves a situation in a harmonious manner. If I allow time to calm down, I can face a situation with greater wisdom. Each situation is different. If I understand their perspective and mine, then I can often resolve a conflict in a manner so we both get what we want.

I am having a stressful situation where a couple of tenants are three months behind on the rent. I notice the tenants have cut a six-inch hole in the interior and exterior wall of the rental house. Now, their washing machine water discharges directly in the backyard. My level of stress and anger is starting to rise. It takes months to actually evict somebody according to Vermont rental laws. Of course, they know this and use it to their advantage. They decide to stir the pot by using the devil's favorite weapon: they lie. They tell my tenant living in my lower-level duplex apartment, "We have seen the landlord sneak in your apartment at night. He stands above your bed and watches you sleep."

These tenants cannot afford to move out of my rental unit without the funds to place a deposit to rent another home, so I offer them $500 to move out. They look at me with disbelief and say, "This must be a trick!" It's not a trick. I am willing to purchase my peace of mind. I actually pay them to leave.

Around this time, the septic system at my rental duplex gives out. I am wading in crap, literally this time. I replaced it eight years prior for about $3,500, but since then Vermont has passed a new regulation. I must hire an expensive engineer to approve and design it. What in reality costs $5,000 to replace is lathered into a $20,000 project. I am upset about a variety of ways the cost of living in Vermont has increased, so I write a letter to the editor of the *Caledonian Record*, which is our local paper:

BREAK FREE

There are 3 milestone decisions that changed my life significantly. The first was living without a TV. It set my mind free! The second was selling my car and riding a bike when possible, no guilty acid rain on my shoulders. The third was converting my house to a rental duplex to gain financial freedom.

I am forced to sell my home due to the outrageous costs to live in Vermont; health insurance, heating fuel, and taxes are outrageously expensive, but what broke my back was the new septic regulations requiring a $20,000 mound system. Then a permit arrives after the work is complete stating I may no longer utilize my home as a duplex apartment.

It seems the system is encouraging me to lounge on the welfare system with free food, free medical coverage, fuel assistance, and tax breaks. Why work? For me it's simple, I would rather give to society than be a burden on the system. So I am, like many other middle-aged, skilled Vermonters, moving out of this state. I plan to live in a sustainable community in Costa Rica.

I love this state and this country, but radical change is required. It starts within you. As for those in Government, Lao-Tzu said it well… "If you want to govern the people, you must place yourself below them. If you want to lead the people, you must learn to follow them."

Adios Amigos, 5th Generation Vermonter

BRICK BLOCK

The financial dilemma I am facing is not limited to my rental unit. It seems like every avenue I have invested in is simultaneously draining my finances. My 2nd cousin invented a way to place a simulated brick face with inlaid grout lines on wall and chimney blocks. They are available in all the common block sizes and grout colors and can have the brick face on one or both sides. They can be used in construction for half the cost of bricks, and even up close they appear to be bricks. They are manufactured at cement-block plants, where they produce two or three blocks every five seconds.

Brick Block is a fabulous idea, especially for the United States, Canada, and Latin America. But one needs a team and finances to launch a specialized block like this nationwide. The Lion, along with a great uncle who is an inventor at IBM, and various friends and family members including myself, become board members and investors. Brick Block receives various patents and we manage the business for the next ten years.

Brick Block is unveiled at the New England construction trade show. We are a big hit and have hundreds of leads and prospective projects. A few years later, we have manufacturing plants producing our specialized blocks throughout New England and as far south as Pennsylvania. We ship our product further south. The largest areas for brick construction in the United States are in the deep south.

Brick Block needs to purchase a few new molds to be able to make our products in block plants that utilize a different brand of block production equipment. I take out a $70,000 loan and lend the money to Brick Block. I want them to succeed. To make a long story short, I don't get paid back in cash. I agree to accept stock. In part, I choose to follow the risky financial example set by The Lion. He is in full support of my actions, perhaps in part because he is a major stockholder. In the end, I am responsible for a $70,000 loan to the bank.

THE RAT TRAP

At this point, I have excellent credit, and a dozen credit-card companies have sent offers for cash at 0–5% interest. Like a rat, I take the bait. I am good at playing the credit card game. I pay off the $70,000 loan to the bank in five years. In the process, I accumulate a huge amount of credit card debt. I owe them … $70,000.

After three years, it starts to steamroll, and my monthly payment in loans and credit cards bills are twice what I earn each month. My whole financial world is starting to crumble. I need to make some radical decisions real soon.

I feel like I am running a gauntlet with bill collectors beating me on all sides. They are all demanding that I pay them. I have always paid my bills on time, but I can no longer do it. The thought of not being able to pay all my bills is anxiety-inducing. I constantly feel the stress. I am forced to draw a line, consider my priorities, and decide which bills to pay. There is a bill for the guy who delivered gravel for my septic system. He is fairly low on my priority list until he places a lien on my home.

I am living on the edge of a nervous breakdown. My muscles are wound so tightly that they feel like steel knots. I am in a very dark place. I made some unwise decisions with my finances. Now, I am paying the price. The stress is physically clamping down on my body like a vice. I have to stop and rest every few hours.

In order to keep all possible rental money flowing, I sell *all* personal items of any value: guns and family antiques, like the grandfather clock that my great, great-grandfather assembled. Then I move back into our family home with The Lamb.

To top it all off, I am in the middle of another one of those ugly scenes with a tenant who is behind on the rent. His dad has been a family employee with us for years. Now his son just gave me his spiel, "I am not going to pay any more rent. I am not moving out either." I have already lined up a new tenant to move in at the end of the month. I need him to either pay up or move out. I am angry. I make a big show by banging on the stovepipe. Then I go to punch a cupboard door beside him. As my punch is mid-air, he bends over at the waist. My elbow accidentally hits him in the eye. He gets a shiner out of it. He immediately drives to the police station and presses charges. As part of my retribution, I am ordered to take a series of sessions with a counselor for anger management.

To make matters worse, the tenant never returns to the rental unit. I am told he is afraid to come back. Eventually, I must place all his belongings in a storage unit. I give his Dad the key along with all the food from his fridge and freezer. Just another day as a landlord! ■

CHAPTER 15

The Lighthouse

During all this commotion, I am attending the local Christian church led by Pastor R.I.P. I know if I serve others it's time well spent; plus it makes me feel better. They want a youth-group leader. I want to work with youth, but Pastor R.I.P. will not even consider me as a candidate. I assume it's because I am a yoga teacher.

I have prayed about teaching yoga. It's what the Holy Spirit wants me to do. I have even dissected the components of yoga for myself from a biblical perspective, so I can clearly understand where there are controversies. The Bible is clear about not having idols in the form of statues. Some yoga teachers set up altars with statues of various Gods and Goddesses like Shiva, Ganesh or Buddha. Yoga is traditionally linked to Hinduism, Buddhism, and Jainism, so their concepts are infused. I can empathize how this could make a Christian feel uncomfortable.

CRISTO MORPHO FITNESS

One Easter Sunday, I design a Christ-based yoga class called Cristo Morpho Fitness. It comes as a complete download, before I knew there was any such thing as Christian yoga. It includes a time for prayer, worship music, breathing exercises, and sometimes I read healing scriptures while postures are being held. The big difference between a regular yoga class and a Christ-based yoga class is that the focus is on Christ. During a Cristo Morpho Fitness class, I can feel the presence of the Holy Spirit.

Once I taught Cristo Morpho Fitness to my Integral Yoga class students. They gave me mixed reviews. Jesus brings up strong reactions. Most people either love Jesus or they are radically opposed. Those who are open to a Christ-connection get touched by the Holy Spirit. One woman, who was open, had giggles all through the class. Sometimes the Holy Spirit comes accompanied with tears or giggles.

As a Christ-based yoga teacher, I encounter resistance from pastors who have not experienced a yoga class. They don't want a form of Christian fitness taught in their church. Some fundamental Christians deem yoga as evil. I have heard some outrageously false claims about yoga from Christians. A co-worker, who was a Christian woman in her sixties said, "After attending my first yoga class I felt vibrantly energized, like I was young again. I felt so good that I went out and partied that night and the next morning I felt great." She went on to explain how it was her decision to go drinking, but she thought evil spirits from the yoga class prevented her from feeling the effects of the alcohol. Another Christian proclaimed, "Every yoga pose allows an evil spirit to enter your body." Thankfully, there are some open-minded pastors that welcome yoga or Christian yoga into their church.

THE UNIVERSALIST CHURCH

I visit the local Universalist church. I am introduced to Pastor B. I explain to him that I desire to lead a youth group.

He says, "We have been searching for a youth group leader. You can start next Sunday."

I say, "I would like to offer Cristo Morpho Fitness and yoga classes at your church."

He replies, "Sure! There is a big sanctuary upstairs."

It's an old church with a beautiful sanctuary space with high ceilings, huge windows, and a well-worn wooden floor.

On Sunday, I begin as the youth pastor. There are 10-12 bright kids in the youth group. They paint a wall mural in the space where we gather. Then each kid paints an animal with a musical instrument, such as a cat with a guitar or an elephant on the drums. During the winter we have a sledding party at a nearby steep hill. Of course, it is followed by hot chocolate with marshmallows back in the church kitchen. We also meet here to make homemade pizzas. The kids like to play checkers and other games during our free time. I am discovering that these youths are a talented bunch. One is acting in a play (which we attend), another plays the violin, and a few play guitars or drums. We decide to gather in the sanctuary on a Saturday morning for a music jam.

Before I know it, I am elected to be on the board of directors for the church. I get approval and organize a project to clear out the sanctuary for a week, and we refinish the floors. It's a big project. Some local yoga teachers and church volunteers pull together. Now there is a beautifully refinished floor. It seems like a big leap compared to being reined in at the Christian church.

After four months, I am finding the real challenge of being a youth pastor is dealing with the parents, because the kids are all super cool. There was one incident, regarding a youth being told about an upcoming music jam, that became pivotal. For some unknown reason, his mother was strongly against his attending. When I called to inform the youth, his mother answered so I gave her the message. She said, "Don't contact him about it. He doesn't want to go." What she may not have known was that after he missed the first music jam, he was rather bummed out. He specifically asked me to tell him about the next one. He played an instrument and wanted to participate. So I went against her request. I told him about the music jam. Perhaps if he really wanted to attend the music jam and his mother was against it, the three of us could discuss it.

Once she found out I had contacted her son, against her request, she was livid. She arranged a special board meeting, without my knowledge, to resolve the situation. She had the power to persuade. They had an on-the-spot vote to remove me from the position of youth group leader. What really hurt was that the board did not want to listen to what happened from my perspective before deciding my fate. As a result, I felt banished from their church.

Needless to say, my stint of volunteer service at the Universalist Church came to a rapid end. I was not too upset. Pastor B had done a few things that led me to question his ethics. I left their church for the most part feeling unheard, unappreciated, and unfairly treated.

THE ULTIMATUM LETTER

I never had any reason to question the ethics of Pastor R.I.P., and I hunger to be in a church where I can feel the Holy Spirit during worship again. I humbly go back to his church. After a spell of not attending what they consider "the right" church, I have ruffled some feathers.

Upon my return, a long-time church member gives me a scrutinizing look and sharply says, "What are *you* doing back here?"

Overall, I am welcomed back by the Christian church. I am willing and ready to find my place in this church. I join a home group. It becomes a life support system. I find that the home group is a place to worship with friends, share personal challenges, and recognize how the Bible can guide us through difficult times. I share my financial despair and receive some heartfelt support.

Sometimes I feel uncomfortable at the Christian Church. I don't meet their standards for being a Christian. My spiritual path began with yoga and immersing myself in more of a universal approach. Therefore, I often speak different spiritual phrases. I find it difficult to accept their lack of tolerance toward other religions and the way their leaders verbally bash homosexuals during services and seminars. Basically, I fail tremendously at being what they consider to be a good Christian.

After five years of attending their church, I ask Pastor R.I.P. point blank, "What is it I need to do so you will trust me?"

He says, "I don't believe I can ever trust you. There is nothing you can do." This was quite a debilitating blow. My own father had proven years ago that he didn't trust me, and now my secondary father figure tells me the same.

Their church does assist me in numerous ways, for which I am grateful. I meet with a church elder weekly to receive counsel. He listens, but eventually asks me to stop talking about my financial problems. He doesn't know what to do about my bills or the stress they cause. Finance is not his area of expertise. Then Pastor R.I.P. connects me with a Christian financial advisor, who is monumental in helping me face the reality of my sticky financial situation.

He says, "It's important to tithe and have faith. There is no quick fix when you are in this deep. It could take several years to recover financially."

As fate had it, soon after, on a Sunday, Pastor R.I.P. gives a sermon devoted to tithing.

He states, "When you are facing financial difficulties, it's important to continue to tithe."

I am not convinced that tithing to the church will help my situation when my money is, in effect, coming from a credit card company, which increases my debt. I finally get it while I am driving home. It's about giving regardless of your situation. I turn around and drive back to write out a check for 10% of what I earned that month.

The next time I meet with Pastor R.I.P., he says, "I am doing something this church has never done before. I am returning your tithe check. I feel it was not given with the right attitude in your heart."

This leaves me utterly confused about tithing! It's the beginning of the end. Afterwards, a series of uncanny events unfold at the church. It all ends with what I call "The Ultimatum Letter" from Pastor R.I.P. It is a formal letter that I will paraphrase in a shorter form:

THE ULTIMATUM LETTER

We are requesting that you stand up in front of all the church members and openly repent for three things. If you don't want to comply, then we request that you leave our church, the support group, and any affiliation.

1. *Repent that it was wrong to leave our church and go to the Universalist Church.*
2. *Repent that your letter to the editor stating major milestones in your life should have included Jesus Christ. We feel your reference should have been Biblical scripture instead of a Lao-Tzu quote.*
3. *Repent that one cannot renew their mind through a Christian healing session. Renewing the mind happens over time, through reading the Bible.*

The renewing of the mind has to do with what happened after I went to a session with Charles Guest, a Christian Healer for Spiritual Warfare. During the session we address my fear of older men as an eight-year-old. With the help of Jesus, we were able to connect my heart and my mind. It was a powerful healing session. When I came home my head began to throb and burn. It was hot to touch. I became concerned and put ice on top of my head. Then I heard a soft voice say, "It will go away in one hour", and it did. This was my first real healing with Jesus and I was excited about it.

During a time for open testimonies at church on the next Sunday, I said, "After my spiritual warfare session, I felt my mind was renewed." I chose the word "renewed", because I was trying to use some of their church jargon. I never imagined my ignorant misuse of a word would be critically judged as grounds for my removal.

Well, it's not in my heart to repent the three things that Pastor R.I.P. requested to remain at his church. I did not feel that even one of the three things was really wrong. I feel that I have no option, if I have any self-dignity remaining, other than to leave Pastor R.I.P.'s church. This means I will lose the lifeline of support that I received from the home group.

My boat has begun to sink. In desperation, I abandon it. I swim alone toward the shore, shivering from being wet and cold. I am frustrated with this Christian church; our core beliefs and values are different. It's essential that I am part of a spiritual community where my relationships are based on mutual trust, respect, and understanding. Love and acceptance seem far from my reach at this church, but I believe they exist elsewhere.

These awkward issues are bobbing on the surface, circling around like sharks. I am swimming in treacherous waters: nobody to trust, nobody to understand me, nobody to affirm me anymore. I am going through my darkest night of despair. Part of my underlying hope is that the church will stop singing cheery hymns and cast out a lifeline to pull me back aboard. Their merry rowboat filled with Christian crusaders is rowing nearby. I am floundering in the water. My body sinks, except for one hand that is raised up above my head. They have spotted me and extended out a gift in my direction. I anticipate a life preserver, but instead it is an anchor. They give one last plastic smile and shout out "Halleluiah" before they wave farewell. I am swept down ... down ... down toward the bottom of the deep, dark, blue sea. I feel alone, betrayed, and alienated by yet another church.

I let go of their anchor and come up gasping for air. In the darkness, I locate the shoreline and swim toward it. I crawl up onto the dry land, exhausted. A storm is starting to rain down. The wind blows the rain in sheets off the ocean. After I catch my breath, I begin to walk along a slippery, dark path. The short scruffy shrubs offer no relief from that wind. I find myself standing on a small cliff, peering out toward the sea. There are no boats in sight; there is no shelter. Whichever direction I turn, I am facing the storm. From my despairing perspective, there is nobody left on this earth. I am all alone. Why am I being broken down, crushed, and bruised, lost and forgotten, abandoned and cast aside?

Then, in the distance I see *Him*. There is a lone lighthouse on a distant island. The light shines across the water. A beam of light exposes a desperately lonely man, drenched in rain, shivering from the cold, longing for the comfort of a friend. Then I realize, even in the middle of the storm, I am not alone. I feel the source of the light radiating. It is peace and love. I recognize it. I have felt it before. His silhouette is in the middle of the fog. I know who *He* is, but more importantly, *He* knows who I am. The church may leave, my finances can be a disaster, my body can be battered, but Jesus is still the same. I stare at His silhouette, looming in the distance. He is surrounded by the light. I take a step forward …

JESUS CALLING

I cry out to Jesus. I take another few steps forward, lose my footing, and slip over the edge. I start to slide down the face of the slippery, wet cliff. In despair, I grasp out to reach a branch or a stone — something solid, something real to hold onto. As I fall, I feel my hand wrap around a branch — No it's *not* a branch, it's the wooden stem of my chanupa that I have grabbed. I snap out of the daydream. I am standing on the back porch of our brick house preparing to pray with the chanupas! Spread out upon a table before me are my three pipes and stems, with furs underneath them. The sun is shining down brightly. I can hear the roaring waterfalls from the river below.

I am doing a rather unorthodox chanupa ceremony because I want Jesus to be a part of it; perhaps *His* silhouette from the fog remains with me. I feel it's my last chance to surrender my life to Jesus. I give Him full spiritual authority in all realms. It's a step beyond being a part of any church. It's about desiring a deeper relationship with Jesus. It's a big bold move, which I do willingly. Christ performed miracles, and people are healed by His love, daily. Certainly, Jesus has the ability to straighten out my life. Maybe I need to surrender *completely* before Jesus can fully maneuver in my life.

THE CHANUPA CEREMONY
WITH THE HOLY SPIRIT

I have a four-inch pewter statue of Jesus with one arm nailed to a cross. He is looking toward a dove with wings spread. It is taking flight from His other free hand. This statue represents the peace that Christ brings, along with the suffering He willingly endured. I offer tobacco to the earth and load the three chanupas with kinnikinnick to pray. In my ceremony, I load one pipe to honor the east, one for the south, and one for the west. The statue of Christ stands alone to honor the north for the Holy Spirit.

There is a chickadee sitting in a small pine tree, peeping out a song, calmly witnessing my ceremony. I sing a song to the East, South, and West. I smoke each of the three chanupas ... My Personal Pipe, The Healing Pipe, and The Universal Pipe ... as I say my prayers. When I am done praying with each chanupa, I kiss it.

I think to myself, *How odd is this?*

I just gave each pipe a soft little kiss of affection. It was like what one might give to a friend on the cheek when they depart.

I sing out, "Hallelujah, hallelujah, hallelujah" from Handel's Messiah to honor Jesus for the north. It was fresh in my mind because I had orchestrated our church home group to sing it.

I make a request of Jesus: "Take charge of my life through the Holy Spirit. Rule with your authority over all the aspects in my life ... my finances, my spiritual life, my health, and my relationships." It's a step in faith, for in my heart, Jesus represents my last hope. There is stillness; no visions, no thunderbolts, no tingling in my heart. The ceremony is complete.

But a few minutes after the ceremony, a spirit responds. As I walk back through the kitchen carrying the three wooden stems, I pass the wood stove. There is a roaring fire within it.

A soft whispering voice says, "Throw them in the fire!"

I stop walking. I don't want to listen or obey the voice of

this spirit. I try to ignore it, yet I know it could possibly be the Holy Spirit responding. I had a vision three years earlier of myself smashing my chanupa bowls and burning the stems. Now it has returned as a haunting flashback.

I reply to the spirit in a questioning tone, "Throw them in the fire?"

I think to myself, *Are you crazy? I can't do that.* I tell myself it's the voice of an unwanted spirit attempting to misguide me. I had never heard a soft whispering voice like this one following any other chanupa ceremony. But this is the first time I have ever invited the Holy Spirit to be a part of the ceremony. I am concerned. I place the stems upstairs in my bedroom and go back for the bowls. I carry all three bowls with a fur wrapped around them.

When I pass by the wood stove, the soft whispering voice speaks again, "Smash them with a hammer."

I respond out loud, "I will not do any such thing!"

Suddenly, The Universal Pipe falls out of the fur. It hits the floor and breaks in half. At that moment, I feel disappointed and dismayed; I know, without a doubt, it's the Holy Spirit. If I am not obedient, then the other two chanupas will be taken away. I am reluctant, but feel I have no other option. I must obey the Holy Spirit. I did ask the Holy Spirit to take control of my life, but this is not what I expected. I grab my Bible to find some confirmation.

"I have a message from God in my heart concerning the sinfulness of the wicked: There is no fear of God before their eyes. In their own eyes they flatter themselves too much to detect or hate their sin. The words of their mouths are wicked and deceitful; they fail to act wisely or do good. Even on their beds they plot evil; they commit themselves to a sinful course and do not reject what is wrong. Your love, Lord, reaches to the heavens, your faithfulness to the skies. Your righteous-

ness is like the highest mountains, your justice like the great deep. You, Lord, preserve both people and animals. How priceless is your unfailing love, O God! People take refuge in the shadow of your wings."

(Psalm 36:1-7 NIV)

A SACRIFICE FOR THE ALTAR

Of course I am reluctant! But I have faith that The Holy Spirit is taking control and making this request for my own benefit. I'm not in a position to judge whether praying with the chanupa is a sin. I have seen plenty of good results from my prayers. Perhaps the Lord is jealous enough to want me all for himself, in His own way. I am willing to comply. Actually, I feel I have no other option than to be obedient, even if it means laying down my chanupas. If I must do it, I prefer to do it with my own hands, rather than having each taken away by some other means. The Holy Spirit, for reasons unbeknownst to me, has made a clear request. I know what I must do.

"They say to wood, 'You are my father,' and to stone, 'You gave me birth.' They have turned their backs to me and not their faces; yet when they are in trouble, they say, 'Come and save us!' Where then are the gods you made for yourselves? Let them come if they can save you when you are in trouble...."

(Jeremiah 2:27-28 NIV)

I take my personal pipe and the healing pipe and do as I am guided. In a ceremonial manner, I carefully wrap them in red cloth and tie off the bundle. I bury them each underneath a sweat lodge altar.

MY ESCAPE TO YOGAVILLE

I need to leave this town, this church, and this situation. All I feel here relates to misery and pain. A friend is traveling overnight in a van destined for Virginia. I arrange to travel with him. I made arrangements to volunteer at Satchidananda Ashram, better known as Yogaville, for a few months. Afterwards, I hope to start taking classes at the nearby Liberty University, through a Vermont state grant. I have faith in God to provide a way to pay the bill.

Yogaville gives me a chance to pull myself back together. As part of their volunteer program, I am a LYT (Light) serving for thirty hours a week, usually in the kitchen or housecleaning. There is plenty of structure and discipline built into my routine. I go to daily yoga classes and meditations. Our group meets weekly for scripture studies and community Satsang, and we share as a group, which provides the needed support. I find the teachings from Swami Satchidananda very inspiring.

He says, "The aim of all spiritual practices is to know the real Self, to know the Knower. A very healthy and relaxed body with a calm and serene mind will allow the true light or the true nature of the Self within to express itself without any distortions."

My favorite part of the Integral Yoga classes is the long, guided, deep relaxations. They provide detailed step-by-step instructions on how to relax. They leave my body refreshed and renewed.

The presence of Swami Satchidananda is still here guiding people even after he has left his body. He gives encouragement to his devotees, the yoga teachers, volunteers, and visitors. He helps build up people's confidence in themselves. I never met him in person, but I can feel his peaceful presence.

I often take long walks in the woods. One day, I go to meditate in a cave on a trail near a brook. Before I know it, I find myself rolling in the brook in my underwear grieving, crying, and yelling out in anger to God, "Why did you take away my chanupas?"

In general, a man or woman receives a chanupa when they are ready for it. If it's misused, it can be taken away. I heard of a circumstance where a misused chanupa was even stolen. I understand the immense power in the chanupa. It should be honored and respected.

I wonder, *Was I worshiping the chanupa as an idol?*

Certainly, it's not meant to be worshiped as a God. It's a grounded way to pray from the heart. I feel constantly humbled by not having my chanupas.

Swami Satchidananda says, "All that happens is God's will, not even a speck of dust can move without God."

Eventually, I start to let it go.

The chanupa is one way I found inner peace. Through them I came closer to understanding God, life, and myself. This Spirit of God still lives in me. I am still intact; my heart is still beating. I am still alive. I can live with or without them. Making them taught me lessons, but losing them was a tougher lesson. It forced me to realize that my power to pray resides in my heart and in my intentions, not in the chanupa.

FEARLESS FAITH

At this point, I don't really know Jesus or what He is all about. If I want to get to know somebody, I spend time with them, but how do I do that with Jesus, who is not in the flesh? I have asked Jesus to come into my life. I am ready to explore the Bible and to start a personal relationship with Him. I feel the best environment for this to happen is a place where I can immerse myself in a "Jesus culture." My Vermont grant for classes at Liberty University is approved. God is faithful in providing the funds.

Liberty University is located in Lynchburg, Virginia. The university is a small city with paved streets. There is a huge dome-shaped arena that has a basketball court in the center filled with folding chairs. I gather here with 10,000 other students for assembly twice a week. We begin with several worship songs led by students playing guitar, drums, and keyboards. It has the same rock beat as a concert, but there are some noteworthy differences. The words are to glorify Jesus and God.

At Liberty University, as with most churches, we begin with songs of praise and worship. It's a way to synchronize in harmony with each other. Even more importantly, we get closer to God or Jesus. Many students have their eyes closed. It allows them to focus more on the feelings in their hearts.

Occasionally, I get tears in my eyes during worship. I become overwhelmed by feelings of love toward Jesus or God. It's mixed at that same moment with the love that I receive. God and Jesus continually love me. But during worship I can feel it and taste it.

When I listen to worship music with 10,000 other people or on my own, it forces me to move beyond my thoughts and worries. I rest in my heart. There is a difference between listening to music and feeling it. Worship music is meant to be felt in your heart. We sing with our voices, but if a song is received or stems from the heart, it becomes a deeper spiritual experience.

I often receive personal guidance through the worship music, through the reading of a scripture, or from those sharing a testimony. I am touched when someone gets up to share how Jesus made a difference in his or her life. There is passion in their voice. *How can I get that kind of passion for Jesus?*

FAITH IN THE BIBLE

My relationship and faith in Christ was shaky until I accepted that the Holy Bible, especially the New Testament, was the truth. I was stubborn and questioned if parts of the Bible were irrefutable.

Jesus said,

> *"Do not think that I have come to abolish the Law or the Prophets (referring to the scriptures of His time); I have not come to abolish them but to fulfill them."*
>
> (Matthew 5:17 NIV)

Reflect upon what that means!

Jesus is saying, "The scriptures are true and I am here as part of the proof."

I have studied and contemplated The Yoga Sutras, The Bhagavita, the Toa Ching, and the Sufi writings of Hazrat Inayat Khan. As far as I am concerned, they all speak the truth. The primary reason I went to Liberty University was to find out what Jesus was really about. What sets Him apart from other spiritual teachers? In the Bible, Peter and John write that Jesus lived a perfect life, without sin. Jesus made some preposterous claims about Himself:

"The Father and I are one."

(John 10:30 NIV)

"You are of this world; I am not of this world."

(John 8:23 NIV)

"Before Abraham was born, I am."

(John 8:58 NIV)

I understand why some people don't believe in Jesus or what is written in the Bible. What Jesus says seems crazy! Jesus does not claim, as do other spiritual teachers, to show a way to salvation. He states He *is* the way to salvation. (John 14:6) Then there are all the healing miracles and His resurrection. After I pieced together what Jesus did and said, along with a lot of soul-searching, I came to the conclusion that there is no other possibility: Jesus *is* the Son of God.

I don't expect everyone's view on Jesus or the Bible will drastically change overnight. It's my desire that some readers will gain a new perspective and a few eager souls will further investigate the Bible or explore what Jesus is really about from followers who know Him. The foundation that I build upon is that the Bible is true. If you do not believe, and you want to position yourself to better understand my viewpoint, then entertain the possibility that it could be true, for the next few chapters.

Many people have experienced an overzealous person trying to evangelize in a judgmental or unwelcome manner. Why do they do that? Well, they are passionate about Jesus and want to share it, but often they take the wrong approach. I believe what most people who know Jesus desire is for you to experience a relationship with Him. The Bible is certainly a relevant starting point for learning about Jesus. An alternative approach, which I advocate, is to speak about their relationship with Jesus. It's interesting to learn another's heart-felt experience and less offensive to show how scripture relates or provides proof. This is the approach I take.

I find some parts of the Bible, especially the Old Testament, hard to comprehend. In these areas, I ask the Holy Spirit for guidance. Often, what I don't understand is made clear through a sermon, a song, or a casual conversation with a friend. For example, I don't understand why I should "fear God." I was afraid of my real father for years, and don't want to fear God. I have some issues around it and pray to the Holy Spirit for an answer. The Bible uses the word "fear" at least 300 times in reference to God. If God is my creator who loves me, then why should I be afraid of Him?

In the article, *What does it mean to fear God?* by JoHannah Reardon, she writes,

> "*Fearing God is good because it saves us from caving in to our own sinful nature. That's why hearing someone is God-fearing actually makes us trust that person more. If they fear God, they are more likely to keep their word and treat others with kindness. In fact, Romans 3, a classic chapter on sin, says that our chief sin is that we 'have no fear of God at all' (Romans 3:18).*
>
> "*So how does fear of God, who is perfect love, take away fear? William D. Eisenhower puts it this way in his article Fearing God in Christianity Today:*
>
> "*Unfortunately, many of us presume that the world is the ultimate threat and that God's function is to off-set it. How different this is from the biblical position that God is far scarier than the world .... When we assume that the world is the ultimate threat, we give it unwarranted power, for in truth, the world's threats are temporary. When we expect God to balance the stress of the world, we reduce him to the world's equal .... As I walk with the Lord, I discover that God poses an ominous threat to my ego, but not to me. He rescues me from my delusions, so he may reveal the truth that sets*

me free. He casts me down, only to lift me up again. He sits in judgment of my sin, but forgives me nevertheless. Fear of the Lord is the beginning of wisdom, but love from the Lord is its completion.

"And, of course, the ultimate example of fear and perfect love working together is Jesus Christ. He warned us at every turn to fear God, not men — and he confirmed that in everything about his life and death. He spoke lovingly but frankly to all and didn't mince words when people needed to face their sin and repent. But he also demonstrated love beyond human understanding when he lived out his words, 'There is no greater love than to lay down one's life for one's friends (John 15:13).' With love like that, what is left to fear but God?" (12)

HOLY SPIRIT GUIDANCE

If I want to get to know Jesus, then I need to get to know the Holy Spirit. Jesus sent us the Holy Spirit as a way for us to stay in touch with Him. This is no ordinary event. The Holy Spirit was sent because Jesus loves us. He can't be on this earth, not right now. Jesus is ruling over the Kingdom in heaven. (Remember, we are all believing the Bible.) Through the Holy Spirit, Jesus and His followers also have power upon the earth.

"But very truly I tell you, it is for your good that I am going away. Unless I go away, the Advocate will not come to you; but if I go, I will send him to you... But when he, the Spirit of truth, comes, he will guide you into all the truth. He will not speak on his own; he will speak only what he hears, and he will tell you what is yet to come. He will glorify me because it is from me that he will receive what he will make known to you."

(John: 16:7,13,14 NIV)

The Bible explains that The Holy Spirit has characteristics similar to any person. I like to picture the Holy Spirit as our living host, a wise and gentle grandfather who provides intimate services and powerful resources. Our living host does what Jesus would want to do if He was on the earth. He has an engaging personality. He has a range of glorious emotions. He is, hopefully, elated and always good-natured. The Holy Spirit has His own will and desires. One is to comfort and care for His family.

I have been let down by men and women, especially when I have built-in expectations. But Jesus, a.k.a. the Holy Spirit, will not, cannot, let me down. He is there with me. When I feel broken and need healing, the Holy Spirit knows it and wants to aid. He is there to listen, encourage, and comfort me. It is a great comfort to know that during my whole life, someone will be present who always understands and loves me.

Often the cause of my discomfort stems from what I tell myself; I have no friends, nobody loves me, I can't do it, I am not smart enough, strong enough, or handsome enough. When I pause and let the Holy Spirit intercede, He reveals them all … as lies.

"Behold, You desire truth in the innermost being, And in the hidden part You will make me know wisdom."
(Psalm 51:6 NASB)

The Holy Spirit crashes over me, "I am so pleased with you." He holds me. His voice keeps me steadfast when I am in over my head. He wants me to give Him all my problems. He wants me to rely on Him. He wants my attention. I believe He wants me to lose control. That way, He can take over. He can handle it; I can't anymore. When I rely on Him, it brings me beautiful joy. He really deserves to have what He wants — me.

Jesus is on earth and in heaven. Jesus knew that He had to die on that cross to allow the Holy Spirit to be with us. Through His obedience, He was able to divide Himself to be able to reign over heaven and earth. He is still alive! I never understood how people could get so excited about Jesus. Now, I am becoming one of them. In my case, I first needed a deeper understanding of Jesus and to experience what it means to actually have the Holy Spirit living inside of my heart. Now, I know how much goodness resides in Jesus and the Holy Spirit. It's hard to understand what that actually means if you have never experienced it. One gets access by asking Jesus, via the Holy Spirit, into your life. He needs permission to operate in your life. One needs to invite Him to take up residence in their heart. It can be that simple. The Holy Spirit is available to counsel, comfort, intercede, guide, and give out spiritual gifts.

> *"To one there is given through the Spirit a message of wisdom, to another a message of knowledge by means of the same Spirit, to another faith by the same Spirit, to another gifts of healing by that one Spirit, to another miraculous powers, to another prophecy, to another distinguishing between spirits, to another speaking in different kinds of tongues, and to still another the interpretation of tongues. All these are the work of one and the same Spirit, and he distributes them to each one, just as he determines."*
>
> (*1 Corinthians 12:8-11 NIV*)

When I have a need for a spiritual gift, I pray for it. I believe that I have received all of the gifts at different times, in varying degrees. Faith dominates as my strongest gift. I have also been given wisdom, but I need to slow down to pray and listen in order to receive it. I often receive my guidance during walks.

The greatest gift is being in His presence. It is a taste of Heaven. We are able to taste Jesus through the Holy Spirit.

When I patiently and persistently pray with faith, God has never failed to provide personal healing. The Holy Spirit wants to protect me from harm and keep me healthy. In order to receive these blessings, I must be obedient to following the guidance given. We often expect a miracle, which does happen on occasion, but more often it requires discipline, patience, and persistence. I believe that being where there is a strong presence of God or Love can bring about healing more rapidly.

When I have a serious problem, I pray. I acknowledge today that I could be more joyful and that I can be more thankful for my blessings. I am writing this because a few people reading this book could be more thankful. You know if I am talking about you because you have goose bumps all over your arms! If that is the case, then right now, put down this book and give thanks for all you have been given. The book will still be here. I had my health, finances, and beloved friends taken away so I could learn to be thankful. Now don't be like me. Just do it.

Pause for a moment and be thankful!

> *"Rejoice always, pray continually, give thanks in all circumstances; for this is God's will for you in Christ Jesus."*
>
> *(1 Thessalonians 5:16-18 NIV)*

DOUBT

After Jesus was crucified, most of his apostles were gathered in the upper room. They were scared for a good reason. They didn't want to be captured and crucified. Thomas ran off by himself. He knew being with them meant a greater chance of being caught. These are the apostles — the ones Jesus hand-picked to follow Him! They saw all His miracles and still they had their doubts. Jesus said to Peter during Passover,

> *"Simon, Simon, Satan has asked to sift all of you as wheat. But I have prayed for you, Simon, that your faith may not fail. And when you have turned back, strengthen your brothers."*
>
> *(Luke 22:31-32 NIV)*

If I understand it properly, Jesus grants Satan permission to sift His disciples like wheat. Jesus knows that Peter must face temptation, but He is praying for him. He loves Simon so much He wants him to reach his full potential.

Even after witnessing His resurrection, they fell back to their old ways. Peter and the others went fishing. Maybe they wanted to return to their former lifestyle because it felt more comfortable. Again and again, Jesus let them know that His life and His resurrection happened to give their life a new purpose and meaning. It was hard for them to change their ways and make their own stand.

But the ascension was the climax of His final forty days. He requested that the apostles gather at Mount of Olives. He told them that it was time for Him to leave this earth. They had witnessed His life and death and resurrection. It was time to receive their final instructions. They were told to be His witnesses and spread His teachings. They were told to stay in Jerusalem until they received the power of the Holy Spirit, which will comfort and guide them in all truth. Jesus explains that He must leave in order for them to receive the Holy Spirit.

The apostles are beginning to understand their purpose or their final destiny. Jesus had shown a living example of how the Holy Spirit lived in and operated through one man, Himself. Jesus declared that anyone who believed in Him with faith would receive authority to heal and perform miracles in His name.

The next book is called Acts for a reason. They finally got it! They began to have real faith. They dedicated their lives completely to Jesus. After they receive the Holy Spirit, they better understood its power and wanted others to receive it. The apostles began miraculously healing people and Peter stood up at Pentecost to say,

"Therefore let all Israel be assured of this: God has made this Jesus, whom you crucified, both Lord and Messiah."

When the people heard this, they were cut to the heart and said to Peter and the other apostles, "Brothers, what shall we do?"

Peter replied, "Repent and be baptized, every one of you, in the name of Jesus Christ for the forgiveness of your sins. And you will receive the gift of the Holy Spirit.... Those who accepted his message were baptized, and about three thousand were added to their number that day."

(Act 2:38-41 NIV)

Great things happened when Peter placed his faith in Jesus. The same can happen to you and me. There will be temptations and we can count on being sifted, just like Peter. But Jesus is there to intercede for your behalf and mine. All we need to do is *believe*.

After the resurrection, doubting Thomas said he had to touch Jesus to know He was real. Jesus complied.

"Then Jesus told him, "Because you have seen me, you have believed; blessed are those who have not seen and yet have believed."

(John 20:29 NIV)

THE MISUNDERSTOOD CHRISTIAN

I am writing this section for Christians who have an understanding of and faith in the Bible. They are often misunderstood by other people who have little understanding of Christian lifestyle or the Bible. My hope is that Christians can be better understood. It's easy to talk to a Christian about Jesus, but I am cautious when I talk about Him with people that don't have a connection with Jesus or the Bible. Some people have a lot of resistance toward God or Jesus. I believe the primary cause is spiritual abuse from church leaders, but it also occurs through authority figures in well-intended Christian families.

Ronald Enroth in his book, *Recovering From Churches That Abuse*, explains,

> "*When our trust is violated by those who have been accorded society's respect because of their special role as spiritual caretakers and shepherds of God's flock, the pain, injury, and disillusionment can be devastating. Juanita and Dale Ryan in Recovery from Spiritual Abuse (Downers Grove, Ill.: InterVarsity Press, 1992, p 9-10.) wrote, 'Spiritual abuse is a kind of abuse which damages the central core of who we are. It leaves us spiritually discouraged and emotionally cut off from the healing love of God.'*
>
> "*Spiritual abuse takes place when leaders to whom people look for guidance and spiritual nurture use their positions of authority to manipulate, control, and dominate. Or, as David Johnson and Jeff VanVonderen describe it in The Subtle Power of Spiritual Abuse (Minneapolis: Bethany House, 1991 p. 20), 'Spiritual abuse is the mistreatment of a person who is in need of help, support or greater spiritual empowerment, with the result of weakening, undermining or decreasing that person's spiritual empowerment.'*
>
> "*Most people who are victims of spiritual abuse are sincerely seeking God, either out of a desire to serve him and know him more intimately or out of a deeply felt need to resolve problems. Being vulnerable in their spiritual journey, they would not knowingly subject themselves to pastoral or spiritual abuse. When they later realize that they have been involved in an un-*

healthy, abusive system, it is understandable that they may harbor resentment and bitterness against the leadership and against God himself. 'Why did God allow this to happen to me when I was sincerely trying to know his will?'" (13)

I try to relate to each person on a level they can understand. I deliberately choose not to discuss Jesus or the Bible with some friends because, frankly, they are not interested or get offended. In this case, it's better that I just show how much I love and care about them. It's not difficult to open up and talk about Jesus after I have established a friendship. Over time, people are naturally curious, and most want to know about my relationship with Jesus, even if it's not their chosen faith. I hope that my actions and the kindness with which I treat others reflects that Christ lives within me.

Imagine how hard it is for a Christian to relate to somebody who has little or no knowledge of the Bible. The Bible addresses almost all of the major issues of life. The Bible is a Christian's foundation of evidence; one who does not accept the Bible as the truth will at times contradict the Bible with their words and corresponding actions. Those who are not Christians will validate their evidence based on their worldly reasoning. Jesus was not of this world. Christians must at times have faith that goes beyond understanding. To debate with a Christian without accepting supporting evidence from the Bible or being of the opinion that part of the Bible is not true, never goes over well.

Once you have established that somebody believes in the Bible, you generally know a lot about their beliefs. At times, it's a real challenge for a Christian to live out Christ's commandments. If you want a genuine eye-opener, then the next time you interact with a Christian, ask him or her to open their heart and tell you what Jesus has done in them or who is Jesus to them. If they have a personal relationship with Jesus then you will know by their experience that Jesus is the real deal. Christians will be delighted to share in this way.

> *"As a prisoner for the Lord, then, I urge you to live a life worthy of the calling you have received. Be completely humble and gentle; be patient, bearing with one another in love. Make every effort to keep the unity of the Spirit through the bond of peace."*
>
> *(Ephesians 4:1-3 NIV)*

JESUS IS MISUNDERSTOOD

There is a force out there that makes it difficult for some people to accept and understand Christ. Can you feel it? It's rooted in a dark misunderstanding and carries a history of false accusations, prosecutions, and violent acts that claim to be done for Christ. Gandhi said, "I like your Christ, but not your Christians. Your Christians are nothing like your Christ." Jesus knows which actions are acts of love and those that are not. It's no surprise that Christians sometimes feel misunderstood. Jesus was misunderstood almost all the time, by most people, including his twelve disciples.

Jesus loves me and I love Him. Sometimes I talk to Him as a friend and I feel His presence. Other times, I feel all alone, but Jesus is nearby. I know Jesus has the capability to heal the trauma in my heart because I have experienced it. Jesus is a big part of my life and good things keep happening. I am glad about it and our relationship keeps deepening. But my Savior, Jesus, is still a mystery. He operates from a completely different dimension.

When I speak with Jesus in quiet times, He talks back. Once Jesus said, "I am not in love with you." I thought to myself, *What a bummer!* Then, He continued, "I am *madly* in love with you and any person that is making an attempt to follow me."

I asked Jesus, "What do you want to tell people?" Jesus said, "I have five things...

1. "Don't be afraid of me. I am not the (misguided) church."
2. "I am sick of people pretending they know me more than they do."
3. "I would like there to be more hands-on healing in the U.S.A."
4. "If a Christian kills himself, he will not come to me."
5. "Love one another."

Knocking on Heaven's Door

If you surrender to Jesus, then expect to slowly transform into a new creature. It's a process of surrendering one's life to Christ. I believe there is always a little more I can surrender. In my spiritual vision, I go to Jesus and find a door. I knock on it, just like knocking on heaven's door. At first, He does not open the door or respond, but Jesus knows I am there.

I say, "Jesus, I want to have a deeper relationship with you. Will you be my teacher, my guide, and my friend?"

Eventually, the door opens and Jesus says, "Will you die for me?"

Wait a minute. That's a bit too heavy. I visualize myself dying as a martyr for Christ. Ouch! I am not ready to stand up for Jesus to *that* extreme. My life is a precious commodity. In reality, there are few who are willing or able to completely surrender their whole body and soul to Christ in an unharnessed and unashamed manner.

I say, "I am not ready to die for you, but if I get to know you better, then one day I may be ready."

Jesus says, "Come back when you are ready." I leave a little disappointed. I can't explain Jesus in a candy-coated way. Perhaps it is best if we take a look at His words and you decide what He really means. Yes, we need to creak open that old dusty Bible and look at the words in red. The Jesus I am getting to know is not a gentle lamb. He is a fierce lion.

"Do not suppose that I have come to bring peace to the earth. I did not come to bring peace, but a sword. For I have come to turn 'a man against his father, a daughter against her mother, a daughter-in-law against her mother-in-law; a man's enemies will be the members of his own household.' Anyone who loves their father or mother more than me is not worthy of me; anyone who loves their son or daughter more than me is not worthy of me. Whoever does not take up their cross and follow me is not worthy of me. Whoever finds their life will lose it, and whoever loses their life for my sake will find it."

(Matthew 10:34-39 NIV)

This sounds pretty harsh. Jesus wants a serious commitment.

"Not everyone who says to me, 'Lord, Lord,' will enter the kingdom of heaven, but only the one who does the will of my Father who is in heaven. Many will say to me on that day, 'Lord, Lord, did we not prophesy in your name and in your name drive out demons and in your name perform many miracles?' Then I will tell them plainly, 'I never knew you. Away from me, you evildoers!'"

(Matthew 7:21-24 NIV)

You mean I can go to church and tithe and read the Bible? But once in heaven, I might not be let into the Jesus club. That is an upset! What do I need to do?

"Therefore go and make disciples of all nations, baptizing them in the name of the Father and of the Son and of the Holy Spirit, and teaching them to obey everything I have commanded you. And surely I am with you always, to the very end of the age."

(Matthew 28:19-20 NIV)

A disciple is one who will embrace and assist in spreading the teachings. If I believe in the teachings of Jesus, that seems pretty reasonable. I will gladly share His teachings with others. What is the best way for me to go about it?

Jesus picked out twelve ordinary men that were willing to follow Him. Life unfolded; Jesus was Himself. He often taught the disciples and other people during ordinary everyday events: they ran out of wine at the wedding; He meets a woman at a well, because He is thirsty; the temple taxes needed to be paid; a woman was caught in the act of committing adultery; and His friend, Lazareth, died. My point is — opportunities arise.

Now, about baptism. Jesus is asking us to dunk underwater in the name of God, Himself, and The Holy Spirit. To a conventional adult, this ceremony might seem bizarre. But Jesus also told us we must look at everything with fresh eyes like innocent children.

> *"And he said: 'Truly I tell you, unless you change and become like little children, you will never enter the kingdom of heaven. Therefore, whoever takes the lowly position of this child is the greatest in the kingdom of heaven. And whoever welcomes one such child in my name welcomes me.'"*
>
> *(Matthew 18:3-5 NIV)*

When I take a childlike perspective, I am ready to dunk in the pool. It helps knowing Jesus did it first. There was also the criminal being crucified next to Jesus, who was not baptized. The fact that one believes in Jesus seems more important than the baptism.

> *Then he said, "Jesus, remember me when you come into your kingdom."*
> *Jesus answered him, "Truly I tell you, today you will be with me in paradise."*
>
> *(Luke 23:42-43 NIV)*

I felt the reasons for my being baptized were more symbolic. Let's seek an answer from Got Questions Ministries. *What is the symbolism of water baptism?*

> *"Water baptism symbolizes the believer's total trust in and total reliance on the Lord Jesus Christ, as well as a commitment to live obediently to Him. It also expresses unity with all the saints (Ephesians 2:19), that is, with every person in every nation on earth who is a member of the Body of Christ (Galatians 3:27–28). Water baptism conveys this and more, but it is not what saves us. Instead, we are saved by grace through faith, apart from works (Ephesians 2:8–9). We are baptized because our Lord commanded it. (Matthew 28:19).*
>
> *"Water baptism is a beautiful picture of what our Lord has done for us. As we are completely immersed in the water, we symbolize burial with our Lord; we are baptized into His death on the cross and are no longer slaves to self or sin (Romans 6:3–7). When we are raised out of the water, we are symbolically resurrected — raised to new life in Christ to be with Him forever, born into the family of our loving God (Romans 8:16). Water baptism also illustrates the spiritual cleansing we experience when we are saved; just as water cleanses the flesh, so the Holy Spirit cleanses our hearts when we trust Christ."* [14]

LOVE YOUR ENEMIES

In order to learn or teach all of Jesus' commandments, we need to study the Bible. Let's examine a few of His principal commandments.

> *"'Love the Lord your God with all your heart and with all your soul and with all your strength and with all your mind'; and, 'Love your neighbor as yourself.'"*
>
> *(Luke 10:27 NIV)*

One imperative reason He came was to show us how to love one another and how much He loved God.

> "You have heard that it was said, 'Love your neighbor and hate your enemy.' But I tell you, love your enemies and pray for those who persecute you, that you may be children of your Father in heaven. He causes his sun to rise on the evil and the good, and sends rain on the righteous and the unrighteous."
>
> *(Matthew 5:43-45 NIV)*

Jesus introduced a new paradigm. The workings of God are a mystery. If God really sent Jesus, as His son, in the flesh, don't expect to be able to figure out Jesus. That is not what it's all about. There is a bigger purpose. God wants us to know how much He loves us. Jesus came to show us how much He loves God and us. The Pharisees, and many of us, from pride, fear, or ignorance, do not want to accept Jesus or His love.

I believe the broken ones were healed by Jesus because He loved them. His love was directed at the broken ones for a reason: They were open and able to receive it. Actually, He was overwhelmed with compassion. Love emanated from His presence, healing manifested because sickness and disease were obstacles in the way. The woman with the bleeding traveled thirty miles to touch His cloak and then she was healed. Many people went out of their way to seek out Jesus, probably because they heard about the miracles. But what Jesus was and still is offering is healing through His love.

If you have been broken or suffered immensely, you are a prime candidate to receive His love. It will probably not manifest in the way you expect. In all honesty, you may need to be broken down even more before you are ready. One must be ripe. Most of the hardcore followers of Jesus have been broken down, beaten, and pummeled. The Holy Spirit or the love of God flows through the cracks and scars in their bodies, just like Him. These Brothers and Sisters that specialize in love, naturally spend their time with the broken-hearted, those inflicted with diseases, the homeless, prisoners, widows, and orphans. When Jesus said, "Love your enemies", it was meant to include your extended family, the clerk at the grocery store, your local police officers, and any annoying coworkers. In short, every single nasty person who crosses your path. If you really *love* them, you no longer see them as being nasty. You sympathize with them; you treat them with kindness.

We can't impart the teachings of Jesus unless we are living in the light of Love. As I get closer to this light, the line of religion and people's everyday (non-violent) actions being right or wrong begins to fade. It is more about loving people for who they are, not what they do. People raised in other cultures have different values and customs. We should expect them to think and act differently. It is the sad truth; many Christians are not fully living in that light. But it's essential that we learn to revere God and cherish each other.

WORLD HARVEST OUTREACH

I want to share an example of a church that I attend in Chambersburg, Pennsylvania, that has successfully fostered an environment of love. Relationships with each other and with the Holy Spirit and Jesus are their primary focus. They go on regular missionary trips to the Ukraine and Costa Rica, where they have established some beautiful relationships.

There is no need to state their rules. They live them and you learn their protocol after attending a few gatherings. Only a few guidelines exist. One is to be yourself. It takes some people a year or more to be comfortable in their own skin. Their second rule is no coffee in the sanctuary. They don't want to stain the carpet. They enforce it in a light-hearted way with the coffee police. They don't need a lot of rules or a complex governing structure, because the Holy Spirit rules over this place with love.

Their worship team resembles the Bethel Church format. Each gathering for worship or a discussion is fresh and alive, because they follow the Holy Spirit's lead. It's not always apparent what will happen next, but a theme generally appears. It is common to see a man or woman step up onto the stage during worship to share a word, a personal breakthrough, or join in a song. Actually, the whole church is part of the worship team. There are many from the younger generation. They are usually up front by the stage doing lively dancing and dynamic praising. It can become blissfully ecstatic. Sometimes they spill up onto the stage. They become united, as one spirit in worship.

Occasionally, someone in the worship team or the multitude breaks down in tears. A lot of stuff comes up when you are in the presence of the Holy Spirit and this much love. Those in need are soon surrounded by hugs and caring, warm hands. I recall one of the young female singers weeping, because of what the Holy Spirit was pressing upon her to deliver. She is given fortitude by a few young women who run up and place hands on her back. She knows what she has to say is significant. Once she regains her composure, she valiantly grabs the mike and screams, "YOU'RE NOT DEAD! YOU'RE NOT DEAD!" When you have been really broken, it feels like the life has been sucked out of you. I was feeling bleak and lifeless. She went on to remind me, along with the whole worship team: *We are Alive!* Jesus gives us life and He is alive in us. Sometimes, we need a slap to wake up, so we can fully live and love as intended.

For many people there is fear of being intimate. As babies, we were hugged and held by our mother. We loved being intimate. We cried out for it sometimes. Touch is essential for our being able to thrive emotionally as a child, and as an adult. Along the path, some of us were taught that being close is forbidden. We are sometimes told in a relationship: You can't touch me, you can't be near me, you can't speak to me, and you can't hug me. Maybe it was another church or a community that sent the message: "you don't fit in" or "we are not comfortable with you". I believe after it happens a few times, we start to lose hope. It sends a message that "you are not worthy of being loved" and "you need to stop being intimate". In order to break the chain of lies, we need to be able to trust and respect other people, our church community, and be confident in ourselves.

At World Harvest Outreach, the leaders or "Fathers" set an example for all the "Sons". They are the first to repent and ask for forgiveness. Jesus wants to annihilate the wall of judgment we have created. In most cases, the wall was unknowingly built through society. As children, we learn to emulate our parents and friends. People still discriminate against race, religion, and women. It often reveals itself in the form of sarcasm or bias jokes. We need not blame ourselves, but if we are aware of our own blemishes, we can take responsibility. That means we need to learn to love every single person for *who they are*; not how they look, what they do, their different beliefs, or their past.

Take a moment and consider whether you have shown favoritism or resistance to people according to: gender, race, religion, age, physical features, income, intelligence, opposing beliefs, or temperament.

If we are able to selflessly give and receive love, it will be reflected in our traits as described in "the fruit of the Spirit". In other words, don't try to be kind, just be loving and you will possess kindness.

"*But the fruit of the Spirit is love, joy, peace, patience, kindness, goodness, faithfulness, gentleness, self-control; against such things there is no law.*"

(Galatians 5:22-23 NASB)

The King James Version uses the word longsuffering. It's an excellent word. We can show our love by hanging out with friends and family when they are hurting. We don't need to teach them, preach to them, or try to fix them. All we need to do is be with them, with love in our hearts. The secret is to focus on loving them so much that we forget about ourselves. Just remember, we are not trying to heal ourselves or them.

RENUNCIATION AND ATTACHMENT

It seems like I had everything good in my life taken away. Maybe it was to make space for something better (like God or Jesus). Perhaps, I needed to learn to not be so attached. Renunciation is all about relinquishing or surrendering something that you once enjoyed. The ultimate renunciation is of self, one's separateness from others and the world.

Let's seek an explanation from a teacher close to my heart, Swami Satchidananda. He is the founder of Integral Yoga and Satchidananda Ashram. Swami Satchidananda writes,

> *"Either you renounce completely, or lose everything. Both are the same. If you don't renounce and you are a sincere seeker probably the world will temporarily take all away from you. That is another reason why people who are really after God suffer so much and seem to lose everything one by one. Don't think by wanting God, you will have everything. No, if you want God be ready to lose everything. He will take it away because He wants you totally. He doesn't want you to run after other things."* (15)

I believe that is what happened to me. God wanted me to surrender everything, in essence my whole life, to Him. I am pretty stubborn. It took fifteen years to break me down.

God took it all away: My finances, my wife, my health, my

cameras, and even my cat. My, my, my, this all seems about me, doesn't it?

Swami Satchidananda writes,

> "To keep the mind tranquil, we have to free ourselves from anything that we might call ours. It includes the body, mind, intelligence, ego, everything. Nothing is mine. Nothing belongs to me. It all belongs to God. And ultimately, I, Myself belong to God."

When I first read this quote and contemplated surrendering myself completely to God, I began to cry.

I thought to myself, "What good will my body be to God?" I cannot sit down for very long; it causes pain in my back. Well, God knows about my back, and He will accept me or you in our currently-perceived, pathetic conditions. Through His love we can find healing and a purpose. His love is everywhere, especially inside Jesus and the hearts of other people. But finding love never happens as we expect. God has a tailor-made plan for each of us. Jesus is part of God's plan for me.

Swami Satchidananda continues with this subject in a booklet called *Everything Will Come to You,*

> "Renunciation means 'well given up.' But in this case, it's not that you give up completely. What you give up is the notion that you are this and you are that. It's an understanding. You don't have to become somebody. You don't have to get it from somebody. What it means is that you come 'to know yourself' who you really are. This understanding cannot be given to you by somebody else."

At this moment, I am in Costa Rica and a fabulously brilliant colored Toucan has perched a few feet away on a tree limb. I am in awe of the pure majestic beauty in the rainbow of colors on his chest and tail feathers. God is always this close. When I focus on God or my inner peace and let go of anything that I call mine, then I am a more compassionate and loving person. God, peace, or truth reside deep within me; sometimes it gets covered up.

Swami Satchidananda continues,

> *"Attachment is based on just you and yourself. This is selfishness. When you are free from selfish attachment, you become a better instrument to serve everybody. Because you see yourself in everybody, everybody's pain is yours, everybody's suffering is yours. A total unattached person is one who can best serve, because he or she doesn't think of personal gain in doing anything."*

Swami Satchidananda encourages his students to give up their attachments to everything (not necessarily things) for a reason.

> *"You get the Kingdom. Because you left everything and got the Kingdom are you poor? No. Then you become the owner of everything. The Bible assures you, if you stop running after things, you will get the Kingdom and everything else will be added too. What a wonderful teaching. Everything will be automatically added. You don't have to ask, 'Can I get this? Can I get that?' No. Everything will come to you."*

SEEING THE LIGHT

Surrendering my all to Jesus is probably not as demanding, after I have had everything taken away, because I feel less attached. But the thought of allowing Jesus and all His love to shake up my world is still frightening. Despite all my hardships, the Holy Spirit has led me through safely to Jesus. He must have been present during my darkest moments, when all my spiritual battles took place.

Jesus has done the work for me. He died, in part, to forgive me for anything that violates the ideal relationship between myself and God. The Bible is clear about deterring those methods that I thought were giving me power. Some call it sin. It's an old archery term that means "to miss the mark." I am going to take aim at Jesus. His terms are crystal clear … Take all of me or nothing.

> "Whoever is not with me is against me, and whoever does not gather with me scatters."
>
> (Matthew 12:30 NIV)

The words of Christ seem unrelenting. Jesus draws a line, and those who dare cross it step into a new realm; they will never look back. He is radically bold and in your face, but His love for God and the diligence He shows for us and for His followers is exemplary. Jesus is serious about His request. I need to be willing to give up my life. I think about when Jesus said, "Come back and knock on my door when you are ready."

Only a king with the authority and power to offer something more valuable would dare make such a bold statement. It truly is a narrow gate, and few can pass. I think of all the healing that took place in my heart through Jesus. I know I can trust Him more than any earthbound man or woman. I know Him well enough to make this decision, but my ego still doesn't like the idea of losing my life. Am I willing to serve Jesus all the days of my life? Will my new "Life in Christ" be better? My mind keeps coming up with excuses.

I shift gears and focus on the *love* in my heart. I extend trust and humble myself, even though I don't fully comprehend Jesus, the Messiah, Son of God. I am going to have faith in Him so He can live, breathe, and operate through me. My answer resides in my heart. Yes! I am willing to give my life for Jesus. I love Him and I know He *madly* loves me. I know He is willing to die for me. In fact, Jesus died for us all, so in effect He has already died for me. He has already done it! Why am I hesitating? If I must die for Jesus, God please let it be a noble death: not an aneurysm, a car wreck, or slipping on a bar of soap in the bathtub.

I am ready to return and knock on His door. I stand outside and proudly say to Jesus, "I will die for you."

The door opens and I step inside. Then the door shuts with me on the inside. It feels different. He really is the King of Kings. Jesus is a tough Master.

I let go of my thoughts about how a relationship with Him should appear. I surrender my hopes, dreams, and ambitions into His hands. If I can do this, then I am free. I do feel lighter, like a burden has been lifted. Jesus is in the spirit, and I am in the flesh. It is kind of exciting, like a first date. All I need to do is be myself. I have given Him my all. I must be patient. Jesus is working in my life. He knows what I want and what I *really* need.

My new plan is pretty simple … I will follow His plan. I pray and quietly listen. I sense the presence of Jesus and keep Him in the corner of my eye.

Jesus says, "You will feel no more suffering or pain." I believe it's true. Once in His world, I feel that I can rise above my pain and suffering. Standing inside the quiet place near Jesus, I can sense that one day a fierce battle will unfold. Jesus will be riding on that white horse. I will be charging in on Jesus' side.

Perhaps the battle has already started. Actually, it was going on inside of myself for fifteen years. Thankfully, I saw the light. I realize now; it's easier to join Him than to resist. Today is a good day to join with me on the same side as Jesus.

If you believe in Jesus and want the Holy Spirit, just ask Him.

THE GUIDE

We all attain spiritual growth by living in this world. It is enhanced if we live with love in our hearts and cultivate awareness. Relationships of love may, in fact, be the greatest teachers. When love is the main focus, spiritual growth is a side-effect. God gave us roles as a mother or father, grandmother or grandfather, boyfriend or girlfriend, brother or sister, friend or co-worker for a well-intended reason: to experience being loved and to express our love toward each other. Most of us need not venture on a quest to find more spiritual growth. We just need to pay careful attention to the beloved ones in our lives. Part of our journey in learning how to love one another includes feeling pain and suffering. Our losses allow us to feel human vulnerability.

The Swan Song section is a love story. The gamut of emotions I felt during that relationship included: envy, rage, panic, guilt, playfulness, bliss, affection, and compassion. We all go through an array of feelings in relationships. At one point in my relationship with Swan Song, I was experiencing a lot of confusion, so I went on a ten-day silent retreat. It led me to a place of peace. Afterwards, I had more confidence in myself. My faith in Jesus also brought me comfort. I made a bold decision I had not even considered prior to the retreat, because I was able to listen to my heart.

What if, during those transitional points in our life, we took a pause and went on a guided retreat? What if we just set an intention to be in our heart and just listen in silence for 3 or 5 days? What if we press in closer to our chosen faith and do spiritual practices that assist us in receiving guidance with clarity?

An ideal time to do a retreat is before or after a life transition. You could be facing an illness, heading into a new job, moving to a new location, or contemplating your next step in a relationship. If one clears their slate and gets a fresh perspective, they will better know who they are, what they need, and what their attitude is. Through proper guidance and prayer, one attains mental clarity, a deeper emotional connection, and spiritual preparation. By contemplating a future or past scenario, without being emotionally attached, a degree of insight is revealed. Often we don't grant ourselves enough silent time to absorb the current feelings in our body, heart, and soul. We plug into the next project or relationship and then wonder, *"Why am I in this same sticky situation again?"* It is better to face our inner fears while peaceful and relaxed during a safe retreat setting. Then we build up resilience to face the stress-dragons with courage.

A spiritual retreat can be a time of advanced spiritual growth through introspection, awakening, or letting go. The key components are silence, meditation, relaxation, and spiritual practices. One intentionally changes their patterns and detaches from the world, which leads to a fresh perspective. This is a time for transformation and to gather inner power and fortitude.

GUIDED RETREATS

My favorite type of retreat is a personal guided retreat. I prefer these because they provide one-on-one guidance, but if one does not want to fly solo, then group retreats can be satisfying. It's recommended to have a guide while on retreat because one can enter into altered states of consciousness, and deep emotional issues can surface. Besides, it can be overwhelming for the mind to be silent for an extended period. A guide will offer instruction, support, and act as a protective spiritual shield. The best retreat guides will work with your intentions and choose practices to reinforce them. The most common length for a retreat is 1, 3, 5, or 10 days. It's best to start with a one or three-day guided personal or group retreat. After several shorter retreats, spread out over a few years, then consider a five or ten day. One can even be guided on a thirty or forty-day retreat. That takes considerable preparation. During a longer retreat one can dive beneath the surface and examine their core beliefs. When one gains an understanding of why they made certain decisions and how their beliefs led them in a direction, it can shake up their whole world perspective.

Autumn is my favorite time for a retreat. Nature is shifting and letting go of the leaves before the stillness of winter. There is a personal rhythm that one can tap into during a retreat that entices a deep personal connection with nature. Being in nature is the ideal environment for a retreat.

Hazrat Inayat Khan wrote,

> *"To the eye of the seer every leaf of the tree is a page of the holy book that contains divine revelation, and he is inspired every moment of his life by constantly reading and understanding the holy script of nature. When man writes, he inscribes upon rock, leaf, paper, wood or steel. When God writes, the characters He writes are living creatures."* [16]

I experience regular guided retreats at The Abode of the Message in New Lebanon, New York. Their retreat guides are familiar with all the major religions and accommodate to allow one to deepen their own chosen spiritual path. They have wooden huts with heaters, excellent food, and enjoyable walking trails. During a retreat, there are no outside conversations and no writing in journals. The reading of a few spiritual passages is encouraged and often revealing. The focus during a retreat is an inward moment-by-moment journey into the heart. It may sound simple, but a lot of internal shifts transpire and it can be a life-altering experience.

The standard retreat includes a morning and evening meditation; a time for slow, mindful walking in nature; a check-in time with your guide; breathing practices; and usually, chanting a few selected names for God.

REMEMBERING THE NAMES OF GOD

Wazifa is the Sufi practice of reciting and meditating on one or more of the 99 names of God. It's a Sufi tradition, and the words are Islamic. Yet, we all know and hold the names of God in our hearts. Repeating these names of God aloud or silently is a powerful healing tool. For example, Ya Nur means "light." When this word is spoken, whispered, or thought, it manifests. As you remember the name, its divine transmission flows into your heart. It can deeply transform and heal. It's a powerful practice to promote the conscious emergence and continual awareness of those divine qualities in one's own life. It's a means of connecting to, and being a vehicle of, the divine presence. Pir Vilayat Inayat Khan, in his book *Awakening*, explains,

> "If a peaceful person comes into the room, someone might say, 'It is wonderful to see a peaceful person.' The dervish, however, would say instead, 'Isn't it wonderful to see Divine Peace coming through this person?' What they mean by this is that the human personality has the potential to become the vehicle of the Universe's archetypes. This is the intention behind the practice of wazâ'if... to connect a specific quality in oneself to its source..." (17)

When I repeat a wazifa, I speak the word from my heart and recall the meaning. The depth of my intention is more important than the number of repetitions. It's a different way of praying. When the proper wazifa is chosen, I often experience a feeling of ecstasy. Sometimes there are uncontrollable tears which correspond to blissful joy or act as a channel for an emotional release.

In yoga, they repeat a mantra, and Catholics repeat the rosary. It's a similar ritual; I hope that people of different religious traditions can acknowledge our similarities instead of dwelling on the differences. It is incorrect thinking to believe there is only one right and acceptable way to pray. God didn't just create one religion, one language, or one color of skin. But we are all one human tribe.

MAKING NATIVE AMERICAN CRAFTS

During my retreat, I like to do some light stretches in the morning sun and take a catnap after lunch. I also find it brings me inner peace to make a Native American item. Usually, I know well in advance what I will make and gather all the supplies before my retreat. Sometimes, someone will give me an item from nature, like a turtle shell. Often, I will be inspired to make it into a gift, such a turtle-shell rattle. When it's done, I give it back to them. I like to make Native American crafts and give them away as gifts.

As a guideline, I make Native American crafts with hand tools — no power tools — so my energy goes into it. I start by offering tobacco and then sage myself, the tools, and the pieces. The sage is used to purify everything. Each piece of leather, bone, stone, shell, or wood tells its own story. As the designer, I bond the pieces together; I am a part of it. Once it's complete, I smudge it again with sage. But this time, my intention with the smudging is to make it sacred. A sacred item should not be set upon the ground. It should be respected. Usually it is stored in a box, basket, or suitcase surrounded with sage, cedar, or sweet grass. Otherwise, there is no wrong way to make a Native American craft item. Anyone can do it. Just listen to your heart.

Each Native American craft I make represents a stage in my life. During one of my first retreats, I made a rattle from a small branch that fell from the giant sycamore tree I call the Almighty One in Shakomako. The wooden handle is covered in black leather, and the shakers are made of large, ear-shaped pods with seeds inside. They fell from a tree that I stood under during my initiation into the Sufi order. The Sufi order does not insist that one initiates; in fact, they don't even suggest it. When I felt ready, I asked an accomplished Sufi teacher I admired to initiate me.

I remember staring intensely into the eyes of the Sufi teacher, Aziza, as she said the opening invocation created by Hazrat Inayat Khan as part of my initiation:

Toward the One,
The Perfection of Love, Harmony, and Beauty,
The Only Being,
United with all the Illuminated Souls,
Who form the Embodiment of the Master,
The Spirit of Guidance. [18]

In a mystical way, I could see the past lineages reflected in her eyes. There was a vast spaciousness that went back in time. Deep calls to deep. It is a bit spooky, but rather cool. When I use the rattle, it reminds me of my initiation.

During another retreat, I attain 99 round, stone beads of amethyst, malachite, and smoky quartz to make prayer beads. I chose each type of stone for certain qualities it possesses. The amethyst is for healing. The malachite reaches the inner feelings of a person and reflects what is there, be it negative or positive. The smoky quartz is commonly used as a powerful Native American stone to protect and clear negativity. At the starting bead, I attach an eagle-head bead carved by an Alaskan Native. I purchased it during the summer I was a canoe guide. When I use these prayer beads, they are more powerful than anything I could buy.

THE GOOFY SUFIS

It's common practice to keep to oneself what transpires during a retreat. One can never fully express with justice the magnitude of a self-transformation experience with mere words. Attempting to describe it may actually take away from the experience. It was my nature to break or bend every retreat's rules, perhaps to better understand it, or it might have been just for fun.

There are various denominations of Sufis. I am part of the Sufi lineage called the Chishti. The tradition of this order is traced from the time of Abraham. But within the larger Sufi circles, we are called the Goofy Sufis. When I first met the mountain-retreat coordinator, Nevin, he came up to shake my hand, dragging one leg and groaning. He was just kidding around. He would greet me and other coworkers by waving his hands on his head like they were moose antlers. I am well-accomplished at, and proud to uphold, our reputation for goofing off.

During retreats, I have spoken when I needed to be silent, read a book, received a massage, entered a sauna, ridden a bike, checked my email, and traveled to town. Afterwards, I realize all these retreat guidelines are for my own benefit. I have grown to respect them. This said, I, the rule-breaker, will break the rule again and share glimpses into my personal retreats.

WISE WOLF ON RETREAT

It's the break of day at the top of the mountain. I walk slowly along the forest trail. I am observing the great oaks and the mostly-bare maple trees and how they are spaced apart symmetrically, like soldiers dressed in camouflage. A gray squirrel and a few blue jays are in the tree branches, part of the costume worn by the forest. I feel that the trees can sense my footsteps as I tread on the dark brown earth beneath them.

I inhale and take a step. With my exhale, I take the next step. I feel my heel and toe touch the earth. My steps are like whispers. I am still enough to hear my heart beat four times between each step: *thump ... thump ... thump ... thump.* The orange sunrays peek through the leaves, and a few golden beams spotlight down upon overzealous grass patches. The shadows near the tree trunks show a dark contrast, and broken twigs lie randomly scattered about. I can smell the moss draped on the northern side of each tree. I slowly step forward on the path out into the rays of sunlight. It shines on my hands and cheeks. I pause to feel the warmth and welcome it on my skin.

In the distance, I hear the gentle, deep tone from a set of wind chimes. *Ding ... dong. Ding ... dong.* There is a gigantic set of chimes dangling at the top of the retreat mountain. They are here to represent the elements of the wind. I see the four shining, silver bars, like elephants' tusks, hanging down from forty feet above, where they are tied to a branch of a giant oak.

I slowly, step by step, make my way to the giant chimes. I stand underneath them and slowly gaze up. The gigantic chimes are suspended directly above me. The sound reverberates through my cells. When I move slightly to the right or left, the perfectly resounding tone is distorted. I remain still in my chamber. The energetic tone is thick, like warm chocolate being poured on my head. I feel it drip down my arms and chest before it forms a small puddle around my feet. I am tempted to stoop down and take a lick. But I remain still.

I look down another trail. There is the silhouette of a man walking in my direction. As he comes closer, I can distinguish that he is wearing slightly weathered jeans, leather work boots, and a blue sweatshirt with the hood over his head. The cloth veil over his face glistens. It is tucked in under his hoodie to cover his face. But I know him by his walk. One hip is tighter and slightly pulls out. His short steps, combined with his white beard behind that veil, resemble that of a wizard. He is my mentor, Wise Wolf. I am glad to see him here. He is on the mountain as a participant in his own ten-day retreat.

As he approaches, I smile and expect him to acknowledge me. He knows I am here. It is obvious. I hold back the urge to give him a big bear-hug. That is how he usually greets me. Yet, Wise Wolf peers straight ahead; he is focusing intensely within. Perhaps this walk in his heart is melting the trauma and stressful hours he spends as a hospice worker. His retreat time is precious. He holds every drop of energy compassionately. He continues to deliberately step forward, as if a cement statue has broken free from the mold to take its first few slow, silent steps. There is not so much as a nod as he walks past. I am mesmerized by his slow, mime movements. Or is it the inward concentration?

I reminisce about our past mentor meetings; how he would sit on the edge of a chair, listening intently. Once he said firmly, "Why are you beating around the bush? If you have something to say to me, just say it!" He was right. After that day I did. He was the first man older than myself that didn't scare the crap out of me. I felt he trusted me, and I trusted him. I was comfortable enough to talk about anything with him. This meant a lot. It was a breakthrough, because both The Lion and Pastor R.I.P. had instilled the belief that they would not trust me.

Wise Wolf was there to listen during my darkest moments. I confided in him that I sometimes had mixed feelings about being on a spiritual path that involves yoga, Native American traditions, and Jesus. I find that many Christians are offended by my involvement in Native American traditions or yoga. They expect me to follow Jesus, exclusively.

Wise Wolf said, "All these paths come together within you."

I desire to obey the Holy Spirit. When I participate in yoga or Native American traditions, Jesus and the Holy Spirit are right beside me. If I am not sharing them as part of my truth, then I am offending myself. The Holy Spirit wants me to be myself. Some people may not be pleased with my not following Jesus, exclusively. It is not my role to make them happy. Regardless of what others think, I need to respect and love myself, every day. The real question is: *Can they love me for who I am?*

When one initiates in the Sufi order, they are supposed to have a guide for life. At one point, my guide said she would guide me on retreats, but could no longer be there for personal advice. After that, Wise Wolf unofficially took over. It was clear that he cared. He was more than just a mentor. He is a friend who shares wise counsel. He teaches me more with his silent intention than he could with words. During the moment Wise Wolf passes, I realize the levels of depth that one is capable of attaining on a silent retreat. I continue to watch Wise Wolf out of the corners of my eyes, without turning my head, until he disappears.

SILENCE

Silence is mystical. It's rather ironic that I am attempting to convey the deeper meanings of silence with words. Imagine a house with a family in the country. During the day, they are all active and talking. At night, on the outside, the surroundings become quieter and darkness settles in. The stars appear above and some creatures, like the owl, start hunting. This owl is not hunting mice; it is swooping in to gather up their words. Now, the family is cozy and asleep in their beds. They are all giving their bodies and minds a chance to rest. While asleep, they are all at peace. Silence is touching the recesses of their souls. While being silent, they let go of their worries from yesterday and plans for tomorrow. They all wake up refreshed and ready for another day.

Silence is always there, even during the daytime, sometimes trapped beneath the commotion. During a silent retreat you retain the silence from the night all through the next day, even while you are awake. Wise Wolf was holding silence, even on the inside, deep within his organs. Without being weighed down by thoughts, words, and concepts on the inside, one can live more in the present moment. When inner silence is achieved, retreatants become more curious about their surroundings. They move more slowly, with fresh eyes to examine the outside world. Something as common as a fern blowing in the wind becomes fascinating.

Our inner heart resides with God in stillness. In this place, we are unified through a deeper sense of knowing. We are able to know and love ourselves. We gain a fresh perspective. Our attitude shifts. What we thought were problems are no longer such a big deal. When silence is held for extended periods and contained properly, it shatters our preconceived notions. ▪

The Forty-Day Retreat

I follow in some big footsteps when I commit to a forty-day retreat. In the Bible, Elijah (1 Kings 19:8) and Moses (Exodus 24:18) fasted for forty days. Moses did two back-to-back, and at least during the second one, had neither food nor drink. But probably the most renowned forty-day fast was done by Jesus.

Immediately after being baptized with the Holy Spirit by John the Baptist, Jesus fasted for forty days and nights in the Judean Desert. The temptation of Christ is told in the Gospels of Matthew, Mark, and Luke. During his fast, the devil appeared to Jesus and tempted him three times. Jesus refused each temptation and the devil departed.

> *"Then Jesus was led by the Spirit into the wilderness to be tempted by the devil. After fasting forty days and forty nights, he was hungry. The tempter came to him and said, 'If you are the Son of God, tell these stones to become bread.'"*
>
> *(Matthew 4:1-3 NIV)*

It is important to note that the devil remarked, *"If you are the Son of God"*. He wants to question the identity of Jesus. Jesus is solid in His identity. If we understand our true identity, then the devil has no recourse. Satan's power is limited and temporal. He really only has power when we give him the authority. I believe this happens when we exhibit a lack of faith or believe his lies. Jesus has authority over Heaven and Earth.

If we realize how the Cross, the Incarnation, the Resurrection, and the Ascension set us all (not just Christians) free, then we can live and love, fearlessly.

THE HOLY SPIRIT AS MY GUIDE

As a 44 year old, life is a dream. My beard is turning white. I felt the desire to do a forty-day retreat for three years before it manifested. When the time came, I sought out a Sufi guide. There are only a few qualified to guide a forty-day retreat. One qualification is they need to have been guided on a forty-day retreat themselves. When I contact one and get no response, I take it as a sign; I should seek alternative forms of guidance.

I know it's imperative that I have a guide, or at the very least, check in with somebody regularly. I speak with my two mentors and they make themselves available by email or phone, but neither is officially qualified to guide a forty-day retreat. I decide to check in once a week at a men's support group for sexual integrity at a local church. I can share with them. But I stay mindful about not talking too much.

I am not expecting my forty-day retreat to be easy. The devil, or undesirable spirits, tempt me. Jesus, Moses, and Elijah were guided by listening to God. I will do the same, but I will rely heavily on the Holy Spirit as my primary guide.

How will the Holy Spirit guide me? Certainly, I will pray and listen. I always pay attention when a similar message appears through three independent sources. When this happens, it's probably the Holy Spirit or God. I trust the Bible and other spiritual scriptures as confirmation. I find that wisdom and a compassionate heart join together as a team for my final filtering process. That is how I get my guidance.

There are different levels of intensity when I feel the Holy Spirit, but usually it's a tingling sensation. I often sense the presence of the Holy Spirit during worship or when I receive guidance in a prayer or passage. When I give a person a message directed by the Holy Spirit, I feel the presence. It does not need to be a Christ-related connection. The Holy Spirit often works through me when I teach a yoga class or participate in a Native American ceremony. I conclude that the Holy Spirit or God's presence guides us all, regardless of our religion or beliefs. Jesus broke down many barriers. God's truth, light, and love are available for every soul to claim.

I need to remain firm in my own identity. I have an identity in Jesus. I have an identity in Native American traditions. I have an identity in yoga. If I am to deny any part of who I am, then I am not living my truth. But a controversial question that some Christians ask... *Does Jesus condemn those who practice yoga and participate in Native American traditions?* Jesus broke down walls of intolerance. He has room for everyone. In the past, I tried to deny or conceal parts of my identity from others who may not appreciate how it melds together within me. I know some people will love and accept me for who I am, others will not.

ANGER SURFACES

The night before my retreat begins, anger starts to surface. There are three professionals that I felt did me wrong. I had an unnecessary hiatus hernia operation. I blame it on the surgeon. Then, I was given antibiotics for six months by another doctor, to eliminate the *possibility* of Lyme disease. The antibiotics raised havoc with my stomach, immune system, and liver. The last professional was a healing-touch counselor in New York. I went to him for healing. He diagnosed that I had a male/female energy imbalance. At one point, he asked to rub my sexual organ. I awkwardly consented. Afterwards, I felt I had been sexually molested. It left me feeling even more confused.

I turn a leaf and accept full responsibility. I ask Jesus to help me find forgiveness to heal the anger. My mind slips to view past relationships, financial insolvency, emotional turbulence, and sexual abuse. I grieve for deceased family members, pets, and friends.

In our culture, it's not commonly acceptable for a man to cry. I take thirty minutes to consciously cry out my pain. It starts off with a fake sob that grows to be a deep, heartfelt, genuine cry, with tears. I regret that I am not utilizing my God-given gift to take more photographs. After all the crying, I feel better. Now I am ready to begin my forty-day retreat.

MY DAILY RETREAT PRACTICES

I will be doing this retreat in my home. I place a sign on the door that says "Observing Silence" for any visitors. I spend much of my retreat time in a spare bedroom. It resembles a retreat hut. There is a large white candle on a shelf, blue carpet on the floor, and two windows, but otherwise the room is empty and free from any clutter. The wall is tongue and groove pine boards. Some of the knots in the boards resemble distorted ghost faces.

I set a strong intention to do specific retreat practices every day. Each evening, I cover my head with a veil to keep my focus inward. I light a thick, white candle and repeat my two chosen names for God from the Sufi tradition. My index finger and thumb roll over the 99 stone prayer beads that I made. I repeat the first wazifa: "al-Qahhar," the one who overcomes all obstacles and is victorious over any opposition. It is to encourage the pursuit of one's purpose by practicing mastery.

My head is facing to the right side. It begins to roll downward, with my chin near my chest, then up and over to the left. Next, I glance up toward the ceiling. The cycle ends with me facing downward in the direction of my heart as I say the last wazifa: "al-Ghani," the one who is self-sufficient, without need of anything and completely satisfied. It is to encourage creativity and to be confident in one's abilities.

I transition from saying my wazifas out loud (Dhiker), to saying them more softly, as a whisper (Fikr), and as the ultimate variation, I repeat the words in my mind, as a thought (Fikr-Asir). I can feel a subtle resonating vibration generated, even after the words and thoughts have ceased. This is the energy and power in a wazifa that resides beyond the sound.

The third chant I repeat two or three times a day. It's the word "Cristo Morpho." I define it to mean, "Christ Transforms." "Cristo" is Christ in Spanish, and "Morpho" is from the Blue Morpho translucent butterfly that frequently meanders along the brooks on our property in Costa Rica. I say "Cristo Morpho" as I walk slowly in a circle around the room with the 99 stone beads in my right hand, as an abacus, counting out the repetitions. I listen to the words and feel the sound vibration, which resonates from my throat. My goal is to repeat "Cristo Morpho" 10,000 times over forty days. It seems insurmountable, but little-by-little, day-by-day, from December 12th to January 20th, I persist.

THE COMPASSION OF BUDDHA

The Holy Spirit is my main guide, but I also pick out forty universally-known spiritual teachers. I request guidance from one each day. On the first day, it's Buddha. I call on Buddha to be present as I sit to meditate for thirty minutes. During my meditation, I feel intense peace like never before. I am held in the silence and stillness of pure compassion. When standing under a starry sky, one gets a sense of the vast expanse of the universe. The stars spread out beyond our vision, but one can grasp that stars exist in other infinite galaxies. Imagine this comprehension of the stars as compassion that extends towards every blade of grass, insect, and life form on the earth. This is how much compassion resides in Buddha.

On day 3, my guide is Swami Sri Yukteswar. He is The Guru that entered me for ten days. He says, "Christ is your chosen guru."

On day 5, I pray with Angel Ariel about how I can help the environment. I send a $25 donation that goes toward the release of wild wolves in New England.

On day 6, the Sufi teacher, Hazrat Inayat Khan, is my guide. The focus is on healing. He says, "Focus on the cure; never the illness or pain, for then it will only grow. Genuine healing requires confidence, concentration, and faith."

I begin to allow ten minutes each day to focus on the gold cross that The Lion gave me, as a way to build up my power of concentration. I spend some time each day affirming that I have a strong vibrant body, a good memory, plenty of energy, and the ability to express my emotions.

MY REQUEST TO MAKE A CHANUPA

As I mentioned, I like to make Native American items during my retreat. I would like to make a new chanupa under the authority of the Holy Spirit. I need to have a dialogue with Jesus and the Native American chiefs before I begin such a controversial undertaking.

I have a large piece of black pipestone and one piece of a cherry limb left from a tree on my property that I cut down and milled. I made a promise to that tree that I would use all the wood. I made a chest the same dimensions as the Ark of the Covenant to hold my sacred items, and the remaining lumber was used to build two large bookshelves.

I gather in a spiritual powwow with seven respected Native chiefs. It may be a vision in my mind, but each event has a purpose and I take seriously the signs given through my visions. This group is called together to decide if it is in my best interests to make and own a chanupa again. In my inner vision each chief rides in on his horse. They travel from different regions of the United States and Canada. I place nine different animal skins for seats around a fire circle. Red Cloud leads the horses to the water and comes to the circle. He stands in front of the buffalo robe. Ten Bears, who is covered in black body paint, goes to the bear fur. Shooting Star, who represents the Northern Alaskan region, chooses the cougar. Black Elk goes to the elk skin. Last of the Mohegans, who represents tribes that have already vanished in this country, prefers a bobcat. Red Cluster goes to a fox skin. I tell the chiefs we are expecting Jesus and the White Buffalo Calf Woman to arrive, but we can all sit down. There are two furs remaining; one is a white rabbit fur and the other a sheepskin.

A thunderbolt strikes the ground and Jesus is walking toward us across a field. Then a White Buffalo appears near him. He turns to face what has changed into the White Buffalo Calf Woman. They walk solemnly together to our circle and sit down. All those gathered are fully present and listen intently as I explain how my three chanupas were taken away when the Holy Spirit was invited to rule over my life during my last chanupa ceremony.

Jesus explains, "This act was requested to show obedience to me." Jesus knows of my love for the Native traditions, the chanupa and the White Buffalo Calf Woman.

Jesus asks, "Can a man have two masters?"

I make my request to the group to make another chanupa. I explain that I desire the power of the Holy Spirit to reign as the ultimate authority over and through it. Red Cloud protests and is not in agreement to give their power over to Christ's authority.

The White Buffalo Calf Woman speaks, "The power of Jesus is greater than our medicine. We know that when the third White Buffalo appears, our Native nation will shift. It is a merger so our people and their wisdom will live on."

She takes the bracelet I had purchased for her off her wrist and passes it to Jesus.

She continues, "My allegiance is with Him. Under His love is the power we all feel for one another, as a brother and sister."

She passes a chanupa around the circle. Each Chief smokes the chanupa and then in turn, speaks to the group, while they hold it. They decide as a group to allow the Holy Spirit pipe to exist. I can make another chanupa and be a pipe carrier, but there are certain stipulations. Chief Shooting Star blows the pipe smoke across the stars in the night sky.

Jesus, who is last in the circle, speaks, "God willing, the Holy Spirit will live in this pipe and I will rule as an authority. If at times, I do not act, then the White Buffalo Calf Woman shall, as in the past."

I offer the skins each is sitting on and a bundle to each, as a token of my appreciation and respect.

(I had a longstanding debate with myself about including the making of the new chanupa. I will receive condemnation from some Christians for being a pipe carrier again. For me, it is more important what Jesus wants. He wants me to be free; that means fully being myself. Jesus fully respects and honors Native Americans and all of their traditions. The greater tragedy is for me to conceal my truth. I need not hide any part of my identity. I am not the man I once was. I am a son of my Heavenly Father; I am that I am.)

QUALIFICATIONS TO TEACH

On day 8, the yoga guru, Neem Koroli Baba, is my guide. It's amazing how the character and personality of some guides comes forth. I spend about one hour each day as directed by the guide of the day.

Neem Koroli Baba says in a grumbly voice, "Chant for one hour, then seek my guidance."

I chant along with music by Krishna Dass and Snatam Kaur. They both chant from the heart, and one can feel a loving vibration in their voices. His guidance reveals that whenever I want it or need it, I can take in a loving vibration through chanting.

I feel that this forty-day retreat is a prerequisite for becoming a spiritual teacher. During this retreat, I plan to complete my last requirements to become a certified yoga therapist. My desire is to teach people with chronic conditions.

I ask Neem Karoli Baba," What must I do to be qualified to teach people?"

His response is, "Listen to God."

I decide to ask the same question to some of my other guides. Swami Satchidananda says, "Speak the truth and care deeply for others; live in a high state of consciousness; have an area of spiritual expertise."

Another says, "Do not be attached to your results; live as an example of your teachings; and be there when you are really needed."

The yoga teacher, B.K.S. Iyengar, says, "It's important to have a lifelong commitment."

They all have slightly different perspectives; when taken as a whole, they all add a piece to make the pie complete.

On day 11, I begin to work on the new chanupa. It shall be called "Quddus". The word Quddus comes from the Arabic root Qadusa. Qadusa carries the meaning "to be pure, holy, and spotless."

There are going to be three bowls in this one pipe. One large bowl in the middle I will call the "Holy Spirit" section, and one smaller one on the end I will call the "God" section. A cross will be mounted on top of the "God" bowl. In one of the T intersections forming the cross, will be the third bowl, which represents Jesus. In effect, this one pipe will have the trinity of the Father, the Son, and the Holy Spirit. I will attach the pewter statue of Christ on the cross. It is the statue of Christ I had on the day of the ceremony, after which the three chanupas were taken away. I feel joy that what was once taken away by the Holy Spirit will now be returned, not as three separate chanupas, but three chanupas in one. It will be better than I could have imagined.

In my agreement with the Native chiefs, there are conditions to allow Christ and the Holy Spirit to operate through my chanupa, such as, "I will not touch my lips to any other chanupa." Jesus requests that I read the gospels while I make the bowl, to absorb them into my heart and transfer them to the pipe. The elements are strongly under the direction of this pipe, and I believe the "God" bowl has the innate ability to control the weather, if I am ever guided to pray in that manner.

On day 12, I feel emotionally and physically wiped out. Thoughts and speech make no sense. I want to cry.

On day 19, I burn a hole through the piece of cherry wood for the pipe stem. My metal rod is not long enough to reach the full length, so I need to come at it from both ends. I use the wood stove in the kitchen once the coals are red hot. I am questioning if I can be precise enough to meet in the middle with a straight hole. These things cannot be rushed. It is cozy to have a fire, with snow on the ground outside. There is the smell of smoke, because I have the front door of the stove open. When I break through, I peer through the stem hole as a telescope to view the full moon. It is perfect.

On December 24, Swami Shivinanda is my guide.

He asks, "If you are told a lie by all, why will you believe me when I tell you differently?" He has a good point. I allow myself to question whether what I have been told by other people is true.

I want to do something special for Christmas Eve, so I repeat all of the 99 beautiful names for God 17 times.

On Christmas Day, my guide is Mary. I want to honor the

mother of Christ. She guides me in her way to honor my own mother. I told The Lamb I would visit with her on Christmas Day for a few hours. She comes to my home, and we have a cup of tea and play Scrabble, her favorite game. I have a great meditation on Christmas Day, perhaps because the world is focusing on Christ and giving in the spirit of love.

A MILESTONE

Day twenty is a milestone. It's New Year's Eve. I am halfway. I have a dream about my past wife, Forevermore. We are sleeping together in my parents' bedroom in our brick home. She talks about teaching Spanish students how to dance the tango, and then leaves the room. I wake up distraught and all emotional. It has been fifteen years since I have seen her. I thought I had worked through all my stuff with Forevermore. Now she comes back in a dream.

My intention is to go deeper in the remaining twenty days of the retreat. I want the stuff to surface that is lodged deep down in the crevices. It seems to have already begun to surface around my separation with Forevermore.

As a way to express what I feel and find closure, I write a letter to Forevermore and send it to her mom. I would prefer to send it directly to her, but I have had no contact with her for the last twelve years. I don't even know where she lives. I have doubts that her mom will even give her the letter. Regardless, I feel it will bring some healing to share how I feel with her mom.

I explain in the letter what went on in my head and my heart … how it all led to our divorce. This happened fifteen years ago; I guess it took me a long time to process it. I can't change my past, but I can live and heal in the present.

We both took what we thought was the easy way out. It took years for me to move on. I can't remove every trace of Forevermore from my memory. Actually, I still love her in my heart. I find comfort in knowing it's possible that I could feel the same intensity of love again, even if it's not for her. There is grace enough and time enough in this life for a second chance.

CARING FOR THE HEART SESSIONS

During the second half of my retreat, I do one session a day in a Christian counseling workbook called *Caring for the Heart* by John Regier.

The big session for me is on bitterness. Can I actually forgive The Lion? What I hold against him is damaging to my body and spirit. I need to find inner peace around it. It's not hurting him one little bit. Jesus comes to heal my heart. When this happens, I feel lightness in my shoulders as my burden lifts and floats away.

"Bitterness is like drinking poison and waiting for the other person to die."
— *Joanna Weaver*

NANI AND GLITTER

I do sessions for every woman with whom I have had a relationship. During my college years, I had two girlfriends simultaneously, Nani and Glitter. I told each of them about the other, but I downplayed the situation.

Nani lived in Vermont and was a sweet country girl. She liked to babysit, bake cookies, and wear flannel button-down shirts. Glitter lived for the bright city lights. She was the life of the party and wore the latest trendy black skirts. I met Glitter at college.

Once Nani came to visit me at college, and while we were eating in the dining hall, Glitter spotted us and cruised over to our table.

With a big fake smile she said, "Hi, I am Glitter," as she nonchalantly threw a glass of water in my face.

She continued to express hostile and jealous feelings.

Nani gave me a stuffed rabbit named Hoppy. When Glitter found out it was from her, Hoppy's fate was sealed. The first time I came home to rescue Hoppy, he was tied around the top of the chimney. The next time, my roommate's Ford pickup, which he called the Demon Dog, had a rear tire parked dead-center on Hoppy, squashing his rabbit body as flat as a pancake. The last time Glitter took Hoppy, it was as a hostage; I never saw him again. He was given to some neighborhood kid that passed by on a bike.

I juggled two girlfriends for more than a year. I found no good reason to change my wicked ways. I thought I had the best of both worlds, but I was being insensitive to their feelings. I lacked integrity in my relationships with women. In my conscience, I felt it was wrong, but inside my head, my father gave me his approval through his actions.

During that summer, I met Forevermore. She said, "Listen Jack, you're not going to date me if you have other girlfriends."

I got the message fast. I was not going to let what happened with Julia, whom I had a crush on in the seventh grade, happen again. There was no hesitation. I immediately went and told Glitter and Nani that we were over. I was extremely fond of Forevermore. I wanted to be with her. I thought we would last forever.

Glitter and Nani both deserved better treatment from a man. We were all young and naive. I didn't know I was instigating a messy triangle, but as I reflect back, it's clear. After my heart-healing session, Jesus cleared away the debris. I sympathized with how my selfish actions hurt Glitter and Nani. I contact them both to ask their forgiveness for treating them with a lack of respect. Now they are both married and have kids. Nani responds, "You are forgiven! It was over fifteen years ago. We have all moved on."

On my wedding ring, Forevermore personally had engraved the words "friends forever." The engraving deeply touched me. I had the thought ... *Once she was my wife, and now she does not even want to be my friend.* When I realized this a few years ago, I became angry. I took a hammer, and with tears in my eyes, pounded my wedding ring until it broke in half. This was the first time I really began to process and feel the pain from our divorce.

In my sorrowful, brokenhearted condition, I mailed the two broken pieces of my wedding ring back to Forevermore. In my warped way, I wanted her to know how much it hurt not being her friend. I didn't consider how it would make her feel when she received it. It's one of the few actions I truly regret. If I ever speak with her again, I will ask for her forgiveness. But after that incident, she ceased all communication.

In my "Caring for the Heart" session, I get in touch with how she probably felt when she received the pounded wedding ring pieces. On this day, I cry uncontrollably for a few hours. The sadness that resides in my chest found a way to release after I began to care more about her feelings. It's a little late, but now I understand why she stopped communicating with me.

While I am crying, The Lamb attempts to call me, even though she knows I am on a silent retreat. She leaves a message inquiring how I am feeling. It's her nature to care about others. She could sense that I was feeling some intense emotions. God knows everything that is happening. He cares and loves me as a loving parent. God lives in The Lamb's heart.

After my session with Forevermore, I feel the whispering voice of God say, "Your time with her is done. There will be another that you will love as dearly."

During the course of the "Caring for the Heart" sessions, I work to remove the dark spirits of envy, pride, lust, lying, stealing, deception, sarcasm, and hypocrisy. I become aware of the spiritual battle and how I was influenced in subtle ways. I have my own inner battle between the darkness and the light. The light beckons with a kind and loving smile. The darkness seeks to manipulate and control. The problem is pretty common; I like to do what makes me feel good. I need to be able to discern what is actually beneficial. In small doses, acts that are not beneficial seem harmless, but once the door is open, it does not shut as easily. Over time, they compile together and it can destroy the person I was meant to be.

We have the freedom to choose our own destiny. What we think are trivial decisions may actually be more important than what we consider to be the crucial ones. I ignorantly gave over my power to the darker spirits through inappropriate thoughts, desires, and actions. I was oblivious to how pornography, inappropriate music, and dowsing were affecting me. When the veil was lifted, it was a revealing moment. I took control and reclaimed my power.

This battle takes place in my home, on retreat, and out in the world. I choose what I want to watch, read, or take in through my senses. When I watch a movie or go to a concert, I am influenced by it. I delete songs on my computer or throw away the CDs with any lyrics that reinforce these darker forces. Artists like Jim Morrison or Bob Marley, who openly promote drugs as part of their image or in their lyrics, are no longer welcome. One song can trigger that old familiar feeling of going to a party or getting high. Christians call it a familiar spirit. I don't need it or want it anymore.

We all want to be happy. I rely on an array of addictions when I am deficient in pleasure. I may crave certain types of food or have a desire to shop, watch a movie, or be online.

It's scary to face my own demons, but if I don't confront them today, they will continue to rule over my life. In order for me to find harmony and conquer this adversary, I need to get grounded, draw a line, slip into the flow, reclaim my identity, get closer to nature, and enjoy intimate relationships. It includes sharing and caring for others. If I want to be loved by my family and friends, I need to treat them accordingly.

"Treat others the same way you want them to treat you."

(Luke 6:31 NASB)

I give thanks to the Holy Spirit for insights into how I had been led astray. The scriptures and spiritual teachers are here to guide us toward the truth. The enemy's favorite tool is to lie. You can count on it. The whole glorification of alcohol, drugs, sex, cigarettes, and violence is an illusion created by the dark forces. If I had lived without any alcohol or drug use, I would be healthier, richer, and wiser. How can people say it's alright for them and then not expect their kids to be like them? If one lives their own truth, then their kids have a genuine example. Let your actions glorify those around you. (It is easy to say, but not so easy to do.)

APHRODITE, GODDESS OF PLEASURE AND PROCREATION

I am tempted by one undesirable spirit. It's my own fault. I invite her in. If the devil is going to tempt me, it will be with a sexy woman in a red dress. On day 28, I choose Aphrodite as my guide. She is the Greek Goddess of love, beauty, pleasure, and procreation. Her Roman equivalent is the Goddess Venus.

You might ask, "Why in the world did you pick the Goddess of pleasure and procreation as your guide?"

Yes, I should know better. It's like my subconscious secretly leads me to find new forms of sexual temptation. It's relentless.

Aphrodite does not guide me with love and beauty, as I desire. She comes as a wild sexual fantasy. She wears no red dress. I am unable to resist her.

Luckily, I am getting vital support from the men's sexual-integrity group at the church. It is way too agonizing for me to explain Aphrodite to my brothers in Christ, but even if they didn't understand, they would have given me support. It's best that I just don't visit Aphrodite, ever again.

SEXUAL INTEGRITY FOR MEN

By attending a men's sexual-integrity group, I am waging a personal battle. When I realize other men face similar sexual challenges, I empathize, and my situation becomes more ... human. We each write a purity statement. Some guys carry their purity statement in their pocket or repeat it when facing sexual temptation. It's a powerful tool that draws the boundaries. It's your personal beliefs, affirmations, and intentions that revolve around sexual integrity. Words are more concrete than thoughts when it comes to a spiritual battle. I memorize my purity statement because each sentence has power and a purpose. When I am being tempted, I would like to say I always wield it like a sword. But the truth is, I don't always wield it. When I do, it helps.

MY PURITY STATEMENT

I resolve to do God's Will.
I am protected by God's grace.
I am pure in my thoughts and actions.
I will fear no evil, for God is with me.
The male and female body is a sacred temple.
Sexuality is a gift from God,
for a man and woman to express their love.
I will set an example of how to live the truth, as guided
by the Holy Spirit, the Bible, and Jesus Christ.

Each person is different, and there are different triggers or patterns that emerge in every addiction. An alcoholic or cigarette smoker will feel the urge for a fix when stress increases. My triggers can be stress, boredom, success, isolation, or watching a movie with a sensual scene. I do my best to avoid or be cautious during these times. At these times a blinking yellow light flashes:

$$* * * * * WARNING * * * * *$$

It means I am near the point of no return. If I reach this point, then I most likely can't turn back. When lust hits hard, I need to get my fix. It's the point after an alcoholic takes that first drink. Sexual addiction can be confusing because sex is a natural act. But when one seeks sex for anything other than a way to express love to a partner, it becomes distorted. This is what leads to sexual addiction. It's all about having a pure intention. For example, a side effect of sex is that it can relieve stress, but if your reason for having sex is to relieve stress or fall asleep, it indicates a problem.

The hard part about an addiction is when I fall off the wagon. I need to get back up with my pride all bruised and climb back on. I may go years without a problem and suddenly.... *WHACK!* It happens. I may think I am beyond needing support and get careless about my triggers. To retain my stronghold, I need to keep the door with the beast locked and bolted shut. In effect, I slam the door on lust. I vow to change my ways, but in the real world, that door can wiggle open with time. One day, there will be a knock, knock, knock on my door, probably when I least expect it.

THE LION'S DEN

Three years later I am at The Lion's house for ten days as he stays at his summer camp on the lake. It seems like a good quiet place to write a few chapters of my book. My landing in The Lion's Den is not a random occurrence. It has happened for a reason. I have not seen him much over the past few years because I felt a need for space to heal with minimal stress. My life has been fairly peaceful. As I settle into The Lion's Den, some of my childhood memories come back to haunt me.

I look at a large wall hanging of an English hunting scene. When I was a child, it hung on his office wall at home. In this scene, four men are sitting around a table drinking coffee and enjoying breakfast. They are dressed in red suits and tall black leather riding boots for fox hunting. One man stands apart from the others. He is leaning against the fireplace. As I look closer, he resembles ... The Lion. He holds a whip under his arm. His conversation commands the attention of the other men in the room.

The scene of the men reminds me of our hunting camp, more so when my grandfather, Buck, was alive. Family and friends were welcome to visit, and often they would end up spending the night. In the morning, there would be a big breakfast with bacon and eggs, toast cooked over the fire, fresh coffee, and tall tales. Stories at camp followed a natural progression; the last story told is slightly more impressive than the prior. The stories tended to be exaggerated over time, and the facts inflated exponentially by the number of beers consumed.

REMINISCING ABOUT THE LION

I reminisce about my interaction with The Lion during my younger days. When I was eighteen, I packed my 1937 Pontiac full of my belongings, including a drum set, and headed out to travel across the USA. It was a time when one would expect some encouragement from a father. I was heading out as a young man to explore the world, on my own, for the first time.

The Lion's parting words were, "You won't make it on your own. The world is a cold and cruel place."

That statement made me angry. But I dared not show it in front of him. I took it as a challenge. I could survive in this world. I clenched my jaw and made a vow. "I will work hard enough, long enough, to be rich enough and tough enough to survive in this world." The Lion probably made a similar vow as a young man. I was told that after he quit college, his father told him to move out of their house, go get a job, and make something of himself. The Lion used to say, "I will outdo my father."

After high school, I was persuaded to go to college to get a business degree. The Lion promised I would have a huge yearly income. He told me the exact amount I would be making. He did the same thing with Gadget when trying to persuade him to attend Vermont Technical College, but he declined the offer. He didn't want to have to pay back the loan. In my case, he wanted an heir to take over his empire: the family business. At the time, I was slightly hesitant and did not want to go to college. For many years, he tried to sell me on the concept, "Money is the most important thing in life."

The Lion did pay for my first four years of college. His car was used as collateral when I went for a semester abroad in Australia. I was responsible for the loan payments. While living in Seattle with Forevermore, I was struggling to find a decent job, and The Lion wanted to purchase a new car. This meant both of our loans needed to be refinanced. He said, "I refinanced *our* loan to help you out. Now you can pay it off faster." I was not involved in the decision, and found out that my loan payments were doubled. I took on a night job counting inventory in order to make the payments.

My grandfather Buck was always helping people. He would deliver items, and as a mechanic, he could fix about anything. He was so accustomed to helping others that he made up a few funny quotes. One is, "If you help somebody out, then the next time they need help, they are going to think of you." Buck had another quote that applied to my loan situation, "If you *really* want to help me, then don't help me."

Most of the real problems my brother and I had with our father revolved around money. The Lion was a businessman, and it was his nature to make a profit. Family was not immune. Gadget purchased a home in his late twenties, and The Lion was the cosigner. Then The Lion convinced him to switch roles and become the cosigner so he was listed as the owner. He explained it would benefit Gadget's taxes. When The Lion was in financial trouble, he sold Gadget's home. According to Gadget, he had made $35,000 in payments but never received any cash from the sale of his own home. The Lion could be underhanded in a subtle way. Gadget was rather pissed off about that one, but eventually he forgave him.

Once, I could not come up with the money to pay my property taxes. I knew The Lion had loaned $700 to another manager. I figure being his son and an employee for the past eight years has built up some goodwill. I work harder and am paid less than the other managers.

I ask, "Dad, can I borrow $1,000 to pay my taxes?" He replies, "Son, these times are hard and life is tough!" Then, as if to console me, he repeats a Shakespeare quote from Hamlet. He says, "Neither a borrower, nor a lender be." I knew what he really meant. He was a big-time borrower. At one point, he owed over three and a half million dollars to various banks. And he was also a lender. He was just not a lender to me.

If I had been given time to make a decision as to my inclination, I would have probably studied photography. God gave me a gift for taking pictures. I recall a moment when I was in Kluane National Park, high on a mountaintop with a herd of wild Dall sheep. The lighting was perfect, so I was able to position the Dall sheep with snow-capped mountains in the background. When I have a camera, I see life's beauty through God's eyes and I can capture it. I want to do it so I can share the photos with others. The camera and I had a sacred contract. It allowed me to express creatively who I was. For me it's as natural as the way a niece or nephew grabs hold of your leg and gives it a hug.

I must pay my taxes! The only asset I have is my camera equipment. It breaks my heart to sell it, but I feel like I have no other option. I place an ad on the Internet. It sells fast to a Chinese buyer. Then the camera equipment is stolen on route. It never reaches its intended buyer. Insurance pays for it, but I feel like God took it back. Our contract was broken. I make another vow: "I will never borrow or ask for any assistance from The Lion for the rest of my life."

THE SOFT SIDE OF THE LION

Many years after I sell my camera, The Lion starts to acknowledge that I have talent as a photographer. And The Lion graciously, without hesitation, has offered his home. He says, "I am glad to have you come stay in my house; while you are there, feed my dogs." It has worked out so far. I really need a place to stay, and I like to write when nobody is around. Maybe The Lion is being human and his heart is not all stone.

Once, he purchased hip waders for Gadget and me to go fishing with him and Buck. It was probably Buck's idea. We went to a secret spot known as Horn of the Moon. The Lion is not the type to walk in the woods, and I never saw him hold a fishing pole. But he bought us hip waders and went with us. Horn of the Moon requires a hike up the brook to reach a mountain pond. We were instructed to walk slowly in the marshy bog. One wrong step and you will slip out of sight in the muck. Buck had a fly-fishing rod. I watched him pull in a nice rainbow trout. I didn't catch a fish, but it was a memorable day.

If I think hard, I can recall family trips and other fun times, but these did not leave deep ruts in my mind like the painful memories did. Once I was working for the family business as a manager, he made it a point to share all his challenging business scenarios. He would call me first thing in the morning. He wanted me to learn how to deal with similar problems if I ever took over the business. His heart was into teaching me. Once, I asked him how he was going to deal with a difficult situation. He replied, "I don't know." I was dismayed; how could he, The Lion, not know the answer? He had never been this vulnerable or this honest before. It did not show weakness, but wisdom. His decisions were a matter of the right timing, and sometimes he just needed more information before he could make a good decision. He was a sharp businessman for many years.

In his behalf, The Lion and I would often play ping-pong in the basement or toss a baseball in the front yard. He even helped coach the peewee baseball team in our hometown; underneath his rough coat, he cared for and loved his kids.

THE BRADY BUNCH

I am rudely awakened to another part of his underlying nature, and mine, while I am thumbing through the channels of his television. I stumble upon the Playboy channel on his satellite network. I am surprised there are not any blocks or codes.

Anybody can watch it. Of course, I immediately stop on *that* channel.

The scene starts off innocently. It is a take-off on the Brady Bunch. Cool. There is a funky, multi-colored van and the whole family living together, but the actors are all over 18. I am intrigued. I used to watch the show. So far it's clean. There has not been any flesh shown. It quickly shifts when Greg brings his girlfriend up into his groovy bedroom with the lava lamp, and they undress.

Cindy is in a high-cut skirt with her trademark pigtails. She is out in the front yard flirting with the milkman. I want to change the channel, but I cannot do it. The hook is sunk into my flesh. After a few minutes, Cindy is having sex with the milkman on a lawn chair. Why am I watching this?

I can't bring myself to change the channel. Instead, I detach and observe my feelings. I really feel for the women and men that work in these porn flicks. I wonder, what do they tell their spouses and kids? Love is lacking. Their acting is cold and uninviting. The sad truth is I have gone for years without watching any porn and today I watch it for 20 minutes. The inevitable *knock, knock, knock* came on my door. I opened the door and invited *lust* to come sit beside me in the living room.

RETAINING SEXUAL INTEGRITY

I set up my home to remove these fleshy temptations. I don't even own a television. Now, porn is staring me in the face. I am right back in The Lion's Den, where it was first conceived. I should have expected it. The Lion may not be aware or willing to acknowledge that porn is an issue. I am not blaming The Lion for my sexual addiction. Every man is accountable for his own actions. But now that porn is readily accessible, I must dance with the devil. I don't have many options. I turn to a Christian friend who is aware of temptations that exist in pornography for support; otherwise I will be hooked and reeled in again and again.

I phone up Cowboy, who was my housemate when I attended Liberty University. He understands my helpless feeling and situation. I desperately ask, "Will you be my accountability partner?" He replies, "Yes, of course." It's a simple but powerful solution. I call him each night and let him know if I did or did not turn on the Playboy channel that day. He prays for me. I know my limits and prepare myself for a weeklong battle. I have numerous reruns of the Brady Bunch scenes stuck in my mind. Of course, I have the desire to turn back on the Playboy channel, but I don't do it. It would be awkward and embarrassing to tell Cowboy that I turned on the Playboy channel.

Soon after watching the Brady Bunch porn flick, I feel shame and guilt. It happens every time. I compassionately forgive myself. I pray to Jesus for strength to overcome my addiction. I think of the women in my life that were affected by my past sexually addictive behavior. How much did the pornography magazines and movies affect my failed marriage?

John Regier, the Christian counselor who created Caring for the Heart Ministry, says that a man involved in pornography is only capable of loving his wife at a 3% level. One will not give or receive love normally until they get adequate counseling to heal any trauma received or inflicted as physical, emotional, or spiritual abuse.

A good wife or a woman with integrity will keep her man accountable. She will have the courage to speak out against porn and will not tolerate movies with strong sexual content. Recovery from an addiction can be a long process. For me, it requires spiritual transformation and faith in the healing power of Jesus Christ.

I pray that Jesus will help me avoid pornography. Part of me desires to watch porn, while another part despises it. I need to be strong and make a stand for myself. My accountability partner and men's support groups have a vital purpose, but more important are my own actions. Joe Zychik writes,

> *"If you want to overcome sex addiction, don't expect a group to save you. You overcome sex addiction or any other problem through your own, independent, self-reliant choices."* [19]

All week long, I face the beast. I slay and conquer it. It is a victory!

T.C Ryan's says,

> *"I worked long and hard at recovery before experiencing the sustained sobriety and growing serenity I longed for. To overcome my intimacy wounds, I focused on interpersonal relationships. I had two sponsors and worked with two therapists. I attended sex-addiction recovery groups, and I began a confidentiality group for clergy. I discovered how important being part of a healthy community is for genuine life change."*

He goes on to explains what the sexual addict needs,

> *"Something greater than reasoning, something stronger than self-will, and something more interventive than messages to make different choices. The addict needs truth and community, support and love, and the healthy reintegration of their life."* [20]

VISUAL STIMULATION

Women and men are programmed differently. Most women desire intimacy and affection from a man, especially before becoming involved in a relationship. That means a guy who genuinely listens and cares. Most men are visual creatures; all it takes is a flash of some bare skin, and the primitive triggers get activated. Because of my past programming, I am hypersensitive to any female flesh, be it on paper, video, or on a woman. As a man, I must be extremely disciplined and careful about what I place in front of my eyes if I want to live a pure life. It took me years to reprogram my lustful thoughts. Now I look upon a woman as a sacred creature with a divine spirit, mind, and body.

In Costa Rica, I go to the R rated *American Pie* movie with a date. I have no clue what the movie is about, but it's the only movie that we had both not seen. When it starts to get raunchy, I begin to writhe in my seat. I can't stand watching it. I awkwardly tell her I want to leave the movie and invite her to go with me. She does not want to leave the movie, which is her option, but she feels greatly insulted because I did. After I leave the movie, I wait outside of the theater for her. Later, once she has cooled down, I explain why I loathe sexual scenes and how they are disrespectful toward women, but she really doesn't get it.

I share this example because it's hard for a woman to fully understand sexual addiction and how lust can adversely affect a man. I urge women who believe their partner is struggling with sexual addiction to listen to them. Allow some compassion and forgiveness. Pray for and encourage your partner to make decisions and actions with sexual integrity.

THE CHAINS THAT BIND

I forgave The Lion for most of what happened in my childhood, but I still have some bitterness around how I feel he took advantage of The Lamb. After he moved out, he gave the family brick home to his wife. He agreed to make the remaining payments and provide her with a car and some spending money. When his business was expanding, he asked her if he could refinance the house for an $85,000 loan with the remaining equity. When I asked The Lamb about the loan, she replied, "I was led to believe that you would take over the business. I think you were led to believe that, too! Had I known that would not happen, I would not have gone along with the loan." In the end, she gave her consent, and also allowed The Lion to charge on her credit card.

He paid $15,000 toward the loan but eventually fell months behind and then stopped making the house and credit card payments completely. The bank started to foreclose on her home. She needed to sell her home to get out of the mess. The only way The Lamb could stall for more time was to file for bankruptcy.

"For the married woman is bound by law to her husband while he is living; but if her husband dies, she is released from the law concerning the husband."
(Romans 7:2 NASB)

Let's get a visual image: two ships, one is a man and the other is a woman, both sailing along. They sail where they want and when they want. They get married because they want to sail together, as a team. The symbol of the spiritual bond of marriage between the two is a ring. There is a ring on the foredeck of one boat with a long chain bolted to the stern of the other. It is a commitment. They need to sail in the same direction. One cannot head into a storm and the other head away. They both either weather a storm or avoid it. One ship may take a hit and the other may remain unscarred, but it will slow them both down. If one ship is hit hard and begins to sink, then the other boat can still float around, happy as a clam — until the chain pulls tight, and then ... *plop!* They both go out of sight.

Given their situation, I encourage The Lion to divorce The Lamb. He says, "I can't do it. Half of all I own would go to her." Well, spiritually they are bound and they both sink. The Lamb might have gone down harder than The Lion because she could not see the chain being pulled tight.

The Lion's pride never allowed him to file for his own bankruptcy. But his actions placed his legal wife in a position where she had no other option, even though she only owed a sliver of his total debt. During his financial crisis, he borrowed from a half dozen friends and made it a point to pay them all back, with interest.

I unexpectedly run into The Lion in town. We have lunch together. His face is weathered; he's heavier set around the middle; and his stature resembles a battle-worn king sitting down to dine. We talk about the last episode of his burdensome financial saga. He tells me that his financial situation has improved. It takes some gumption, but I ask, "Have you considered sending $50 or $100 a month to The Lamb for the money that you owe her?" He flies mad, "I don't owe her anything!"

He does not show any remorse or any intention to ever pay her back. He justifies not owing her by explaining that he provided for her financial needs for many years. (Isn't that what a husband is supposed to do?) Anyhow, it breaks my heart and God's. Marriage is meant to be a vow to protect, support, and honor your spouse. Now that his fortune is basically gone, he has no good reason to not divorce her.

It's a difficult situation. It is probably not my business, even as a son, to try and fix what I perceive as my parents' problems. Perhaps it is better that I pray for them and hand their situation over to a higher authority, like Jesus. He shared His view on marriage and divorce. Jesus was *not* in favor of divorce, at all. But He makes an exception in situations where there has been sexual immorality.

> *"Some Pharisees came to him to test him. They asked, "Is it lawful for a man to divorce his wife for any and every reason?"*
>
> *"Haven't you read," he replied, "that at the beginning the Creator 'made them male and female,' and said, 'For this reason a man will leave his father and mother and be united to his wife, and the two will become one flesh'? So they are no longer two, but one flesh. Therefore, what God has joined together, let no one separate." "Why then," they asked, "did Moses command that a man give his wife a certificate of divorce and send her away?" Jesus replied, "Moses permitted you to divorce your wives because your hearts were hard. But it was not this way from the beginning. I tell you that anyone who divorces his wife, except for sexual immorality, and marries another woman commits adultery."*
>
> *(Matthew 19:3-9 NIV)*

THE PURE HEART FORGIVES

God's grace helps those who help others with a pure heart. The Lamb spent most of her life serving her family faithfully.

Family members and relatives loan her some money to help her get by until her home sells. Three different family members offer to let her live with them. Against all odds, in a slumping market, her big brick home sells for a fairly decent price in the middle of the winter.

She immediately pays back about $120,000 for the loan, interest, late fees, credit cards, and bills accrued from her bankruptcy proceedings to clear the debt The Lion imposed upon her. The Lamb has a humble amount of money left over after selling her home, but it's not enough to buy a small home, which was her dream.

She sent The Lion a statement, but makes no legal attempt to get reimbursement from him. She paid his bills after losing her home, going through bankruptcy, and absorbing a ton of stress and emotional pain.

When I ask her about it, she smiles and says, "I have forgiven him." I say, "Are you serious?" She says, "Yes, I have forgiven him for his actions, but I have not forgotten his debt."

The Lamb has put into action what is probably one of the most important teachings of Jesus and I can't get it! I am blown away. I have not yet forgiven The Lion for what he did to her.

I watched all the suffering The Lamb went through. I even went to a bankruptcy lawyer with her. I saw her cry and I did my best to give her emotional and financial support. Even when The Lamb had to live frugally, she held her head high. She possesses real inner nobility. I am immensely impressed because she is beyond allowing money, or the lack of it, to affect her personality.

As her son, my perception is that she has been taken advantage of and treated unfairly by The Lion. I know The Lamb and The Lion, and I have completely different perceptions. The Lion holds a grudge and has a mental list of people who he feels did him wrong. This method devours the spirit. This is how everybody lived before Jesus came along. Then He set an example of a higher order of truth called forgiveness. Jesus was faithfully obedient to God's will to demonstrate divine forgiveness. He embodied it when his blood was shed on the cross.

There is power in feeling wounded and betrayed by some act that happened in the past, but healing cannot exist on that plane. Forgiveness is much more powerful. It leaves behind all the blaming, guilt, and excuses. Forgiveness happens in the present moment, and when you forgive somebody, for whatever reason, you crucify the perception of feeling betrayed. This allows one to ascend to a higher order of truth.

I feel rather humble because The Lamb naturally knew how to forgive. I ask myself, *"Why is it harder for me to forgive The Lion than it is for her?"*

I guess my pride stems from being her son. I perceive there was a great injustice done to my mom. Perhaps I need to learn to love myself on a new level. The Lamb is teaching me a big lesson. I know if I do not forgive The Lion then it will only hurt me. Maybe forgiveness is more of an act of self-love.

THE LION'S LESSONS

Once, while at a retreat, I sent The Lion a letter expressing how I experienced some deeper healing around father and son issues. I wrote how I forgave him for ignoring or not allowing me to express my emotions through my childhood and adult life. I wrote about the importance of being honest to his children and how the lies he told me were traumatic.

I ask him on Father's Day, "What are your thoughts about the letter I sent you?" He replies, "I thought it had some emotional stuff in it, so I never opened it. I threw it away without reading it."

Of course, I feel rejected and hurt. When I was younger, my father seldom showed that he cared about how I felt emotionally. I believe it was difficult for him to feel or express emotions toward certain others in his life, primarily his wife and two sons. The Lion was not always shown much compassion or understanding from his father. I feel for him. I know deep down he loves and cares for my brother and me.

A shift occurred after he became semi-retired. He began to soften. He even said, "I did some immoral things in my past." Acknowledging this is a big step for him. Now that we're both grown adults and live far away, he wants us to come and spend some time with him at camp. We both do. There is hope for my Dad (and other parents), but I needed to come to accept him, as he is. Now, he even says, "I love you, Son" when I am leaving.

I believe one big factor is that he gets regular practice expressing how much he loves his girlfriend and his daughter. He proclaimed, "My priority during my financial crisis was to save my home and the camp on the lake, so my (current) family can enjoy a quality life."

I recently learned that when he was a senior in high school he had a scary dream about his best friend, Egils Aivars Mezaraups. Egils had dropped out of high school to join the Marines. In his dream, he saw a huge wave spill over the deck of a ship and slam Egils around on the boat before sweeping him overboard. The Lion was shocked when he found out … it actually happened. Egils was dead! They found his body near Bermuda. He was only twenty years old. It shook The Lion up immensely and his death had a huge impact upon him. The Lion felt depressed for several months afterwards and attended few classes during his senior year.

Life sends each of us different challenges, and we must bear them with the fortitude and patience, as Jesus did. Even now, I don't fully understand all the hardships The Lion has endured. I had idolized his high school years. I thought of him as a great athlete and leader, who never let anything phase him. In reality, he went through some tough emotional times. He actually was dealt and felt more pain then most kids, and that somehow makes him even more human. It is easy to preemptively pass judgment, even though I don't know all the facts. I know that life's trials test the character of a man. We must each carry our own cross.

> *King Solomon wrote, "In this meaningless life of mine I have seen both of these: a righteous man perishing in his righteousness, and a wicked man live long in his wickedness. Do not be over righteous, neither be overwise — why destroy yourself? Do not be overwicked and do not be a fool — why die before your time? It is good to grasp the one and not let go of the other. The man who fears God will avoid all extremes."*
>
> *(Ecclesiastes 7:15-18 NIV)*

God is at work and He shines hope on every soul. The Lion's younger girlfriend is the primary provider financially. Now it's his role to take care of their daughter. I commend him because he affectionately loves and cares for them. He has even started to take better care of his health. He stopped smoking, drinks less hard liquor, and is eating better. He goes to his daughter's basketball games, a softball tournament, takes her to dance classes, and joins her to play the piano for a duet recital. He has the time, being semi-retired, but in this new family scenario, he has made family a priority over money. He *wants* to spend his time with them. Perhaps he realizes his time with his daughter is limited.

I admire his example of a better functioning family. This second time around, God is in The Lion's life teaching him how to love and care for a family. Having found *real* forgiveness for The Lion, I see him in a new light. There are many good qualities in The Lion that are noteworthy.

THE LEGEND OF THE LION

The Lion is a beast of power,
A formidable king that rules over his land.
Have no fear, he is glad to meet you at any hour,
He is the first to extend out his mighty hand.
Chairman of the Red Cross, Leader of the Band,
he hands out opportunity, as a job, which will be grand.
Owner of the fancy bistro, lakeside camp,
and shiny Cadillac,
he is the growing envy for what most men's lives do lack.
He trained me, with rigid discipline, as a Lion would,
showing there is no difference, between the bad and good.
Learn to hire, when to fire.
Find out every person's niche,
Let them do it, delegate.
Run the meeting, don't be late.
Interrogate, when the facts are fresh and new.
Read every paper, dissect every word, as a clue.
Don't hold back on greasy food, fickle friends,
or having fun.
Be in the parade, join that club,
hold a barbeque out in the sun.
He gave to me a snowmobile, motorcycle, bike, and car.
Taught me how to drive,
shift the gears, without letting them jar.
Weekend travel, dinner out, and vacation trips.
He was the one to provide the funding and pay the tip.
He coached me in baseball, taught me how to dive.
If it were not for him, I would not be alive!
I take for granted my good life. College bills paid,
clothes appear, an invite to camp,
where friends all hunt deer,
(Wait, that's not what I meant, in our case,
friends all drink beer.)

The Lion shows me how to live on top, appreciate classical
music, don't sweat the car dents; learn of life from our past
presidents: Roosevelt, Kennedy, Hoover, and Abe.
Each left an impression, which for the Lion is sharp.
All worthy men leave behind, as he will, his mark.
I often feel I stand, as the Lion once did,
ready for battle, ready to give.
It used to upset me, but now I don't mind.
I've placed our past where it should be: behind.
I am the son of a Lion. It's my fate.
There is no need to falter. I accept it as great!
He claims to never get enough in this life.
The woman you love need not be your wife.
Better, he says, to go without sleep,
than miss one moment, which is profound
or stirringly deep.
He is my father. I am proud.
I let him know, in his way,
for a Lion is born to roar out loud!

The Final Guided Meditation

In the beginning of the book, I asked you to set an intention as you read the book. If you have read every page, now is the moment for you to receive a word of wisdom, a vision, or healing. Words have the power to heal, but combined with our intention, they are more powerful. My prayers are with you and I have faith that you will receive. Create a sacred space for yourself. You may want to start with soft music, but allow there to be silence during the final five-minute meditation. Perhaps dim the lights or light a candle, wear special jewelry or clothing, or smudge yourself with sage.

First, stand up and say aloud: "Holy Spirit come fill me. Allow the words I read in this book to fully absorb in my heart. I ask you to send me a word of wisdom, a vision, or heal me in whatever way I need."

Place your hands over your heart, pause for a moment, then breathe deeply three times. Pause again. Now sit or lie down. Don't have any expectations about how your healing will happen. You have full permission to express any emotion, such as crying or laughing. Trust the Spirit of Guidance in the form it chooses to manifest. It may be a vision; you may hear guidance as a soft voice or feel a shift in your body, heart, or soul.

Close your eyes and, if you can, have someone read the Guided Meditation slowly to you; otherwise read it slowly to yourself and follow the directions the best you can. If you want soft music, turn it on now, before you continue.

GUIDED MEDITATION:

Sit comfortably with your spine erect and your bare feet solidly on the floor. If you would be more comfortable, you may lie down and close your eyes, but remain awake. Now, take your time to slowly relax the muscles, starting at the top of your head, face, jaw, back of the neck, tongue, chest, shoulders, arms, each individual finger, the full length of your back from top to bottom, abdomen, hips, pelvis, thighs, hamstrings, knees, calves, ankles, bottoms of the feet, and each individual toe. Feel the surface under your body and feel your skin relax. Focus on your breath for a moment.

Now, when you are ready, slowly take three deep, slow breaths a few inches on each side of your heart center. It is three fingers above your sternum. Focus on the area, in this order: right and left, front and back, top and bottom. Afterwards take ten slow, deep breaths directly in your heart center. You may touch that point with your left index finger to help you stay focused.

After the ten breaths, lower your hands with palms down if you are sitting or palms up if you are lying down. Stay in your heart until you sense that you are being held. It's subtle; trust yourself. Stop doing anything. Just breath normally, in and out, through the nose if possible. Let go completely. Be held. Remain here with silence for five minutes. Allow yourself to receive. Trust any guidance given.

Let's finish by reading aloud the Healing Prayer called Nayaz, by Hazrat Inayat Khan:

Beloved Lord, Almighty God!
Through the rays of the sun,
Through the waves of the air,
Through the All-pervading Life in Space,
Purify and revivify me, and I pray,
Heal my body, heart, and soul.
Amen. [25]

AFTERWORD & ACKNOWLEDGMENTS

I would like to thank all my friends and the professional editors ... Nick, Nicole, and Claire ... who edited my book. Rebecca did an elegant job with her editing skills in the prologue and first few chapters. A special thanks to Chitra, Amber, and Janet, who all provided valuable editing assistance. Nancy's editing skills were worth far more than six pineapples. Joan W. fearlessly told me which sections to cut. Rahan shared his perspective on silence. Sue gave Holy Spirit insights. Freedom reviewed my poems. Virginia ensured accuracy regarding SunDo. Sarada reviewed information about Baba Hari Dass. Rev. Prem Anjali, Ph.D., manager/editorial director at Integral Yoga Publications, reviewed all quotes by Swami Satchidananda. K'shatria reviewed the chapters on guided retreats. Vi Waln (who was an editor for the Lakota Country Times) and Swan Song reviewed parts of the Native American section. Pastor Tim and Bokton reviewed the sections on Jesus and scripture.

I want to extend a special thanks to Pastor R.I.P. for his testimony. May Jesus receive glory from our testimonies! All the major characters (whom I could locate) were sent the sections about themselves to review. My mom, The Lamb, as always, went far above the call of duty. She was there to offer her support, editing skills, assisted with research, improved my grammar, and kept me honest. I would like to thank my mother, who teaches me about kindness and compassion; my father, who taught me about business and matters of the world; my grandmother, who shared with me her passion for Jesus. Lastly, to all my friends and family who read the book, I love you.

Just for Laughs

Editors' murmurings and correspondence

"You're not in a position to speak on the scriptures with authority, "Thus saith the Lord," so don't try."   — Bokton

"Yoga is not Christian. It is evil"   — Pastor Tim

"Words like "unusual" or "unexpected" will draw the readers in. Words like "crazy" or "bizarre" could lead people to think you are a "nut" and not be as likely to be interested in the story."   — Rebecca (regarding The Guru)

"You have certainly lived an exciting life, and you do a good job of expressing your deepest feelings in this story. I was particularly interested in the section on The Guru; it was exciting to read and really made me question my own ideas about spirits. I believe that by reading your story and relating it to their own experience, you will be able to help many readers."   — Nick

"Take it easy on me!"   —The Lion

RESOURCES

The Author, Randolph C. Phelps
P.O. Box 255, Danville, VT 05828

Cristo Morpho Inc.,
Email: cristomorpho@gmail.com
Website: www.cristomorpho.com
Facebook: Cristo Morpho Community

SPIRITUAL RETREATS AND EDUCATIONAL LINKS

SunDo Retreat Center,
45 South Main Street, Suite 90,
West Hartford, CT 06107-2402 (860) 523-5260
Barnet, VT www.sundo.org (802) 748-3371

Omega Institute,
150 Lake Dr., Rhinebeck, NY 12572
www.eomega.org (845) 266-4444

Abode of the Message,
5 Abode Rd., New Lebanon, NY 12125
www.theabode.org (518) 794-8090
Saluk Academy www.sulukacademy.org

Himalayan Institute,
952 Bethany Turnpike, Honesdale, PA 18431
www.himalayaninstitute.org
(800) 822-4547 (570) 253-5551

Satchidananda Ashram (Yogaville)
108 Yogaville Way, Buckingham, VA 23921
www.yogaville.org (800) 858-9642

Mount Madonna,
445 Summit Rd., Watsonville, CA 95076
www.mountmadonna.org (408) 847-0406

World Harvest Outreach,
Chambersburg, PA 17201
www.whocenterpa.com (717) 709-1129
Online Gatherings: youtube.com/whocenterpa

Caring for the Heart Counseling Ministry,
Colorado Springs, CO
Email: caringfortheheart@msn.com (719) 572 5550
Website: www.Carefortheheart.com

The Experiment in International Living,
PO Box 676. 1 Kipling Road Brattleboro, VT 05302
www.experiment.org (800) 345-2929

Bibliography

(1) The Vermont Historical Society. (2010) *The Abenakis & the Europeans*. Permission granted by Vermont Historical Society, Barre, VT https://vermonthistory.org/explorer/vermont-stories/ becoming-a-state/the-abenakis-the-europeans

(2) Marquardt, E. (2014) *Children deeply shaped by divorce*. Permission granted by Marriage Missions International, Oro Valley, AZ http://marriagemissions.com/ children-deeply-shaped-by-divorce

(3) Ryan, T.C. (2013) *Where lust leads. Ashamed no more.* (2012) Downers Grove, IL: InterVarsity Press http://www. christianitytoday.com/le/2013/fall/where-lust-leads.html www.tc-ryan.com.

(4) Zychik, J. (2002-2012) *The Most Personal Addiction: How I overcame sex addiction and how anyone can.* Permission granted by Joe Zychik. Internet source: SexualControl. com p. 63.

(5) Got Questions Ministries (2002-2016) *What does the Bible say about an unhappy marriage?* Internet source: www. gotquestions.org Permission granted.

(6) Zychik, J. (2002-2012) *The Most Personal Addiction: How I overcame sex addiction and how anyone can.* Permission granted by Joe Zychik. Internet source: SexualControl. com pp. 41-43, 46-47.

(7) Didjshop.com. (1993-2014) *The Rainbow Serpent Story.* Internet source: www.didjshop.com/stories/rainbow.html. Permission granted.

(8)   Yogananda, P. (1946) *The Autobiography of a Yogi*, First edition, New York, N.Y.: The Philosophical Library, Inc. p. 5, 14-15.

(9)   Khan, H.I. (1978) *The Sufi Message of Hazrat Iniyat Khan, Vol IV, Mental Purification and Healing, Part I, Health.* Farnham Surrey, UK: Sevir p. 19.

(10) Bradley, D. (2009). *Native Americans of San Diego County*. Charleston, SC.: Arcadia Publishing. p. 35. Permission granted.

(11) Lame Deer, J., & Erdoes, R. (1972). *Lame Deer, seeker of visions; The life of a Sioux medicine man.* New York City, NY: Simon and Schuster Publishing. pp. 262–263.

(12) Reardon, J. (2013). *What Does It Mean to Fear God?* Carol Stream, IL: Christianity Today International. ChristianBibleStudies.com. Permission granted. http://www.christianitytoday.com/biblestudies/bible-answers/spirituallife/what-does-it-mean-to-fear-god.html

(13) Enroth, R. (1994) *Recovering From Churches That Abuse*. Grand Rapids, Michigan: Zondervan Publishing House, p 16. Permission granted by Zondervan. www.zondervan.com

(14) Got Questions Ministries (2002-2016) *What is the symbolism of water baptism?* Internet source: www.gotquestions.org Permission granted.

(15) Satchidananda, S. (1988) *To Know Your Self: The essential teaching of Swami Satchidananda*. Buckingham, VA: Permission for all quotes by Swami Satchidananda granted by Integral Yoga Publications.

(16) Khan, H.I. (2007). *The Sufi Message of Hazrat Inayat Khan Vol. I, The Inner Life, Sufi Thoughts*. The Netherlands: Servire, Katwijk, and Zee. p. 16.

(17) Khan, P.V.I. (1999). *Awakening: A Sufi experience*. New York, NY: Jeremy P. Tarcher / Putnam, a member of Penguin Putnam Inc. Copyright held by Zenith Institute. p. 24.

(18) Khan, H.I. *The Sufi Invocation*. Internet source http://wahiduddin.net/dance/harmony.htm. Permission granted by Omega Press.

(19) Zychik, J. (2002-2012) *The Most Personal Addiction: How I overcame sex addiction and how anyone can*. Permission granted by Joe Zychik. Internet source: SexualControl.com p. 35.

(20) Ryan, T.C. (2013) *Where lust leads. Ashamed no more.* (2012) Downers Grove, IL: InterVarsity Presshttp://www.christianitytoday.com/le/2013/fall/where-lust-leads.html www.tc-ryan.com.

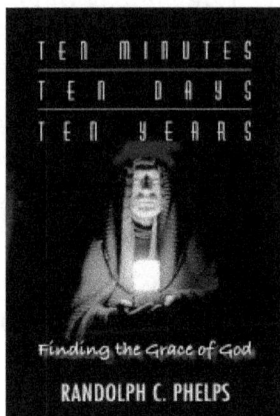

Ten Minutes, Ten Days, Ten Years
Finding the Grace of God

This is a brilliant melding of three intriguing stories. It will fill your soul with joy and substantial inner courage. Each character is given a fun, revealing pseudonym. Over a span of years, their insights and behaviors reveal a steady advance toward spiritual maturity. You learn how their lies and deceptive ways are uncovered and the merits of cultivating intimacy and integrity. Along the path, you discover how they face the challenges of personal addictions, triangle relationships, and emotional anguish.

> *"This book took me on a ride though different metaphysical planes, past lives, and dimensions."*
> — *Natalie Nichols*

This book is a compilation that includes *The Cosmic Guru* and *Swan Song*. It includes the final guided meditation where the reader is guided to receive a word of wisdom, a vision, or healing.

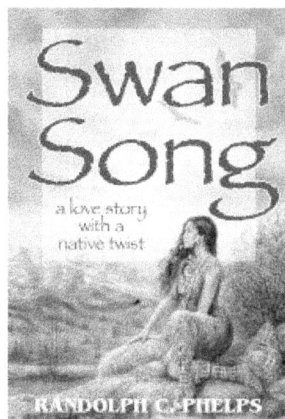

SWAN SONG:
A LOVE STORY WITH A NATIVE TWIST

Swan Song mysteriously enters my life. Through a series of dreams and visions, I realize that our life together has begun where our previous Native American life left off. From our past lives, we encounter My Native Brother, and our two children, Lost Son and Feather Maker. They each have serious life-lessons to convey. Whenever Swan Song and I are together, magic manifests, but trouble is brewing. Chief Thunder Cloud and I were in a spiritual duel over Swan Song's affection in our past lives. Once again, Swan Song and I weave a web of deception through a secret love affair. When Chief Thunder Cloud uncovers the truth, it leads to a showdown.

"Swan Song is a riveting story about a conscious relationship in which the veil of love is torn wide-open."
— *Debbie Bohland*

Swan Song is also available in the book *Ten Minutes, Ten Days, Ten Years: Finding the Grace of God*. There is a final guided meditation in *The Cosmic Guru* or *Ten Minutes, Ten*

Days, Ten Years where the reader is guided to receive a word of wisdom, a vision, or healing. The meditation is intended for those who have read *Swan Song* and *The Cosmic Guru* or *Ten Minutes, Ten Days, Ten Years.*

Samples from Swan Song

MY DEATH SONG

I appear on a dirt road near an old white farmhouse. Behind it, there is a large, circular, back field that scales up the hillside. Floating in the middle of the field is an island of tall striped birch trees.

Sadness for the death of the warrior in my dream still lingers. I am trying to figure out why his death is so significant. We feel connected in some arcane way. That warrior was close to me.

Suddenly, my eyes lock on a coyote walking down the middle of the road, heading in my direction. They usually run away. But something is peculiar about this one. He stops to stare in my direction. Perhaps this coyote can sense my sadness. I am not a threat and I am not afraid. He angles off up into the field. Then he walks a wide half circle and sits down on his haunches, a mere thirty feet away.

Now I am feeling even more sadness. It is becoming overwhelming. I squat down by a small pool in the brook. At that moment, I realize why Wicahpi Ska was so devastated. The warrior who died was her husband, Cetan Luta.

But, wait a minute! She was my past wife. It was me that died. I sense that Cetan Luta was my same age, in a past life, at the time of his death. The medicine has been waiting to reveal his death on the exact day it happened.

I sense the whole tragic scene from my past life. It all happened dreadfully fast. I was following deer tracks into thick brush. The grizzly bear was startled. It came rushing toward me. There was no time to react or defend myself. I felt a sudden shock as it clasped around my back. Then it gouged me with its huge front claws. My life ended swiftly — too swiftly. Something was missing!

In a ceremonial manner, I take mud from the brook and smear two lines down the sides of my face. I begin to chant in a Native language. As I do, the coyote in the field throws his head back and begins a series of yelps, then he opens his mouth wide and lets out a high-pitched howl. A bush is lined up directly between us, so I only see glimpses of him.

I believe this coyote actually wants to join in my ceremony. A coyote will sometimes howl when they are alone and searching for the pack, but joining me is inconceivable. What an amazingly-bizarre honor to chant with a wild animal, especially a coyote. But I am too caught up in my chanting and feeling the emotions to be overly concerned with the coyote.

My whole universe is opening. I am in a surreal, dreamlike state. I have somehow overlapped another dimension of time. Every sound is magnified. The songs of the birds in the far corner of a field fill my ears with angelic voices and a sweet golden harp. I am smothered with the smell of spring flowers. My vision is soft and blurry. It feels like I am in two different places. One is definitely not in this earthly realm. There is a timelessness. It feels like a curtain has lifted and I am in heaven.

As the warrior Cetan Luta, I never had a chance to sing my death song. I died too suddenly. Yes, that's it! I need to sing my death song. A death song is to take away fear and give courage when a warrior is facing a deadly situation, usually before heading into battle or during a severe illness. Maybe there are other reasons for it in the Native afterlife. This is what he needs. That is what he is missing! I start to chant Cetan Luta's death song in his Native American tongue.

While I slip into this microcosmic universe, Cetan Luta's soul finds solace. I believe this window in heaven has opened up on earth to allow his soul to freely pass. Now he can continue to travel, as intended. I am assuming he is on a beautiful journey back to the happy hunting ground. I can sense the presence of a medicine man entrusted to watch over Cetan Luta's soul. He is more than a witness. He is calling forth medicine to make all of this happen. I believe that he is somehow connected to that coyote. I can't see him, but I can feel him. It is possible he could even be … inside that coyote.

OUR CAMPING SPOT

Tucked into the woods off the hiking trail around a quaint pond, is a three-sided lean-to made of large, pine logs. There is a stone fire pit directly in front of it and a weathered picnic table off to the side. There are pine planks on the floor and it all smells like pine inside. Someone had used a knife to carve, in old English script, five of the seven deadly sins. On the three surrounding walls are the words GREED, WRATH, and ENVY. PRIDE hangs overhead. LUST finds its place on the floor directly in front of our tent opening. How appropriate a reminder. (If you're racking your brain, gluttony and sloth are the two missing deadly sins.)

The opening faces toward the pond, which is no more than 25 feet away. In the late afternoon, the ducks come in for a landing as a marmalade sunset engulfs the horizon. At night the frogs near the shore create a chorus of peeps and chirps with the exceptional, resounding, deep croak from a bullfrog.

When I am here by myself or awaiting Swan Song, I always find peace looking at the reflections in the pond. There are tall grasshopper-green grasses and gnarly tree limbs half submerged in the water. They make an ideal place for the turtles to rest while bathing in the last glistening rays. If I move suddenly or a hiker passes on the trail, the turtles plop back into the water. A moment later, a head slowly appears and stretches out before its cautious return.

During our first autumn together, we claim this site as our camping spot. We stick a red prayer flag filled with tobacco high in a tree overhanging the pond directly in front of our camping spot. When we return the next summer, we are glad to see it still hanging, though it has faded. There is an old John-Deere-green hand pump not far away. It provides our drinking water. We take turns pumping the handle as the other rinses the dishes or takes a quick shower.

From near the hand pump, we can watch the smoke from our fire and look down the length of the pond. We gather firewood together before dark. Swan Song loves to sit and stare into the fire. On the cold, fall nights, we are cozy and sleep deeply as we hold each other beneath my buffalo robe. She always sleeps on her left side. I spoon her. If I'm not close enough, she wiggles herself backwards to fill in the crevice. My right arm rests comfortably upon her waist. My hand cups her small, soft fingers. The nostalgic smell of smoke mixes with the smell of the buffalo leather and the scent of our skin. At night when we first bed down, a silhouette from the flames dances on the side of our tent. Later we hear the crackling and popping of the fire as it peters down to form red-hot coals.

We both cherish our favorite camping spot. In the fall, we wear jeans and cuddly, wool sweaters. I remember the comfort of her leaning her head onto my chest while we lay on a woven blanket in the sun. It's as much about the warm, glowing feelings of being together in nature, as being in love.

The timelessness of the breeze gently blows the leaves. I gaze at her watching the clouds. She notices and smiles, returning my glance.

About The Author

Randolph C. Phelps is a native Vermonter and a resident of Costa Rica. He is the founder of the Vermont nonprofit, Cristo Morpho, which established a sustainable, spiritual community located on the Caribbean side of Costa Rica, called The Cristo Morpho Community. During winters, he hosts visitors and directs the Cristo Morpho Volunteer Program, which focuses on immersion into the community through individual service projects, and fostering spiritual growth.

Randolph was a wedding and stock photographer, traveling to Alaska and Australia to photograph the natives and wildlife. His photographs have been published in magazines such as Faces, Challenges, and vacation guides for Alaska Tourism Council and brochures for The Experiment in International Living. His poems have been published in the Green Mountain Trading Post and in the book *Nothing hardly ever happens in Colbyville, Vermont* by Peter Miller.

Randolph has a B.A. in Business Management and was enrolled for a Masters degree at Saint Michael's College in Colchester, VT. This included one semester abroad at Melbourne University to study Australian culture. He is certified by the American Sailing Association for Basic Coastal Cruising. He is a certified Integrative Yoga Therapist specializing in chronic conditions and restorative postures, an Integral Yoga Teacher, and a Thai-Yoga bodyworker. He is also trained as a "Caring for the Heart" counselor.

He has given his time to volunteer at Northeast Vermont Regional Hospital, The Hudson Valley Rapture Center, and the Nature Zone, an educational exotic animal park in Lynchburg, VA. For ten years he was a regular volunteer during the summer months at various spiritual communities. He served the wellness center at Omega Institute in Rhinebeck, NY and assisted with mountain retreats at The Abode of the Message in New Lebanon, NY. He has also been a volunteer at Satchidananda Ashram in Buckingham, Virginia.

I hope that my book touched you in some way. If it did, I am asking that you contact me and share the details. Nowadays, a book is usually a stepping stone to something more grandiose. I believe The Guru or Swan Song story has great potential to be made into a movie. I am seeking a spiritual-based organization to produce this movie. Contact me if you want to sponsor *The Movie* or would like to be updated about the progress.

My spiritual journey ultimately led to establishing the Cristo Morpho Volunteer Program and Cristo Morpho Community. We are located on nearly one hundred acres of rain forest in the mountain village of Buena Vista on the Caribbean side of Costa Rica. I am seeking individuals, families or a spiritual organization that would like to establish their own community or assist in taking our community to the next level. The fruit trees, vegetable gardens, and hardwood trees on our land have been designated to serve the needs of a medium-sized community. This rainforest location is a perfect place to offer spiritual retreats.

We need pioneers willing to commit their time and energy. Perhaps it is your desire to help preserve the rainforest or reduce your stress level by getting back to Nature. Part of our vision is to fulfill the dreams of individuals and families that resonate with our core values. They include respect toward all people and cultures, honoring family and relationships, and living a healthy drug-free lifestyle. Please contact me if you desire to become actively involved in a sustainable community. I am here to serve you.

May peace be with you,

Randolph C. Phelps
P.O. Box 255, Danville, VT 05828
cristomorpho@gmail.com
www.cristomorpho.com

www.ingramcontent.com/pod-product-compliance
Lightning Source LLC
Chambersburg PA
CBHW060231050426
42448CB00009B/1395